Faculty Work
and the
Public Good

Faculty Work and the Public Good

Philanthropy, Engagement, and Academic Professionalism

Edited by
Genevieve G. Shaker

TEACHERS COLLEGE PRESS
Teachers College
Columbia University
New York and London

Published by Teachers College Press, 1234 Amsterdam Avenue, New York, NY 10027

Copyright © 2015 by Teachers College, Columbia University

Permission to reprint material by Elizabeth Lynn for "An Ongoing Experiment: State Councils, the Humanities, and the American Public" © 2013 by The Kettering Foundation.

Library of Congress Cataloging-in-Publication Data available at www.loc.gov

ISBN 978-0-8077-5617-1 (paper)
ISBN 978-0-8077-5618-8 (hardcover)
ISBN 978-0-8077-7351-2 (ebook)

Printed on acid-free paper
Manufactured in the United States of America

22 21 20 19 18 17 16 15   8 7 6 5 4 3 2 1

For Gail and Bill Plater

Contents

Acknowledgments

This book has a long history, spanning back to a sliver of an idea during graduate school and initial evidence of its viability during dissertation research and writing. From that point to the day the volume came to fruition with a group of committed contributors and ultimately a contract for publication, many individuals gave gifts of encouragement, wisdom, expertise, patience, and support. These gifts were essential for the viability of this project. It is a book that bends traditional notions of both faculty work and philanthropy and asked chapter contributors (and now readers as well) to enter unfamiliar territory.

I must thank professor emerita Nancy Van Note Chism, my dissertation advisor, for showing me the enactment of philanthropy in faculty work, thereby helping to name concepts that explain many of my experiences in the academy. I also witnessed and benefited from the generous acts of my friends and teachers, Megan Palmer and Gail Plater, during this period. Likewise, Professor John Levin was a key collaborator and mentor.

The positive reactions from professor emeritus Richard C. Turner and professor emeritus William M. Plater regarding an edited volume on faculty work and the public good foreshadowed their ongoing interest over several years. Their mentorship, "retired" or not, further demonstrated the philanthropy of faculty, inspiring me to aspire to be similarly generous in interactions with colleagues and students alike.

My colleagues and friends in both the Indiana University School of Liberal Arts and the Indiana University Lilly Family School of Philanthropy at Indiana University–Purdue University Indianapolis (IUPUI) have encouraged me to follow my passion in scholarship and practice, as I seek synergies in my interests and roles. My two deans, William Blomquist and Eugene Tempel, are chief among my supporters and advocates. This book was aided by a grant from the IUPUI Arts and Humanities Institute, graciously extended by vice chancellor for research Kody Varahramyan. The grant facilitated the involvement of Elizabeth Dale, a philanthropic studies doctoral student whose organizational skills, disciplinary knowledge, and editorial expertise were invaluable and warrant significant recognition.

I am grateful to the many scholars who joined in this project as chapter contributors, not only for their intellectual contributions but also for the grace and openness with which they participated in the process. I hope they are as proud of what we created together as I am.

Last, I wish to express my appreciation for my husband, Michael Paredes; our son, Kai; and my parents and their partners, Gayle and Don and Paul and Jan.

Part I

CONCEPTUALIZING PHILANTHROPY IN FACULTY WORK

CHAPTER 1

Seeing Philanthropy in Faculty Work

An Introduction

Genevieve G. Shaker

Although my history with higher education is lengthy and diverse—first as a child of faculty members, then as an undergraduate and graduate student, next as an administrator, and now as a faculty member—the actions of my dissertation advisor first opened my eyes to the philanthropic dimension of faculty work. Now I know that such generosity was there all along, but it had remained hidden until I recognized it.

As a graduate student, I benefited from monthly "motivational" sessions organized by my advisor. At each meeting, students reported their progress and announced a personal goal for the next gathering. We learned from each other's research, and our work was propelled forward by accountability to the group. We helped one another—with tips and resources, reading and editing, network sharing, and social capital. Our advisor made further offers of assistance: gifts of books, one-on-one writing time and mentoring, use of personal contacts to further our research, donation of her office as a quiet place to write, and promises of highly detailed and strategic reviews of our drafts.

Were my advisor's activities simply good practice, part of her job, or an act of generosity? Evidence suggests it was the last, and she was not only exceeding a duty to her students in the form of teaching; she was going far beyond what might be expected of her job. She was neither required nor asked by her colleagues to host the dissertation sessions. There was no place on her annual report for her to record her "work." She was nearing retirement and already a leader in her field; thus, the number of PhDs she successfully trained was not a matter of status, nor was it necessary to further her career or attain tenure. She could have professionally fulfilled her duty as a graduate advisor through periodic correspondence, individual meetings, and mandated reviews of our work. She most certainly could have forgone the substantial extra support she gave us, and few outside our little group would have ever known, cared, or judged. In fact, should she not have provided the extra support at all, we might not have even recognized what was missing. Only when we realized that others did not provide such generous guidance did we recognize her efforts. Later, I realized that my advisor was not alone in her "generosity." For many faculty there is a strong commitment to go beyond requirements to do what is essential for the good of their own students and for the public good as reflected in the preparation of future generations of teachers and scholars who will *make a difference* in the world.

I begin with this story and will return to it because this book requires us to recalibrate our understandings of academic culture to allow for a new way of recognizing, as well as thinking and talking about, faculty work. Our well-honed perspectives—first as students and later as faculty, administrators, and interested parties—usually do not include a provision for acknowledging philanthropic contributions to the public good in faculty work. As a mechanism for constructing initial understandings of concepts, theories, events, and people, stories are a primary tool for making sense of our world. Thinking about my story and reflecting on similar experiences, therefore, is a first step in forming an alternate view of faculty work and discerning whether the lens of philanthropy can change how one considers the professoriate.

Why form an alternative view? A major transformation in the composition, role, and expectations of the academic workforce is under way, one so significant that the long-held view of the professoriate will not long endure. To appreciate what may be lost in this transformation, faculty, administrators, and policymakers might benefit from recognizing what is before them—as I did with the generosity of my advisor. In the context of strong evidence that faculty spend far more hours per week and weeks per year on their academic calling than is required by appointment or contract, what could be sacrificed if the faculty's ability to exercise judgments about the use of their time or to set priorities are eroded along with full-time positions, tenure, and loyalty to an institution? Philanthropy may not be the only lens through which to reflect on what is at risk, but it is a lens that opens new possibilities for naming and valuing something that has long been taken for granted.

Few scholars, and notably Richard C. Turner (2010), have spoken explicitly of philanthropy and faculty work, but the usual assumptions about faculty work often imply both an individual and a collective commitment to serving others that approximates a prominent definition of philanthropy as "voluntary action for the public good" (Payton, 1988, p. 3). Commentators have noted that the educational enterprise is a communal effort undertaken for the betterment of society and others' lives (Boyer, 1990; Kennedy, 1997; MacFarlane, 2005, 2007; Plater, 1999, 2011; Shils, 1997) but have not gone so far as to name this as philanthropy and understand it as a guiding and defining value in faculty work. This volume explicitly describes how and argues that contributing to the public good through philanthropy is characteristic of faculty work, is an important part of its value, and it aims to facilitate an innovative discussion about the professoriate and its priorities. The perspective of philanthropy allows actions like my advisor's, completed for little recognition or reward and at her own discretion, to be recognized and appreciated for what they are—motivated largely by a desire to benefit others and the broader community.

Efforts by Texas, Florida, and other states to track and document faculty productivity (June, 2011) are emblematic of the public debate raging about the work of college and university faculty. Books like *Academically Adrift: Limited Learning on College Campuses* (Arum & Roksa, 2010) have called into question such basic elements of faculty work as the quality of student learning. Faculty are thought to earn too much, work too little, and be selfishly focused on the wrong things (Sykes, 1990). Among the questions being asked are: Should faculty teach more and research less? Should faculty productivity be narrowly measured as expense versus income? Do faculty use their time effectively and appropriately? Should there be less discretion and more direction of faculty work? Should tenured faculty be replaced with contingent faculty, who can, in turn, be replaced as needs shift? In the current context, how politicians, administrators, faculty, and the public address these divisive questions may shape the future of higher education in the United States and most certainly will inform the nature of the faculty profession going forward.

The consequences for the professoriate, already fractured by the turn from tenure and the corporatization of academe, could be severe and could leave the work that faculty do nearly unrecognizable. At greatest risk is faculty work outside of the classroom and the lab, at the intersection of what is required and what is volunteered. Faculty meet numerous operational needs, thereby creating and defining institutional culture, climate, and reputation. Faculty often accomplish these tasks by making unrecognized intellectual and administrative contributions, "giving" more than they must. The frequently unreported but extensive contributions of faculty are apparent to those who choose to look for them, as we do in this book. But even before this work is defined as philanthropic, the invisibility of these activities is evidence of their seamless integration in professorial roles and the assumption that faculty can be relied on to exceed stated expectations.

One principled response might be to say that this work—what is here being considered voluntary, discretionary, and philanthropic—should be properly recognized and rewarded as a formal aspect of faculty work. Such an argument is based on what it means to be a professional (Sullivan, 2007) and is a call to accord faculty the same kind of status as that of members of other well-regarded professions. But the downside of moving this discretionary aspect of faculty work into the score sheet of accountability is that it would have to be assessed and evaluated—as are scholarship, teaching, and professional service. Trading philanthropic work for a more recognized, and perhaps rewarded, classification may offer neither the same incentive nor the same satisfaction as something that is perceived to be not only voluntary but also a benefit to society, to the greater good.

The chapters in this book explore how the philanthropy in faculty work can be expressed to provide a more representative view of faculty, their motivations, the scope of their work, and their values. Professorial portfolios inclusive of their philanthropic aspects contrast with the narrow conception of appropriate faculty work as production of credit hours and research dollars. Making a case for the former approach may encourage a holistic view of teaching and learning, research and scholarship, service and citizenship. Respect for a more complete collection of faculty activities, one that recognizes the philanthropy therein, will perpetuate what makes academic work meaningful and create a higher education sector that is more robust, intellectually rich, diverse, welcoming to new ideas, supportive and engaged with the nonuniversity community, and committed to societal needs. Although not all faculty are philanthropically inclined, attention to those who distinguish themselves in this manner could help preserve valuable aspects of faculty work for all faculty and maintain the latitude to engage in voluntary action for the public good.

DEFINING PHILANTHROPY

Returning to the anecdote about my advisor, one might question the philanthropic nature of her actions, arguing that the meetings were expected as a part of her compensation or assigned duties. In actuality, her activities exceeded her job requirements and therefore were conducted at her own discretion. Some may say that her efforts weren't philanthropic because of the satisfaction she received from seeing her students succeed and the happiness she felt from contributing to their progress, but to be philanthropic by most measures does not require individuals to be purely altruistic (or unconcerned with any benefit to one's self) in their motives or that they receive nothing in return. Instead, it is possible and appropriate that actions to help others also intrinsically benefit the actor by, for example, complementing a sense of identification with an organizational mission (Schervish & Havens, 1997) or satisfying a deep desire to make a positive impact on society, an individual, or a group (Duncan, 2004).

Considering only the action itself, apart from the motive, also supports a philanthropic perspective. In judging actions intended to help others (i.e., the monthly meetings), also known as prosocial behaviors, one might argue that the action itself and its desired outcomes matter most (Eisenberg & Mussen, 1989). Consequently, neither intrinsic nor extrinsic gains eliminate the validity of identifying the philanthropic inclination underlying my advisor's actions. The difficulty, however, in agreeing on whether my advisor's intention was philanthropic suggests the importance of discussing a shared meaning of "philanthropy."

Contemporary dictionary definitions of *philanthropy* typically include language about loving humankind and also include a strong actionable element (Sulek, 2010). *Philanthrôpía*, the Greek origin of *philanthropy*, is composed of two root words (*phileô* and *anthrôpos*), which give us the original and literal meaning of "the love of humankind" (Sulek, 2010). *Paideia*, "education" in classical Greek, is a close linguistic and conceptual sibling to *philanthrôpía*, and a case can be made for the ways in which the dissemination of, creation of, and receipt of education may have been an expression of one's love of people (Sulek, 2010).

Among academics, the definition of *philanthropy* is a source of some debate. Lester Salamon (1992) deems philanthropy to be limited to "the private giving of time or valuables (money, security, property) for public purposes" (p. 10). Robert Payton's (1988) definition, "voluntary action for the public good," on which this book rests most heavily, allows for a more encompassing perspective on philanthropy appropriate for recognizing it in conjunction with one's work. Rather than merely acts of traditional volunteerism or financial giving, as in Salamon's definition, in Payton's view, philanthropy is more nuanced and integrated into personal philosophies and institutional missions as ideas and values (Payton & Moody, 2008). It is for this reason that Payton's definition and those like it (i.e., Van Til, 1990), can help us understand faculty work. Just as those working in nonprofit organizations are working for philanthropic purposes, so too do those in most forms of higher education seek to serve and improve society. Of interest in this project, however, is exploring those elements of faculty work that are self-directed ("voluntary"), seek to attain an ideal outcome ("good"), and encompass an objective act ("action") (Sulek, 2010), those elements completed out of concern for others in addition to and in coordination with the full assortment of faculty responsibilities.

Robert Payton and Michael Moody (2008) tell us that in order to see philanthropy in daily life, recognize its origins, and act in a reasonable and thoughtful way, we must "scrape away the layers of our own experience that prevent us from understanding why we did what we did" (p. 4). That is to say, the faculty profession, rather than behaving as a matter of course, needs to reflect on the how, what, and why of its own philanthropy, in order to put it to its best use. As an expression of one's moral imagination to advance the societal common good through involvement in others' lives, the concept of philanthropy as moral action is implied by the responsibilities and behavior of faculty (Payton & Moody, 2008). Whether stemming from religious values, grounded in liberal education, rooted in cultural traditions, inspired by mentors, or resulting from institutional culture, or other factors, there is a range of possible reasons that faculty are philanthropic with their time, energy, knowledge, and resources.

Yet this connection is rarely made in an overt manner by faculty, universities, government, or society. The enterprise of delineating who does what, why, and where reveals the philanthropy of faculty and why it matters to higher education. It is an opportunity to attract caring and gifted people to the profession and to reassure the public of the value of faculty work in its many forms. It may inspire the hesitant or less generous to rise to the examples set by their colleagues. It will allow faculty and their universities to do a better job of contributing to the public good by making clear their philanthropic motivations, aims, and practices and including these elements in their goals and objectives.

FACULTY WORK AND PROFESSIONALISM

Today, the academic workforce is no longer characterized by tenure, with more than three-quarters of faculty ineligible for its protections (Curtis & Thornton, 2013). Institutions increasingly turn to professional staff and administrators to complete work once done by faculty or to accommodate stakeholder requests and expectations (Ginsberg, 2011). Competition for students and for dollars and the upward drift of institutional missions, along with the already mentioned calls for increased productivity and accountability, affect faculty and what they do. Faculty assignments must be completed in an increasingly complex environment of escalating demands and outdated policies, appointment expectations, and structures of support (Gappa, Austin, & Trice, 2007). Ernest Boyer's (1990) landmark text, *Scholarship Reconsidered*, framed faculty work as research and discovery, integration, application (engagement), and teaching to contribute to the greater good. Taking into account institutional differences, however, most faculty assessments fall back onto the more simplistic (and problematic) delineation of teaching, research, and service—something that scholars have been questioning in its rigidity, albeit with mixed success, for decades (Boyer, 1990; O'Meara & Rice, 2005; Rice, 1996).

Notwithstanding a context of ambiguity, many continue to believe that a shared, albeit strained, academic ethos centering on the discovery and transmission of truth undergirds all activities to which faculty lend their professional expertise (Shils, 1997). The professoriate is not dissimilar from other professions—medicine, law, ministry, teaching—in requiring certain educational credentials, featuring flexibility and autonomy, and expecting a public commitment. As in other professions, maintaining the primacy of sustaining the public good as the faculty's role is at times lost or subverted (Sullivan, 2007). When this happens, the profession, as a "way of life with public value" (p. 39), is threatened and diminished as a calling and vocation. Popular understandings of the professional as merely a receptacle and dis-seminator of expertise rather than contributor of knowledge for the public good signals a weakening of the professional ideal (Brint, 1996). Failure to maintain the civic partnership between professionals and society, William Sullivan warns, would mean a loss in the realm of ethical work and the end of the civic identity inhabited by those in the professions.

Edward Shils (1997) contends that the special relationship of the profes-soriate with the commodity of knowledge and the quest for truth imbues the faculty with a unique role even among professions. Faculty dedication to truth and knowledge is what allows them extraordinary autonomy to pursue their work in the way they believe best, using their own judgment to meet "more than the obligations of the ordinary citizen" (p. 8). Does this mean that faculty work can't be philanthropic because faculty are obligated to serve the public good and are more obligated as citizens than other professionals?

While these special duties may exist conceptually and philosophically, they lack institutionalization within the policies and practices that govern faculty work. Faculty are rarely evaluated on these measures, and they are not told to enact these obligations in carrying out their responsibilities. Philanthropy exists in this space of omission. For faculty as profession-als, the reality is that they possess the discretion to decide whether to be expert purveyors of knowledge who complete the minimum of what their job requires. Or they can decide to embrace the social trust, using the un-regulated space and time left to their professional discretion and outside official expectations, to further the hopes of individuals and goals of soci-ety. The faculty who take the second course certainly appear intrinsically driven by motives that supersede a purely self-interested demeanor.

The faculty responsibility to complete some amount of "service" sug-gests a philanthropic component by its very nomenclature. Philanthropy can be evident in service (the catchall of academic work) as faculty put their knowledge to use for community organizations or sit on university fundrais-ing committees, for example, but it is also integrated across the spectrum of faculty work. From their different perspectives, research, and personal experiences, the contributors to this volume each report whether and where they "see" philanthropy in faculty work and how that conception may or may not be helpful. Whether or not "philanthropy" is accepted as the best way to define faculty contributions to the public good, the chapter authors agree, first, that there is something inherent in faculty work that responds to the public purpose of what they do and, second, that their contributions are at risk for a variety of reasons—all of which may directly affect the quality of American higher education.

THE ORGANIZATION OF THE BOOK

The exploration of philanthropy within faculty work brings a new dimension to conversations about the nature of the faculty profession and aims to help dispel misconceptions about what faculty do and why. The chapter authors are scholars who draw on empirical research, historical evidence, personal experience, and theory to shape essays exploring how faculty contribute to the public good and how philanthropy may be evident within faculty work. Through commentary drawn across institutional type, disciplinary orientation, epistemological approach, and philosophical orientation, a diverse narrative emerges explaining and debating how philanthropic and academic work overlap and may be interrelated. Not every contributor views "philanthropy" as the concept best able to capture the nature of the public good contributions of faculty work, but all use the concept to wrestle aptly and thoughtfully with what is at stake for the evolving academic workforce and the public it serves.

Faculty Work and the Public Good's organizing themes take into account a range of topics including current debates about how faculty spend their time, the diminishment of faculty involvement in their campuses, the pressure for expanded campus engagement with local communities, and conversations about faculty involvement in social movements and politics. The five thematic sections are (1) conceptualizing philanthropy in faculty work, (2) purposes and motivations for faculty work, (3) philanthropy as an aspect of academic professionalism, (4) faculty leadership and community engagement, and (5) the public good and the future of academic work. Some ideas and themes, however, span section divisions, allowing for a breadth of discussion about a diversity of faculty activities. Contributors draw on a varied literature, include contextualization about faculty work, provide implications and advice, and pose questions, testing the relevance of philanthropy to different ways of understanding and supporting faculty work and challenging faculty to adopt this new concept for voicing their values and priorities.

Conceptualizing Philanthropy in Faculty Work

This book argues that by its very nature, faculty work is imbued with, and the faculty profession is grounded in, a responsibility to contribute to the public good. The expectation to meet society's needs for an educated citizenry and societal requirements to advance and disseminate knowledge lend a philanthropic component to the act of being a faculty member. This section, of which this introductory chapter is a part, focuses on the definition and historical meaning of the concept of philanthropy and explores points of intersection for academic professionals.

Returning to his work with Robert Payton on understanding philanthropy, Michael Moody deconstructs faculty efforts in "Voluntary Action for Public Good? Faculty Work and the Broad Definition of Philanthropy." He finds the emphasis on the public good within education and scholarly endeavor and attends to definitional concerns about philanthropy and altruism. Revisiting the first recorded use of the word *philanthrôpía* in ancient Greece, in "Recovering the Original Meaning of Philanthropy: A Prelude to Consideration of the Philanthropy of Faculty Work," Marty Sulek underscores contemporary definitions of philanthropy with historical and linguistic analysis and argues that knowledge, teaching, and education are academe's greatest gifts to society and as such carry forward philanthropy's root meaning.

Purposes and Motivation for Faculty Work

In making choices about time allocation and professional emphasis, faculty must consider job requirements but may also rely on a deeply personal—or professional—sense of doing right by others. Concern for and commitment to society, students, colleagues, and the institution can shape and inform faculty work, enhance its meaning, and influence faculty career paths. This section attends to what leads faculty to be philanthropic and, conversely, how philanthropic values motivate faculty to engage in particular activities.

Ann E. Austin charts her thirty years as a faculty member in "Philanthropy as Motivator and Meaning: Reflections on Academic Work," examining the integration of concepts from philanthropy with analysis of individual professorial activities and the literature of academic work. Faculty time spent voluntarily on pedagogical development and student support is the focus of Thomas F. Nelson Laird's "Gifting Time: Faculty Activities with a Philanthropic Orientation," which considers differences by race/ethnicity, rank/appointment, and discipline. "Philanthropy Without Tenure," by Genevieve G. Shaker, considers the motivations of the non-tenure-track majority as shaped by philanthropic aspects of the academic ethos, evidencing this population's desire to contribute to institutional, societal, and student success and demonstrating an opportunity for extending, not eliminating, concern for the public good among the faculty. Emily L. Moore and J. Herman Blake's chapter, "Inherent Philanthropy in Multicultural Faculty Work at a Research University," describes the philanthropic values that intuitively underpin teaching, research, and service in the academy, based on their experience as Black faculty and on interviews with colleagues from diverse backgrounds. In "Professors Acting for the Public Good: Beyond the 'New Normal' to the Academy We Choose," Gary Rhoades argues that modern-day structural patterns in higher education increasingly challenge faculty who wish to contribute to the public good, while providing evidence of faculty who overcome (or tackle) these patterns by behaving philanthropically.

Philanthropy as an Aspect of Academic Professionalism

The ways in which faculty work may easily be thought of as having philanthropy within it, perhaps most obviously through collaboration on efforts to build philanthropic financial support among college and university supporters and, less easily, through the gifts that practitioner teachers bring to the for-profit sector through their teaching, are aspects of an academic professionalism that defies (and will redefine) the work of modern-day academics. This section puts the concept of philanthropy into consideration in nontraditional and traditional academic settings with their varying expectations and purposes to determine its fit as an aspect of academic professionalism.

Dwight F. Burlingame's "Faculty Behaving Well" hinges on the author's expanded definition of philanthropy, draws parallels between faculty and donors, highlights the role faculty play in gaining external philanthropic support for their institutions, and explores creating an academic culture that supports and inspires a philanthropic community. In "Faculty Work as Philanthropy: Doing Good and Doing It Well," Richard C. Turner writes of the need for academic communities to articulate the philanthropic elements of their contributions, as stewards for the public good. The public humanities movement, specifically the development of state humanities councils, and the involvement of humanities faculty, is the focus of Elizabeth Lynn's chapter, "Toward a More Perfect Union: Thought Meets Action in the Philanthropy of State Humanities Councils," which asks what public goods are served by such activities and where the humanities fit into public life. Considering both the for-profit and nonprofit sectors of higher education, in "How Do Faculty in For-Profit Institutions Serve the Public Good?," Denise Mott DeZolt examines how institutional missions and academic cultures can influence faculty philanthropy as engagement, arguing that faculty at all manner of institutions contribute to the public good.

Faculty Leadership and Community Engagement

Directing and applying their research for public purposes, participating in service learning and developing community-based programming, and lending disciplinary expertise for community needs, engaged faculty express their inclinations to make philanthropic contributions to society. Similarly, faculty express their moral obligation to make the world a better place through their leadership and activities to further particular values. They also act on this obligation by working to improve higher education and enhance its public mission. This section explores the connections between engagement, leadership, and philanthropy and the ramifications for faculty work in the future.

In "Beyond the Ivory Tower: Academic Work in the 21st Century," William G. Tierney and Jason F. Perkins decry the tendency of faculty to remain within the academic community, calling on academic peers to engage in the "inevitably philanthropic" pursuit of advocating for societal improvement and encouraging involvement that can align with constructions of academic work. Whether academics, particularly those in human services, live up to the standards of John Dewey and the Progressives as engaged citizen-academics is the subject of Paul S. Shaker's chapter, "Philanthropy and Education Faculty: Renewing Engagement with Teachers and Schools," which also includes a series of successful community-engaged endeavors. "Faculty Grassroots Leadership as Philanthropy," by Adrianna Kezar and Sean Gehrke, contributes to the discussion of the role of extraordinary faculty leaders in effecting broader social change both on campus and off. Jia G. Liang, Lorilee L. Sandmann, and Audrey J. Jaeger, in "Community Engagement: An Expression of Faculty Philanthropy?," define engagement, provide faculty perspectives on engagement as philanthropy, and discuss how the frame of philanthropy fits with principles of engagement.

The Public Good and the Future of Academic Work

The concluding section features the chapter "Reflections on the Public Good and Academic Professionalism," by R. Eugene Rice, John Saltmarsh, and William M. Plater. This chapter looks across the volume contributions to address public policy and the public good in relation to higher education, assessing the usefulness of the philanthropic lens, and addressing the greatest challenges for faculty and their institutions in the coming years.

CHARTING A WAY FORWARD

Exploring the philanthropy within the work of faculty and their contributions to the public good will bring recognition into the discussion about faculty work at a time of threat and opportunity. It will bring clarity and accuracy to discussions about the professoriate and academe. It will foster cultures of philanthropy on our campuses so that we can see, encourage, and celebrate activities for the public good within college and university life. It will provide new roles for emeritus faculty who seek to stay involved in academia. It will generate a new strategy for recognizing how institutions can be citizens through the efforts of their faculty and the public use of their knowledge and scholarship. It will give scholars tools with which to study faculty and their work that can account for more of what they do. It will provide new language for talking about what transpires within universities. This book aims to create an awareness about philanthropy in faculty work that crosses sectors, disciplines, and perspectives, influencing public opinion and public policy as it is disseminated. The chapters should be taken as a resource to help shape future conversations, as a springboard for new research, and as a consideration for personal practice.

Without paying special attention to the philanthropic dimensions of faculty work, such contributions by faculty to the public good may become either casualties to efficiency or a pretext for laying claim to "voluntary action" as time and effort ill-used. An understanding of the philanthropic value and nature of what faculty do may help sustain the vibrancy of the higher education sector, or it may require a sweeping redirection in thinking about accounting for voluntary efforts that have historically enhanced the quality of education and of society. Such redirection could have unforeseen consequences.

There are legitimate concerns. The expectation, however, that activities with philanthropic dimensions will remain unexamined in this period of hyperattention to higher education's budgets and productivity is unrealistic. Accordingly, the public good within faculty work must not remain an unspoken understanding or loosely held secret if it is to be assessed, valued, protected, and maintained. To re-center the position and authority of higher education in the larger society, a new transparency is required to illuminate faculty activities that are most often forgotten or given short shrift.

Growing up in higher education, I knew philanthropy was a force within our institutions. I didn't name it, however, in the many gifts I received as a student, scholar, teacher, administrator, colleague, and friend until I sat in those monthly meetings with my advisor. I now recognize the philanthropy I see at every turn: from the professor who hosted a dinner party for the last day of class, to the colleague who taught class when the instructor was ill, to the friend who read and reread this introduction. We need to show society how to see philanthropy in the work of faculty and, in doing so, turn the tide of public perception and counter the growing view that faculty are a selfish lot who do little for others.

With the swell of criticism, calls for quantifiable productivity measures, and press of economic constraints, the professoriate may be radically redefined even within the decade. The autonomy and empowerment of faculty work as a profession, as we have known it, may soon disappear. In this emerging era, little room may be left for the meaning and satisfaction derived from helping and serving others beyond fulfilling the basic requirements of one's job. Faculty members are aware that higher education, educators, and they themselves can make society better. But being beholden to a moral imperative to improve the public good and having the language to talk about this charge are not the same. A new assertion of, and attention to, the public good that is implicitly expressed in faculty work will give faculty a new way to talk about their work *and* explicitly demonstrate how generously many faculty choose to give of their time, energy, and resources. Making the philanthropic aspects of the faculty profession better known and elucidated will enable those sitting in judgment of faculty to take into account the full scale of a faculty members' work and contributions while empowering faculty to speak more boldly about what motivates them to act for the good of others. By revealing the philanthropy of faculty and naming it as being for the public good, we can make a new case for higher education's future.

REFERENCES

Arum, R., & Roksa, J. (2010). *Academically adrift: Limited learning on college campuses.* Chicago, IL: The University of Chicago Press.

Boyer, E. L. (1990). *Scholarship reconsidered: Priorities of the professoriate.* San Francisco, CA: Carnegie Foundation/Jossey-Bass.

Brint, S. (1996). *In an age of experts: The changing role of professionals in politics and public life.* Princeton, NJ: Princeton University Press.

Curtis, J. W., & Thornton, S. (2013). *The annual report of the economic status of the profession, 2012–2013.* Washington, DC: American Association of University Professors. Available at http://www.aaup.org/file/2012-13Economic-Status-Report.pdf

Duncan, B. (2004). A theory of impact philanthropy. *Journal of Public Economics, 88*(9–10), 2159–2180.

Eisenberg, N., & Mussen, P. H. (1989). *The roots of prosocial behavior in children.* New York, NY: Cambridge University Press.

Gappa, J. M., Austin, A. E., & Trice, A. G. (2007). *Rethinking faculty work: Higher education's strategic imperative*. San Francisco, CA: Jossey-Bass.

Ginsberg, B. (2011). *The fall of the faculty: The rise of the all-administrative university*. Oxford, UK: Oxford University Press.

June, A. W. (2011, September 23). Florida, with an eye on Texas, readies for next conflict over faculty productivity. *The Chronicle of Higher Education*. Available at http://chronicle.texterity.com/chronicle/20110923a?pg=17#pg17

Kennedy, D. (1997). *Academic duty*. Cambridge, MA: Harvard University Press.

MacFarlane, B. (2005). The disengaged academic: The retreat from citizenship. *Higher Education Quarterly, 59*(4), 296–312.

MacFarlane, B. (2007). Defining and rewarding academic citizenship: The implications for university promotions policy. *Journal of Higher Education Policy and Management, 29*(3), 261–273.

O'Meara, K. A., & Rice, R. E. (Eds.). (2005). *Faculty priorities reconsidered: Encouraging multiple forms of scholarship*. San Francisco, CA: Jossey-Bass.

Payton, R. (1988). *Philanthropy: Voluntary action for the public good*. New York, NY: American Council on Education/Macmillan.

Payton, R. L., & Moody, M. P. (2008). *Understanding philanthropy: Its meaning and mission*. Bloomington, IN: Indiana University Press.

Plater, W. M. (1999). Habits of living: Engaging the campus as citizen one scholar at a time. In R. G. Bringle, R. Games, & E. A. Malloy (Eds.), *Colleges and universities as citizens* (pp. 141–172). Needham Heights, MA: Allyn & Bacon.

Plater, W. M. (2011). Collective leadership for engagement: Reclaiming the public purpose of higher education. In J. Saltmarsh & M. Hartley (Eds.), *"To serve a larger purpose": Engagement for democracy and the transformation of higher education* (pp. 102–129). Philadelphia, PA: Temple University Press.

Rice, R. E. (1996). *Making a place for the new American scholar*. American Association for Higher Education. Forum on Faculty Roles and Rewards. Working Paper Series 1.

Salamon, L. M. (1992). *America's nonprofit sector: A primer*. New York, NY: Foundation Center.

Schervish, P. G., & Havens, J. J. (1997). Social participation and charitable giving: A multi-variate analysis. *Voluntas: International Journal of Voluntary and Nonprofit Organizations, 8*(3), 235–260.

Shils, E. (1997). *The calling of education: The academic ethic and other essays on higher education*. Chicago, IL: The University of Chicago Press.

Sulek, M. (2010). On the modern meaning of philanthropy. *Nonprofit and Voluntary Sector Quarterly, 39*(193), 193–212.

Sullivan, W. M. (2007). *Work and integrity: The crisis and promise of professionalism in America*. San Francisco, CA: Jossey-Bass.

Sykes, C. (1990). *Prof scam: Professors and the demise of higher education*. New York, NY: St. Martin's Press.

Turner, R. C. (2010, June). *Faculty work as philanthropy: Doing good and doing it well.* Paper presented at the AAUP Annual Conference on the State of Higher Education. Washington, DC.

Van Til, J. (1990). *Critical issues in American philanthropy: Strengthening theory and practice.* Glenview, IL: AAFRC Trust for Philanthropy.

CHAPTER 2

Voluntary Action for Public Good?

Faculty Work and the Broad Definition of Philanthropy

Michael Moody

This chapter introduces the broad yet contested definition of philanthropy as "voluntary action for the public good." It explores the complexities and usefulness of thinking about philanthropy in this sense and in the specific professional environment of the university. Along the way, we will encounter some complicated but crucial questions about how this definition can apply to faculty work, questions discussed in much greater detail in other chapters. Those chapters dig deeply into many of the issues raised in brief here.

My hope is that this framing chapter provides a touchstone for you, the readers, as you explore the philanthropic nature of faculty work throughout this volume. I invite you to keep these general definitional considerations in mind and to think carefully about where this conception of philanthropy helps illuminate some philanthropic contribution of faculty work—and perhaps, where thinking of faculty work as voluntary action for the public good falls short. By doing so, we can come to a better understanding of the public good contributions of faculty work, an understanding that can help all of us—faculty, students, administrators, policymakers, and advocates for the public good—on all sides of our pressing issues.

FACULTY AS PHILANTHROPISTS?

To many readers, the idea of considering higher education faculty as philanthropists will seem, at best, unusual. The term *philanthropy* often conjures up images of wealthy people giving money, and so a "philanthropist" is someone like Andrew Carnegie or Bill Gates, not someone like your college professor.

But philanthropy is more than giving money, and more than something only the wealthy do. Philanthropy is a much broader and—if you'll pardon the pun—richer concept. And when we recognize this wider meaning of philanthropy, we can see its utility in helping us think about some of the qualities of faculty work that this book explores. Even if some policymakers, unions, administrators, or faculty themselves ultimately decide it is pushing things too far to recategorize faculty members as philanthropists, I argue that there is undeniable benefit to rethinking faculty work as philanthropic.

The definition of philanthropy that informs this book is one offered by the late Robert Payton: "voluntary action for the public good" (Payton, 1988; Payton & Moody, 2008). This way of thinking about philanthropy emphasizes the social benefits from, and moral intent of, philanthropy, and in doing so it harkens back to the original Greek word *philanthrôpía*, meaning "love of mankind" or "love of humanity" (Sulek, 2010a, 2010b). But the modern meaning also focuses on actions, not just sentiments like love or kindness or compassion.

Voluntary action for the public good encompasses a wide array of activity—from helping to giving to serving to advocating, in ways big and small, formal and informal—and it leaves the specific content of the "public good" open. It does not require that all of humanity agree with the philanthropic actor's vision of what is good for humanity. But it does assert that philanthropy is moral action—that is, it is action that intervenes in our world in order to advance a vision of good. Philanthropy is about good works seeking to create a good society.

Just as the notions of "generosity" or "charity" have many subtle meanings and usages, a broad concept of philanthropy can apply outside the narrow framework of institutional or individual donors giving money. Philanthropic action can involve "donors" voluntarily giving "recipients" all sorts of valuable things—time, talent, treasure, wisdom, hope, love, inspiration, knowledge, moral guidance, and on and on—for all sorts of moral, public good purposes—care for the sick, education for children, clean air, historical preservation, religious freedom, an informed citizenry, and on and on.

Still, applying this "voluntary action for the public good" definition to the work that faculty do every day raises questions that are not quickly settled. For one thing, most faculty get paid—even if not very much in many cases—for teaching, research, student advising, and other activities, so how can this work be called "voluntary?" Also, many faculty work for governmental institutions like state universities, and some even are employed by for-profit educational entities, so how can we label this work with a term used primarily in relation to nonprofits? And as faculty are not elected and formally accountable to the public to serve the collective's best interests, how can they be seen as serving *the* public good? Aren't they just professionals doing a paid job, not gallant, altruistic philanthropists dedicated to achieving the public good above all else?

A BROAD, USEFUL, BUT CONTESTED DEFINITION

Philanthropy is an example of what W. B. Gallie called an "essentially contested concept" (Daly, 2012; Payton & Moody, 2008). According to Gallie (1956), essentially contested concepts are ones in which "there is no one clearly definable general use . . . which can be set up as the correct or standard use" and that "inevitably involve endless disputes about their proper uses on the part of their users" (pp. 168–169). An example of such an essentially contested concept, according to Gallie, is "art," and one can see how claiming that faculty work is "artistic" would raise as many questions as claiming it is "philanthropic."

Gallie's point is not that such concepts, because we can't agree about them, are useless. In fact, he argues the opposite: that in the contestation over such concepts we gain better insight into our own and others' ways of thinking and seeing the world, and better understanding of the complexity of the activities or ideas that might be covered by that concept. Such is the case with debating the meaning and application of the concept of philanthropy.

We should acknowledge that most people—even those clearly working directly in the field of philanthropy, like fundraisers or nonprofit executives or foundation staff—define philanthropy in a narrower way than proposed here. Philanthropy in common parlance often means just (1) giving money or, more narrowly, (2) large-scale giving by wealthy philanthropists or, even more narrowly, (3) giving through formal institutions set up either by these wealthy philanthropists or by corporations.

One problem with such narrow conceptions is that they imply that philanthropy is primarily about money. They also separate the giving of money from the giving of other valuables such as time, or talent, or advice. And they separate the giving of money from the organizational mechanisms needed to make good use of that money. Such donor-focused definitions highlight the distance between givers and recipients, and reserve the positive label of philanthropy only for the former.

The ancient concept of philanthropy has depth and versatility beyond the specific notions of giving, or giving money, or giving only by certain people or certain institutions. A broad definition of philanthropy encompasses voluntary giving of all sorts of valuables, as well as voluntary service (formal and informal) and voluntary associations (big and small). The broad definition gathers givers and recipients together under the umbrella of philanthropy. It also allows us to capture an incredible diversity of activity—many sizes and shapes and styles of voluntary action for the public good—under an encompassing term that can stand alongside something like business, another term that is as indefinite as philanthropy but that has largely become accepted as an encompassing label for a very broad and diverse set of activities, not all of which are economic.

Bringing this diversity together under one tent—even if a lively, heterogeneous circus tent like philanthropy—helps us appreciate better the immense importance of philanthropy in our lives, our cultures, our society's past, present, and future. It also opens the idea up to creative adaptation of this expansive concept to reveal what is "philanthropic" about things we might not initially define in that way—adapting the concept as we do, even more liberally, with business or art. So we can see, for instance, how the work of police officers, or tour guides, or doctors (Gunderman, 2009), or even revolutionaries (McCully, 2008), has a crucial element of philanthropy in it, an element we might not otherwise be able to quite put our finger on but that improves our understanding of that work once we think of it in that context.

Philanthropy will remain essentially contested, of course, and the goal here is not to generalize the term so it loses all meaning. Rather, by applying the concept to faculty work, we are deepening our understanding of that work while expanding our complex thinking about philanthropy. Looking at faculty work through an unfamiliar, yet potentially illuminating, new lens can provide insights, even surprises, about the interactions of the various constituents of higher education and the purposes we ascribe to higher learning. It can perhaps even help re-energize faculty work and offer policymakers new ways of seeing the social value of that work.

Voluntary Action?

It is useful, at the start of this volume, to go through the general definition of philanthropy used here and explore the complexities already found in that definition. I look, in turn, at the two key components of the definition on which the volume is based: "voluntary action" and "public good."

According to this definition, philanthropic action is voluntary action. Primarily, *voluntary* here refers to relatively free and uncoerced action. Philanthropic action is neither mandated by law nor done in response to threats or other forms of compulsion. It is about a gift of money, for example, rather than a tax. If you fail to engage in some philanthropic action, no authority has the right to sanction you, at least legally. This does not mean there won't be some potential negative consequences—social, emotional, other—from failing to give or not choosing to act for your view of the good.

Saying philanthropy is voluntary does not mean there is no sense of obligation involved. Voluntary actions can sometimes—even often—be thought of as morally obligatory. People can feel they *"have* to do something" in response to seeing natural disaster victims or some other need. In many religious traditions, for example, giving to the poor is considered a canonically prescribed duty of all believers, about which they have a "choice" only in the sense of choosing whether to be righteous or immoral (Schervish & Whitaker, 2010). Philanthropy is less than a purely "free" choice in this case. Similarly, philanthropy can feel coerced by social pressures, for example, in workplaces where you are expected to give in some way in order to remain in good standing with coworkers and superiors.

However, choosing to act in these cases is still voluntary in the sense that there are no official or legal consequences for not acting. People still have to choose to fulfill their felt obligation to do good. Of course, when such a choice is externally coerced, as in the workplace example, we usually consider this a less "pure" philanthropic voluntary act. This in itself highlights the importance of the voluntary part of our definition.

Another piece of what is often implied by saying philanthropic action is voluntary is the lack of expectation for tangible return. Philanthropy is supposed to be what Kenneth Boulding (1981) called a "one-way transfer of exchangeables." *Volunteering* and *voluntary service* commonly mean a gift of time or talent without financial or other material compensation, and a voluntary gift of money for charitable purposes is different from a "payment" of money for consumer purposes. While there may be a "return" given back to the donor or volunteer, it should be of a different sort from the exchangeable they gave; it should be, say, a word of thanks, an internal feeling of satisfaction or happiness, or perhaps some kind of special access or thank you gift that is more a gesture of thanks than a quid pro quo. For instance, faculty who donate to their own universities might get a thank you letter from the university foundation—maybe even a nice mug.

Here again we see how the inclusion of voluntary action can cause some complexity. What about people employed in nonprofit organizations, for below-market pay and with a strong commitment to the philanthropic mission of their work? This fits as philanthropy under our definition, yet they are getting paid something—and some people who work in these roles are surely "just in it for the job." Or what about Peace Corps, VISTA, or AmeriCorps "volunteers," who are given some compensation for this service—even if just a living stipend and student loan relief—and whose service is technically "paid" for by the government, not a philanthropic entity?

These examples show again that a strict view of voluntary action is pretty unhelpful in covering the full range of action we want to encompass

under the definition of philanthropy. If only action that is completely uncoerced, devoid of obligation, and without any sort of tangible or intangible
return counts as philanthropy, then philanthropy is a thin concept. It is more
useful to think of nonprofit employees as part of the philanthropic sector,
and to recognize the philanthropic purposes of (at least most) AmeriCorps
members, or Teach for America teachers, or others who work for the public
good for minimal pay. We want to count it as philanthropic when people
give under the coercive influence of felt obligation, or when they get something tangible in return like a tote bag or a donor's reception in the museum
before an exhibit opens to the public. We want to be able to see what is
philanthropic about action in diverse contexts.

This more subtle understanding of voluntary action can help us face
some of the tough questions raised earlier, about whether we can count
faculty work as philanthropic if it is done in a government or for-profit educational institution—instead of a nonprofit—or because the faculty worker
gets paid, which all but a few faculty do. If they were in it for the money
only, and the compensation defined the job, I daresay most faculty members
would not stay in the job long. While a few faculty make high salaries, most
do not, and the burgeoning ranks of contingent or adjunct faculty make remarkably little in most cases. Most faculty members would be able to make
more outside academia, especially given their education and expertise. Instead, they choose to do this work at least in part for what we can consider
philanthropic reasons.

My own experience working in higher education for almost 25 years has
convinced me that many faculty, whether they work for a nonprofit college or
a public university, choose to be faculty because it is good work in service of
a good society, a society of educated citizens in which ideas and reason and
research make a difference. This is demonstrated by many examples of faculty
going "above and beyond" their formal responsibilities by taking students on
alternative spring break trips, or volunteering to facilitate community conversations about rising violence, and so on. Some also feel a professional obligation to do faculty work, to train new entrants into a profession—such as social
work, medicine, and law—that wants to maintain the public's trust. And some
see their research as part of a collective public project, an essential effort to
ensure social progress and to make the world a better place by, for instance,
challenging gender stereotypes or reducing the spread of disease through
new public health techniques. To focus on the compensation of these faculty,
or the sector in which they are employed, discounts the philanthropic values
of their chosen work.

Turning to the *action* part of this definition, we see that philanthropic voluntary action can take many forms. It includes both individual and
organized voluntary action, both what we do alone and what we do with

others who share our purpose. It includes many types of action, from providing services to advocating for a cause, to managing volunteers to training trainers, to raising funds, to giving funds. But is also includes things we do spontaneously, informally, or even without thinking—actions as common as helping a stranger get his or her car unstuck from a snowbank, or as rare as rescuing a drowning child from a pond. This same diversity of action can be seen in the various activities of faculty, from offering career advice to a graduating student, to converting research findings into a report for a city agency on the causes of homelessness.

While many of the actions we think of as philanthropy are organized and formalized, often taking place inside institutions, the notion of voluntary action is broader than just formal action connected to nonprofit organizations. The actions of faculty—teaching, research, and service—can fit this understanding of voluntary action, even though these actions are not what we think of as traditional philanthropic actions like soliciting donations or volunteering time.

For the Public Good?

The preceding explanations have already suggested that, while voluntary choice is important, effectively applying our broad definition of philanthropy often relies most heavily on specifying the philanthropic *purpose* of the voluntary action. Voluntary action is philanthropic to the extent that it is meant to serve or achieve the "public good."

The use of the term *public good* implies, for most people, that there is an absolute good out there somewhere—a single "correct" vision of the good—and that we (or someone) can know for certain what it is. This understanding of the public good is problematic for a few reasons. For one thing, it can feed the belief that philanthropic actors are condescending or paternalistic, imposing what they *know* is "the" public good on those who are affected by their philanthropy. This has been a recurring criticism of philanthropy throughout its history (Friedman & McGarvie, 2003).

Another version of the absolutist view of the public good is that it is entirely separate from any individual self-interest or group special interest. This is how Jean-Jacques Rousseau ([1762] 1987) defined the "general will" and how James Madison ([1788] 1961), in his famous essay "Number 10" of *The Federalist Papers*, defined the interests of "factions" as diametrically opposed to the "permanent and aggregate interests of the community" (p. 78).

But what about a disability rights advocacy group that mobilizes the disabled and their supporters to fight for their rights and, in doing so, helps ensure benefits and a better world for disabled people everywhere? Is this then *not* public good–oriented action because it benefits the actors in some special way? Or what about a political science professor who incorporates a service learning component into an American government course, to serve the community and help create educated citizens to improve our democracy, but then uses data from those service activities to write an article that helps her with tenure and promotion? Are self-interest and the public good two sides of a seesaw (Lichterman, 1996)? Or do we want to allow for the fact that action can be intended primarily to advance a public good, while at the same time benefiting the actor in some way?

Instead of thinking of "the" public good in this pure, absolute sense, it is more helpful to think of the public good as something constantly contested and debated (Mansbridge, 1998), and voluntary philanthropic action as pursuing "a" vision of the public good, not "the" only vision. The public good is an aspiration worth discussing and arguing about as well as pursuing through action but is not a preexisting and fixed standard to be achieved. Philanthropic action is defined by this voluntary pursuit of some actor's vision of the good—even if that vision is more implicit in the action than always explicit in the mind or words of the actor. And this public good mission of philanthropic actors is often mixed in with other, even egoistic intentions or consequences of the action. Think of corporate philanthropy, for instance, which is often seen as motivated by "enlightened self-interest"—giving in the local community helps the community *and* helps the corporation.

Put another way, acting for the public good is not the same as acting altruistically—although of course these are not mutually exclusive. Philanthropy is defined by the public good purpose or moral intent of the action, not by the pure altruistic motive of the action.

The public good intention of philanthropic action does not, of course, guarantee good outcomes in all cases. Donors as well-known as Bill and Melinda Gates have come to realize that sometimes their intended good was not achieved because of a flawed theory of change, organizational mishaps, or other causes (Moody, 2011). What matters—for definitional purposes anyway—is that their voluntary action was intended to advance the public good, that a vision of public good was the goal.[1]

Philanthropy in this sense becomes a way that people affirm and advance their visions of the good. More broadly, the meaning of the public good in any society is determined partly—sometimes primarily—through philanthropy. If the public good is not "found" but "forged" in the public sphere, as Craig Calhoun (1998) puts it, then philanthropy is a chief means by which we as a society contest and create our shared conversation about the public good. Just because different groups or individuals disagree on the definition of the good does not mean that their voluntary actions in pursuit of their particular definition are not philanthropic. Both law professors

working pro bono to get prisoners off death row and criminal justice professors writing op-eds about the deterrent effect of the death penalty fit under
this view of philanthropic action for the public good. Opposing voluntary
actors often advance opposing visions of the good, but both sides are philanthropic in their choice to act for what they think is right. And somewhere in
the middle of this philanthropic maelstrom we forge a contested, evolving
public good.[2]

Philanthropy in this definition is fundamentally *moral* action, in two
senses: (1) Philanthropy is a primary vehicle people use to implement their
moral imagination and to shape and advance the moral agenda of our society; and (2) Philanthropy is about voluntarily intervening in other people's
lives for their benefit, to do them good and to advance the public good. The
moral, public good purpose of a philanthropic action becomes in this view
its key defining characteristic. And philanthropic actors are seen as acting
out their moral imagination, their vision of how things could be better and
how a good society should look and act. As described earlier, faculty often
conduct their work with a definite moral, public good purpose—for example, to advance knowledge that can improve people's lives, to provide the
facts or skills needed to solve tough public problems—so the philanthropic
property of this work is clear.

What about the challenge raised at the beginning that faculty might
be just pursuing their own subjective view of the good, not what is *really*
for the public good? This is in fact one of the more common criticisms of
faculty today, especially from the political right. Faculty are advancing a
one-sided view of what's good, the argument goes, and even indoctrinating
our children in this subjective, partisan ideology. If we think of the public
good as constantly contested, and philanthropy as a primary means for this
contestation that forges our moral agenda, then this criticism doesn't deny
the philanthropic element to faculty work—even by those faculty who *are*
overtly partisan. In fact, by saying that faculty use their position to advance
some set of values or moral creed, these critics are saying what many in this
volume claim: that those faculty are voluntarily acting for (their view of) the
public good.

Taking this a step further, we might even consider faculty work as dis-
tinctively focused on this lively contestation over the public good that is
at the core of philanthropy. Higher education is, after all, where the free
discourse about ideas and visions of good are fostered and encouraged. Faculty engage in this vital questioning and debate about the public good in
the classroom and in their scholarship, as well as when they look outside
the academy and engage in public actions like "thought leadership" on a
social issue or consulting on a community project. The work of faculty often

surfaces the public good contestation underneath our actions, which we often leave implicit. Faculty can even help us reflect on the broader moral conceptions in play when we intervene in the world, and in doing so, they can sharpen our sense of the philanthropic nature of those voluntary actions.

Still, for most faculty the public good they want to pursue in their work is a more general and widely valued one. It is the public good of education in itself, and of intellectual work. They devote their careers to the moral ideal that a good society requires well-educated citizens, thoroughly reasoned ideas, and a commitment to empirical fact. This sense of a higher calling for higher education, and faculty as its leaders, has taken many forms over the years, from Ralph Waldo Emerson's ([1837] 1957) argument about the public duty of the "American scholar" and Woodrow Wilson's (1896) vision of universities "in the nation's service" to Paulo Freire's (1970) "critical pedagogy."

In whatever form, this social responsibility and public role of higher education is a core reason we can consider faculty work as philanthropic work. This faculty work for the public good, or for the "love of humanity"—the original Greek concept of *philanthrôpía*—deserves greater recognition and critical analysis. The following chapters in this volume are a great place to start.

NOTES

Portions of this chapter are adapted from Payton and Moody (2008), used with permission. Thanks to Genevieve Shaker for terrific comments on earlier drafts.

1. Dwight Burlingame, in this volume (see Chapter 9) and elsewhere, has proposed modifying Payton's definition to "voluntary action intended for the public good." Philanthropists like those of the Gates Foundation also extend this notion of intention beyond the initial reason for giving; it includes monitoring consequences and adjusting action to achieve the public good goal better with future actions.

2. Siobhan Daly (2012) explains in more detail how "what the public good is (descriptive aspects) and how it should be served (normative aspects) are inherent to the contestability of the concept of philanthropy" (p. 544).

REFERENCES

Boulding, K. E. (1981). *A preface to grants economics: The economy of love and fear.* New York, NY: Praeger.
Calhoun, C. (1998). The public good as a social and cultural project. In W. Powell & E. Clemens (Eds.), *Private action and the public good* (pp. 20–35). New Haven, CT: Yale University Press.

Daly, S. (2012). Philanthropy as an essentially contested concept. *Voluntas, 23*(3), 535–557.

Emerson, R. W., & Whicher, S. E. ([1837] 1957). *Selections from Ralph Waldo Emerson: An organic anthology.* Boston, MA: Houghton Mifflin.

Freire, P. (1970). *Pedagogy of the oppressed.* New York, NY: Herder and Herder.

Friedman, L. J., & McGarvie, M. D. (Eds.). (2003). *Charity, philanthropy, and civility in American history.* New York, NY: Cambridge University Press.

Gallie, W. (1956). Essentially contested concepts. *Proceedings of the Aristotelian Society, 56,* pp. 167–198. London, UK: Harrison and Sons.

Gunderman, R. B. (2009). *We make a life by what we give.* Bloomington, IN: Indiana University Press.

Lichterman, P. (1996). *The search for political community: American activists reinventing commitment.* Cambridge, UK: Cambridge University Press.

Madison, J. (1961). Number 10. In C. Rossiter (Ed.), *The Federalist Papers.* New York, NY: Penguin Books. (Original work published 1788)

Mansbridge, J. (1998). On the contested nature of the public good. In W. Powell & E. Clemens (Eds.), *Private action and the public good* (pp. 3–19). New Haven, CT: Yale University Press.

McCully, G. (2008). *Philanthropy reconsidered: Private initiatives, public good, quality of life.* Bloomington, IN: AuthorHouse.

Moody, M. (2011). A Hippocratic oath for philanthropists. In D. R. Forsyth & C. L. Hoyt (Eds.), *For the greater good of all: Perspectives on individualism, society, and leadership* (pp. 143–165). New York, NY: Palgrave Macmillan.

Payton, R. L. (1988). *Philanthropy: Voluntary action for the public good.* New York, NY: American Council on Education/Macmillan.

Payton, R. L., & Moody, M. P. (2008). *Understanding philanthropy: Its meaning and mission.* Bloomington, IN: Indiana University Press.

Rousseau, J. J. (1987). *The social contract* (D. A. Cress, Trans.). Indianapolis, IN: Hackett. (Original work published 1762.)

Schervish, P. G., & Whitaker, A. K. (2010). *Wealth and the will of God: Discerning the use of riches in the service of ultimate purpose.* Bloomington, IN: Indiana University Press.

Sulek, M. (2010a). On the classical meaning of *philanthrôpía. Nonprofit and Voluntary Sector Quarterly, 39*(3), 385–406.

Sulek, M. (2010b). On the modern meaning of philanthropy. *Nonprofit and Voluntary Sector Quarterly, 39*(2), 193–212.

Wilson, W. (1896, October 21). Princeton in the nation's service. Commemorative Address. Available at http://infoshare1.princeton.edu/libraries/firestone/rbsc/mudd/online_ex/wilsonline/indn8nsvc.html

CHAPTER 3

Recovering the Original Meaning of Philanthropy

A Prelude to Consideration of the Philanthropy of Faculty Work

Marty Sulek

In order to better understand the philanthropy of college faculty, it is useful to first clarify what, exactly, is meant by *philanthropy* in this context. Contemporary scholars tend to define philanthropy as the private giving of time or valuables for public purposes (see Martin, 1994, p. 246; Salamon, 1992, pp. 5–6; 1999, p. 10). Given the preponderance of this definition within the academic field of philanthropic studies, scholarly considerations of the philanthropy of faculty are bound to focus on how much time faculty members dedicate to their professional activities over and above the requirements of their jobs as teachers and researchers, including their frequent involvement in the fundraising and development activities of the (mostly) nonprofit institutions of higher learning at which they are employed.

This situation naturally raises important questions about the nature of the philanthropy of faculty. Are their discretionary activities in support of their institutions a personal choice to act philanthropically or a professional duty rendered to their educational institutions, an expectation of all faculty regardless of their "choosing"? In order to address this question, it is necessary to first examine the philanthropy of faculty in their principal occupations of research and teaching—in which they ideally make scholarly discoveries that increase human understanding and inspire students to realize their fullest potential through their learning activities—as well as the intrinsically epistemological and pedagogical dimensions of philanthropy itself.

As it happens, the conception of philanthropy as a philosophical ideal informing the pursuit, discovery, and sharing of knowledge through teaching activities has an extremely long history that can be traced back to the very origin of the term as it was conceived in classical Athens. As is well

31

known, *philanthropy* derives from φιλανθρωπία (the nominative noun form of the word in ancient Greek, transliterated into Latin characters as *philanthrôpía*), which literally translates as "love of humanity." As is also generally known, *philanthrôpía* was first employed in a mid-5th-century BCE tragedy titled *Prometheus Bound*,[1] the authorship of which has traditionally been ascribed to Aeschylus, albeit mistakenly.[2] At the very beginning of this seminal play, two characters—Kratos and Hephaestus—indict and punish Prometheus, primarily because of his "philanthropic character" or "way" (*philanthrôpou trópou*, lines 11, 28).

The single most significant manifestation of the Titan Prometheus's philanthropic character is, of course, his well-known theft of fire from the gods, and gifting of it to humans. In the central episode of the play (lines 436–525), though, Prometheus presents a comprehensive account of his gifts to humanity that points to the essentially epistemological and pedagogical nature of fire as a metaphor. There, he first describes how he initially put mind (*ënnous*) and reason (*phrenôn*) in humans (line 444); he then goes on to describe himself as the discoverer and teacher of all human arts (*téchnai broto sin*) (lines 447–506). The philanthropic character of Prometheus, and the gift of "fire" that it motivates, is thus intrinsically tied to his pedagogical acts of having instilled intellect in humans, and having "discovered" and "taught" them all the arts and sciences.

The meaning and significance of the central episode of *Prometheus Bound* has long formed a sharp point of controversy among classical scholars. My own assessment of this episode has led me to conclude that the character of Prometheus, as depicted in the *Prometheia* trilogy, is nothing less than an allegorical representation of Protagoras, widely acknowledged as the first and greatest of the sophists, or professional teachers, in classical Greece (Sulek, 2011, pp. 79–200). The use of *philanthrôpía* in the *prólogos* of *Prometheus Bound*, to condemn the essential character of Prometheus, may thus be plausibly interpreted as having constituted a central value in the philosophical humanism of Protagoras, widely acknowledged as the harbinger of the 5th-century sophistic enlightenment. Recovering this classical conception of *philanthrôpía*, to describe the character of one of the greatest teachers of classical Greece, thus brings the concept of philanthropy into much closer alignment with the work of faculty.

PROMETHEUS'S PHILANTHROPIC CHARACTER

In the opening prologue of *Prometheus Bound*, Prometheus is twice indicted for his "philanthropic character [*philanthrôpou trópou*]" by Kratos (Power) and Hephaestus, the god of fire and craft (lines 11, 28). While both these gods indict Prometheus for his philanthropic character, they also differ in several important respects. Kratos emphasizes Prometheus's theft of fire and disloyalty toward the tyranny of Zeus, while Hephaestus points to how he does not fear the gods and honors mortals beyond what is just. Despite these differences, though, both gods agree that his philanthropic way is a transgression that requires severe punishment. Prometheus, for his part, far from denying his philanthropic character and gifts to humans, trenchantly affirms them shortly after the exit of his tormentors: lamenting his punishment for "bestowing gifts on mankind [*thnêto s gàr géra*]" (line 107) and outright declaring his "overmuch love of mortal men [*lían philótêta brotôn*]!" (line 122). Later, the only human in the play, Io, also addresses Prometheus as "O bringer-to-light [*phaneís*] of universal benefit [*ôphélêma*] to mortals" (line 613). Clearly, then, philanthropy constitutes an integral part of Prometheus's nature and forms the primary motive of the many benefits he has provided mortal humans. In the same way, it is the philanthropic character of Protagoras and all truly talented teachers that forms the primary motivation for their research and teaching activities, as opposed to the job requirements of their profession.

Greek tragedy was often a reflection of, and commentary on, the social, cultural, and political environment in which it was initially performed (Meier, 1993). Assuming this interpretive hypothesis to also apply to *Prometheus Bound*, the question naturally arises: To what or whom does that play's depiction of the philanthropic character of Prometheus refer? The single most obvious piece of textual evidence pointing to Prometheus of the *Prometheia* trilogy as being an allegorical representation of Protagoras is the fact that the Titan is twice referred to as a sophist (*sophistês*) in *Prometheus Bound*, by Kratos in the *prologos* (line 62) and Hermes in the *exodos* (line 944). Employing the word *sophist* to describe a teacher represented a rather novel form of usage in the context of mid-5th-century Greece (Sulek, 2011, pp. 152–156). Furthermore, this novel usage would seem to have been coined by Protagoras, who describes himself as the first and greatest of the sophists (Plato, *Protagoras* 317b-c).

Several other textual clues also support the interpretation of Prometheus as an allegorical representation of Protagoras. When the chorus of Okeanids first encounter Prometheus in the *parados* of the play, for instance, the first gift he describes himself as having given humans is "blind hopes [*tuphlàs èlpídas*]" (line 250). This somewhat positive, albeit ambivalent, appraisal of the status of hope stands in stark contrast to virtually the entire tradition of Greek literature (see Schmid, 1929, pp. 95–96; Herington, 1963, p. 191), beginning with Hesiod's primordial description of hope as the one thing that Pandora retains in the jar after releasing from it all the evils that afflict men (*Works and Days*, 116). Interestingly, though, one of the earliest reappraisals of the status of hope is found in Heraclitus (frags. 18, 27), who is thought to have deeply influenced Protagoras (see Nietzsche, 1968, p. 233; Schiappa, 2003, p. 108). As well, one of the most famous invocations of hope in all of classical Greek literature is found in the "Ode to Man" in Sophocles's *Antigone* (lines 359–367), which has long been recognized as having been decisively influenced by Protagoras (Crane, 1989, p. 109).

Even more decisive than Prometheus's gift of hope in establishing his connection to Protagoras, though, is his gift of fire. As both Guthrie (1971, pp. 63–64) and West (1979, p. 147) note, the single closest parallel to Prometheus's elaboration of what he did for humans, in the second episode of *Prometheus Bound* (lines 436–525), is found in the Promethean myth that Protagoras tells in Plato's dialogue named for the great sophist (*Protagoras* lines 320c–324d). Given these decisive parallels, and many more, it is reasonable to assume that Prometheus is an allegorical representation of Protagoras and that the philanthropic character of the great sophist played a critical role in the formulation and expression of his philosophical humanism.

PLATO'S SUBSTANTIATION OF THE PHILANTHROPIC PROTAGORAS

Corroboration for the hypothesis that philanthropy played an integral role in the expression of Protagoras's ideas comes from Plato's depiction of him in his dialogue named for the great sophist (or teacher). There, Plato depicts Protagoras's prominently referring to "misanthropes" in a manner that not only demonstrates his familiarity with the concept of *philanthrôpía*, but also sheds light on how it likely informed his philosophical outlook. Near the beginning of Plato's *Protagoras*, shortly after Protagoras relates his version of the Promethean myth (lines 320c–324d), in a speech (*epideixis*) that closely parallels the central episode of *Prometheus Bound* (lines 447–506), he further illustrates one of the key points of his myth—namely, that all civilized men have at least some small share of justice—with reference to the "misanthropes [*misánthrôpoi*]" that appeared in Pherecrates's comedy 'Agrioi (*Protagoras* 327d).[3] Protagoras further states that this play premiered the previous year (i.e., in 434 BCE) in the Lenaia, an Athenian dramatic festival mounted primarily for the performance of comedies.[4]

'Agrioi were wild folk, whose appellative means "living in the fields," and who represent one aspect of the antithesis of civilized humanity, as depicted in Pherecrates's play. The other aspect of this antithesis is the play's chorus, composed of a group of misanthropes (*misánthrôpoi*) from the city who, disgusted by the injustice they have experienced at the hands of people there, flee to the countryside. Once in the wilds, though, the chorus of misanthropes find themselves even further dismayed by the outlandishly unjust behavior of the 'agrioi, wild savages who make even the wickedest city dwellers seem positively just by comparison—a situation naturally ripe with comedic possibilities. The misanthropes who flee the city for the wilderness in 'Agrioi may thus be construed as somewhat of a comic inversion of the philanthropic Prometheus, whose gifts of discovering and teaching all human knowledge are what brought about the rise of human civilization in the first place. Pherecrates's 'Agrioi thus appears to be the first in a series of prominent Old Attic comedies that parodied various aspects of the *Prometheia* trilogy, other notable instances of which include Cratinus's *Ploutoi* (429 BCE) and Aristophanes's *Birds* (414 BCE).[5]

Protagoras's reference to *misánthrôpoi* in Plato's *Protagoras* is highly anomalous in the context of extant texts dating to the 5th century. Plato, writing in the early to mid-4th century, is the first Greek writer to employ this neologism in his extant works;[6] and Protagoras's utterance of it in the dialogue named for him is one of the earliest uses of the word within the dramatic frame of Plato's dialogues.[7] Given the novelty of *philanthrôpía* as a word and concept, and its prominence in describing the character of Prometheus in *Prometheus Bound*, plus the anomaly of Protagoras's contemporary reference to *misánthrôpoi* in the course of expositing on his own pedagogical philosophy, these terms may be reasonably accepted as having likely expressed conceptual opposites in the humanistic ideals of Protagorean philosophy and his novel conceptions of human civilization and the gods.

Protagoras's lost book, *On the Original State of Things*, likely exercised a decisive influence on the composition of the central episode of *Prometheus Bound*, where Prometheus describes what he did for humans. In that episode, Prometheus's gift of fire is transformed into a metaphor for having implanted mind and reason in humans, discovering and teaching all the human arts, and thereby acting as the catalyst of human historical progress, from savagery to civilization. As is made clear from the outset of the play, the gifts of Prometheus are fundamentally motivated by his philanthropic character. In a similar vein, Protagoras argues that the sophistic art of educating humans is an ancient one (Plato, *Protagoras* lines 316d–e), that the development and dissemination of the technical and political arts have played a decisive role in the advancement of human civilization (Plato, *Protagoras* lines 321d–322d), and that his own practice of the sophistic art consists of teaching virtue in the form of good counsel regarding both private and public affairs (Plato, *Protagoras* lines 318e–319a).

Protagoras wasn't just a talented pedagogue who taught virtue and good counsel. He also played an active role in politics, serving as a close advisor to Pericles, who commissioned him in the late 440s to write the laws for the newly founded, Panhellenic colony of Thurii, strategically located in southern Italy. The illustrious political career of Protagoras is amply reflected in the depiction of Prometheus in the *Prometheia* trilogy. In the second episode of *Prometheus Bound*, Prometheus describes himself as having once served as a close advisor to Zeus in his war against the Titans (lines 232–240). Only after Zeus resolved "to destroy all human kind and sow new seed on earth," and Prometheus opposed him by freeing humans from death and destruction, was he punished for his philanthropy. The last play of the *Prometheia* trilogy, *Prometheus Unbound*, is also thought to have ended with a rapprochement between Prometheus and Zeus, thus signifying the (re)establishment of the joint rule of power and wisdom.

The need for wise rulers is a theme that appears throughout Plato's works, most notably in the *Republic*, where Socrates calls for the rule of the philosopher-kings, stating that there will be "no rest from ills for the cities" until "political power and philosophy coincide" (lines 5.473c–d). Plato also implicitly associates this idea with Protagoras in *Laws*, where the Athenian Stranger advises an elder Spartan and Cretan on creating the laws for a newly founded city. There, the Athenian Stranger's calls for the worship of a philanthropic god "who truly rules as a despot over those with intellect." This may be read as a rather transparent allegory calling for the philanthropic wise to exercise just rule for the benefit of ordinary humans. At the same time, though, the Athenian Stranger also strenuously condemns the seeming relativism expressed in Protagoras's "Man is the measure" fragment (#1). Shortly after describing the philanthropic god who rules over those with intellect, the Athenian Stranger states that, ideally, "the god would be the measure of all things in the highest degree, and far more so than some 'human being [*änthrôpos*]' as some assert" (line 4.716c). The true measure of what is, then, is not just taken from the perspective of any human being, but is derived, rather, from an intellect that embraces a philanthropic ideal, and characterized as a god-figure, according to the more pious public teaching of the Athenian Stranger.

Not only was Protagoras the first and greatest of the sophists; he also taught his students a unique curriculum that aptly reflected his philosophical humanism. In contrast to his fellow sophists, who expounded on various technical subjects, Protagoras emphatically describes himself as teaching good counsel and civic virtue in ordering the affairs of one's family and city, with the aim of making his students good citizens (Plato, *Protagoras* lines 318d–e). Although generally critical of Protagoras, Socrates took a very similar pedagogic approach to the venerable sophist in his own teaching activities, posing questions to his students, usually on their assumed knowledge of the nature of the virtues, rather than attempting to instruct them in technical subjects. This remains an important point for modern educational institutions that, with the increasing specialization of the disciplines, gravitate more and more toward the teaching of technical knowledge and lack the resources or inclination to teach subjects that would instill more philanthropic skills, such as virtues of character, good judgment, and civic engagement.

Perhaps the single best summation of Socrates's pedagogical philosophy in relation to philanthropy is found in Plato's *Symposium*. There, various luminaries in Athenian intellectual society present several *impromptu* speeches in praise of the god Eros, or Love. In the central speech of that dialogue, Aristophanes praises Eros as

> the most philanthropic [*philanthropotatos*] of gods, a helper of human beings as well as a physician dealing with an illness the healing of which would result in the greatest happiness for the human race. (Plato, *Symposium* lines 189c–189d)

The authenticity of this speech in relation to Aristophanes's own views is corroborated by the parallel wording Aristophanes employs in his comedy *Peace* (premiered in 421) in which the chorus superlatively praises another daemonic divinity, Hermes, as "most philanthropic [*philanthrôpótate*]" of the gods (line 394).[8] A political conservative, Aristophanes was highly critical of Protagoras and the sophists, as demonstrated in *Clouds* (premiered 423) in which the comic poet lampoons their teachings in the character of Socrates. As Socrates demonstrates in his subsequent speech in praise of Eros, though, he is the epitome of the philanthropic teacher, whose highest intellectual inquiry is discovering the causes of growth of the love of knowledge in his students, and whose highest pedagogical aim is to promote their love of wisdom.

As has been mentioned, Protagoras is generally regarded as the originator and most influential proponent of the philosophical humanism that was the hallmark of the 5th-century sophistic enlightenment.[9] A similarly humanistic expression of philanthropy, and corresponding hatred of misanthropic gods, is also found in Plato's *Euthyphro*. There, Socrates is depicted on his way to answer charges of not believing in the gods of the city and corrupting its youth. On the very steps of the courthouse where he is to be arraigned, he encounters a pious priest named Euthyphro, who initially attempts to make common cause with Socrates, on the basis of their mutual relation to the divine; in Socrates's case, a divine sign, or daemon, that occasionally advises him (see Plato, *Apology* line 31d; Xenophon, *Memorabilia* 4.8.1). Socrates, though, sharply differentiates himself from Euthyphro in the following terms:

Perhaps you seem to make yourself available only infrequently and not to
be willing to teach your wisdom. But I fear that I, because of my *philan-
thrôpias*, seem to them to pour out whatever I possess to every man, not
only without pay, but even with pleasure if anyone is willing to listen to me.
(Plato, *Euthyphro* line 3d)

Socrates thus distinguishes himself from the self-declared piety, and
implicit misanthropy, of Euthyphro, who not only seems unavailable or
unwilling to teach his wisdom but also unthinkingly holds up the example
of Zeus's binding his father, Kronos, as justification for bringing man-
slaughter charges against his own father, the legal basis for which is highly
questionable. Socrates's philanthropy, by contrast, not only makes him
seem to share his wisdom with everyone but also makes him willing to do
so without pay, and even with pleasure, if anyone is willing to listen. Not
only that, but he voluntarily obeys the laws of the city and submits himself
to its judgments, even after it sentences him to death.

PERCEPTIONS OF PHILANTHROPY IN THE PROGRESSIVE ERA

While the pedagogical meaning of *philanthropy* has been almost entirely
eclipsed in contemporary usage of the term (Sulek, 2010a), it is nevertheless still strongly reflected in the theory and practice of, for instance, several
seminal figures in the Progressive movement, beginning in the late 19th
century, who advocated a more scientific approach to philanthropy. Andrew
Carnegie, for instance, emphatically counseled prospective philanthropists
to *wisely* administer the distribution of their wealth so as to encourage
self-reliance among their beneficiaries and to not cause "pauperism" (i.e.,
dependence on charitable benefactions) (Carnegie, 1993, p. 9). His adher-
ence to this principle in his own philanthropy may be seen, for instance,
in the vast support he provided for the construction of municipal libraries,
thereby providing people the means to become self-sufficient by educating
themselves, as he himself had done. John D. Rockefeller Sr., by comparison,
founded several institutions dedicated to scientific research and education,
most notably, the Rockefeller Institute for Medical Research (now Rockefeller University) and the University of Chicago. As Frederick Gates (1977),
the chief administrator of Rockefeller's philanthropies, once remarked,
"The values of research are universal values," and the scientific discoveries made by the institute were as universal as the love of God. As Gates
observed, "This philanthropy alone is as wide as the race" (pp. 185–186).

The self-consciously Promethean nature of Rockefeller's philanthropy
is reflected in several other aspects of his life and work. It is aptly reflected

in the mission statement of the Rockefeller Foundation, for instance, as articulated in its founding charter: "to promote the well-being of mankind throughout the world." It is also discernible from the prominent placement given to one of the most famous statues of Prometheus in the world. Commissioned by Rockefeller's son, John Jr., and sculpted by Paul Manship, *Prometheus* was installed in 1933 in the central plaza of the Rockefeller Center in New York. Above this most prominently placed statue is an inscription that reads:

> Prometheus, teacher in every art, brought the fire
> that hath proved to mortals a means to mighty ends.

This inscription paraphrases a passage from *Prometheus Bound* (lines 110–111), where Prometheus elaborates on the good gifts (*géra*) he bestowed on mortals (line 107). In the passage Rockefeller chose to commemorate Prometheus, the first philanthropist, he thus specifically focuses on his role as a teacher of the arts.

From both the explicit statements and actions of Carnegie and Rockefeller, then, it is apparent that these two influential founding figures of modern American philanthropy had far more in mind in exercising their self-described philanthropy than simply "giving away" time and money for public purposes, for their overt acts of philanthropy had an accompanying epistemological and pedagogical purpose that was integral to the fulfillment of the intent directing those acts. Furthermore, the self-consciously Promethean manner in which they strove to administer their philanthropy, in a way that advanced the discovery and dissemination of knowledge, strongly correlates with the philosophical philanthropy of faculty as discussed in this book, understood as both a passion and an ideal that motivates faculty to benefit society by successfully discovering new forms of knowledge, and instilling that wisdom in their students, thereby providing "a means to mighty ends."

FACULTY WORK AS PHILANTHROPY

The Promethean/Protagorean way in which Socrates's philanthropy manifests itself, as a prime motivator of his pedagogical activities, brings us again to consideration of the philanthropy of university faculty. At the beginning of this chapter, I rhetorically posed the question of whether the discretionary research and teaching activities of faculty, over and above what is strictly required of them by their institution, can be considered philanthropy; or is it simply the fulfillment of their duty to the institution? What the exploration of the origins of philanthropy in the philosophical humanism of Protagoras shows, I believe, is that research and teaching constitute the very essence of the expression of the philanthropy of faculty; those activities being the primary ways in which faculty attain their philanthropic aim—the greater realization of human potential in society as a whole—through the discovery and dissemination of new forms of knowledge and the development of their beloved students' intellectual faculties. In fact, I would go so far as to say that the philanthropic duty of faculty to their institution today extends only so far as it, too, manifests these higher goals.

NOTES

1. See Lorenz, 1914; Pearson 1997; Sulek, 2010a, 2010b; Tromp de Ruiter, 1932, 2004.

2. See Griffith, 1977; West, 1979, 1990, pp. 51–71.

3. Protagoras's mention of Pherecrates's comedy 'Agrioi, has presented one of the major impediments to positively establishing the dramatic date of Plato's *Protagoras*. However, the primary ancient source for dating the premiere of 'Agrioi is Athenaeus (fl. late 2nd to early 3rd century AD), who states that it was staged during the archonship of Aristion (5.218d–e), that is, in 421/420 BCE. In making this assessment, Athenaeus likely relied on a *didasclalia*, an official public record of a play's performance. However, he also lived more than 6 centuries after the facts he describes in this case, and thus his assessments should be regarded with caution. From other sources, it is also known that Pherecrates gained his first victory during the archonship of Theodorus, that is, 438 BCE (Anonymous, *On Comedy*, p. 29, as quoted in Smith [1867, vol. 3, p. 257, s.v. Pherecrates]). Given that Aristophanes is known to have revised *Clouds* after it was first produced, in 423, it is not unreasonable to conjecture that Pherecrates could have premiered 'Agrioi in 434 but revised and restaged it in 421/420, when he won his victory with it. The single most decisive piece of evidence in assessing the date of 'Agrioi, though, comes from inscriptions, in which Pherecrates is recorded as having been victorious in the City Dionysia festival in the mid-440s (IG II² 2325. 56), and twice at the Lenaia festival, the first time in the mid- to late 430s (IG II² 2325. 122). It is tempting to conclude that this latter inscription records Pherecrates's victory at the Lenaia with 'Agrioi, as the mid- to late 430s precisely matches the date Protagoras gives in Plato's *Protagoras*, 434 BCE being the year before the dramatic date of that dialogue.

4. Beginning in 432, the Lenaia also began including a competition for tragedies.

5. The scene from Aristophanes's *Peace* (premiered 421) where the chorus describes Hermes, messenger of the Olympians, as "most philanthropic of the gods" could also be interpreted as parodying Prometheus, whom Hesychius describes as the messenger of the Titans (*Lexicon* i387, s.v. "Ithas").

6. Plato employs the term in *Laws* (7.791d), *Protagoras* (327d), and *Phaedo* (89d). The next writer to employ the word *misanthropy* in his extant works is Isocrates, who uses the word a couple of times in a later speech of his (Speech 15, *Antidosis* 131, 135) written in 354 and 353, only 4 or 5 years before Plato's death.

7. Protagoras's use of the word *misánthrôpoi* in Plato's *Protagoras* is likely antedated by the Athenian Stranger's reference to how "extreme, savage enslavement" makes the young "misanthropic [*misanthrôpous*]," rendering them "unsuited for living with others" (Plato, *Laws* 7.791d, trans. Pangle). Traditional scholarship has tended to maintain that *Laws* has no discernable dramatic date (see Nails, 2002). Zuckert (2009, p. 8, 11), on the other hand, dates the dramatic action of *Laws* to sometime between 460 and 450 BCE, based on the fact that it contains many references to the Persian Wars (which formally ended in 449 BCE, with the Peace of Callias), but no references to the Peloponnesian War (which began in 331 BCE). At the same time, *Laws* contains a direct reference to the opening of Protagoras's book *Truth*, in which he states, "Man is the measure of all things" (*Laws*, 4.716c; see Protagoras, frag. 1). *Laws* would thus appear to be an account of pre-Socratic political philosophy, the dramatic date of which occurs shortly after the first arrival of Protagoras in Athens, which West (1979, p. 147) dates to sometime in the late 450s or early 440s.

8. As noted above (note 5), this reference to Hermes, the messenger of Zeus, may be read as a comic reference to Prometheus, who was also known as a messenger, albeit of the Titans (Hesychius, *Lexicon,* s.v. "Ithas").

9. The most succinct statement of his humanistic outlook comes from his book *Truth*, in which he declares, "Man is the measure of all things" (frag. 1). It is also reflected in his agnostic view of the gods, as expressed in the opening line of his book *On The Gods*: "Concerning the gods I am unable to know whether they exist or whether they do not exist, or what they are like in form" (frag. 4). The philosophical humanism of Protagoras is also reflected, of course, in *Prometheus Bound*, where Prometheus declares that he loves mortal humans (line 122) and detests all gods who punish him for the benefits he has provided them (lines 975–976).

REFERENCES

Carnegie, A. (1993). *The gospel of wealth.* Indianapolis, IN: Indiana University, Center on Philanthropy.

Crane, G. (1989). Creon and the "Ode to Man" in Sophocles' *Antigone. Harvard Studies in Classical Philology*, 92, 103–116.

Gates, F. T. (1977). *Chapters in my life.* New York, NY: Free Press.

Griffith, M. (1977). *The authenticity of "Prometheus Bound."* Cambridge, UK: Cambridge University Press.

Guthrie, W. K. (1971). *The Sophists.* Cambridge, UK: Cambridge University Press.

Herington, C. J. (1963, October 1). A study in the "Prometheia," part I: The elements in the Trilogy. *Phoenix, 17*(3), 180–197.

Lorenz, S. (1914). *De Progressu Notionis φIΛANΘPΩΠIAΣ.* Inaugural dissertation, University of Leipzig, Leipzig, Germany.

Martin, M. W. (1994). *Virtuous giving: Philanthropy, voluntary service, and caring.* Bloomington, IN: Indiana University Press.

Meier, C. (1993). *The political art of Greek tragedy.* Baltimore, MD: The Johns Hopkins University Press.

Nails, D. (2002). *The people of Plato: A prosopography of Plato and other Socratics.* Indianapolis, IN: Hackett.

Nietzsche, F. W. (1968). *The will to power.* New York, NY: Random House.

Pearson, B. A. (1997). Ancient roots of Western philanthropy: Pagan, Jewish, and Christian. *Essays on Philanthropy No. 25.* Indianapolis, IN: Indiana University Center on Philanthropy.

Salamon, L. M. (1992). *America's nonprofit sector: A primer.* New York, NY: Foundation Center.

Salamon, L. M. (1999). *America's nonprofit sector: A primer* (2nd ed.). New York, NY: Foundation Center.

Schiappa, E. (2003). *Protagoras and logos: A study in Greek philosophy and rhetoric.* Columbia, SC: University of South Carolina Press.

Schmid, W. (1929). *Untersuchungen zum Gefesselten Prometheus* (Tübiner Beiträge zur Altertumswissenschaft, Heft 9). Stuttgart, Germany: W. Kohlhammer.

Smith, W. (1867). *A dictionary of Greek and Roman biography and mythology.* London, UK: John Murray.

Sulek, M. (2010a). On the classical meaning of philanthrôpía. *Nonprofit and Voluntary Sector Quarterly, 39*(3), 385–408.

Sulek, M. (2010b). On the modern meaning of philanthropy. *Nonprofit and Voluntary Sector Quarterly, 39*(2), 193–212.

Sulek, M. J. J. (2011). Gifts of fire: An historical analysis of the Promethean myth for the light it casts on the philosophical philanthropy of Protagoras, Socrates, and Plato; and prolegomena to consideration of the same in Bacon and Nietzsche. Available at http://hdl.handle.net/1805/2763

Tromp de Ruiter, S. (1932). De vocis quae est φIΛANΘPΩΠIA significatione atque usu. *Mnemosyne, 59*, 271–306.

Tromp de Ruiter, S. (2004). On the meaning and usage of the word *"philanthrôpía"* (M. Sulek, Trans.). In D. Burlingame (Ed.), *Philanthropy in America: A comprehensive encyclopedia* (Vol. 3, pp. 824–839). Santa Barbara, CA: ABC-CLIO.

West, M. L. (1979). The Prometheus trilogy. *Journal of Hellenic Studies, 99*, 130–148.

West, M. L. (1990). *Studies in Aeschylus.* Beiträge zur Altertumskunde, Bd. 1. Stuttgart, Germany: Teubner.

Zuckert, C. H. (2009). *Plato's philosophers: The coherence of the dialogues.* Chicago, IL: The University of Chicago Press.

Part II

PURPOSES AND MOTIVATION FOR FACULTY WORK

CHAPTER 4

Philanthropy as Motivator and Meaning

Reflections on Academic Work

Ann E. Austin

Faculty members in the United States work in an array of institutional types, including research universities, liberal arts colleges, regional institutions, and community colleges. They also hold a range of appointment configurations, including traditional tenure-track positions with considerable employment security, non-tenure-track renewable positions, non-tenure-track appointments with little security in regard to ongoing employment, adjunct positions teaching occasional courses, and part-time positions that can be temporary or, at some institutions, offer benefits and security comparable to full-time employment. While the nature of employment type and the circumstances of work within different institutional types create wide variations in how faculty members experience their work, across academic work experiences there remain some underlying characteristics and motivating values. Many would say that these common values include commitment to learning (one's own and that of others), to advancing and sharing knowledge, and to making a contribution from one's area of expertise that in some way makes the world better.

The theme of this book is that some aspects of academic work may be understood as philanthropy, defined as "voluntary action for the public good" (Payton, 1988, p. 3). That is, faculty members have the discretion and ability to make choices about the use of their time and to participate in activities that benefit other people and the broader society. At the same time, as acts of philanthropy, these contributions are rewarded largely with intrinsic rather than extrinsic rewards. This chapter explores the usefulness of framing academic work as philanthropic through several lenses: an examination of how this perspective can illuminate aspects of my own work as an individual faculty member; consideration of the notion of academic work as philanthropy from my perspective as a scholar who studies faculty careers, academic work, and workplaces; and analysis of the benefits, drawbacks, and research questions concerning understanding, supporting, or engaging in academic work when a perspective of philanthropy is used.

LENS ONE: A PERSONAL VIEW

As other chapters in this book explain, academic work, when defined as "voluntary action for the public good" or philanthropy, might take any number of forms. Faculty members have considerable discretion in how they allocate their time, and much of what they do clearly contributes to their students, colleagues, institutions, communities, and the larger society. Some activities mentioned by others in this volume include professors' spending time improving their course plans, revising learning materials, and learning new technologies to use in their teaching (see Nelson Laird, Chapter 5, this volume). Faculty members help students engage in undergraduate research projects or service learning in the community where students can link theoretical knowledge to practical issues. They serve on committees to recruit and screen potential faculty and administrative colleagues; to make decisions about curricular matters; to decide about priorities of departmental, college, or institutional budgeting; to review and handle instances of academic impropriety; and to engage in matters of institutional governance. They take the time to mentor early career colleagues and talk through projects with peers who are considering new research avenues. They review manuscripts for journals, analyze proposals for foundations, and assess the quality of productivity of faculty members at other institutions being considered for tenure, promotion, or awards. They speak to community groups, translate research findings into language that can be shared with the public, offer advice or serve as evaluators on community projects related to their areas of expertise, and respond to requests by national and international leaders for guidance about public matters.

What examples can I provide from my own experience as a faculty member for 30 years, serving over that time in two public universities and one private university, first as a tenure-track and then tenured professor, of instances where I chose to allocate time to make substantial contributions that benefited others and the broader community? In what ways is the notion of "philanthropy" useful in illuminating the meaning of these activities as part of my role as a faculty member?

One aspect of my work that I take very seriously is my teaching. I teach graduate students in formal classes and through many one-on-one relationships where I advise students as they move through their graduate coursework and conceptualize and conduct their dissertations (my role does not involve teaching undergraduates). As a teacher, I am committed to ensuring that each course is up-to-date in its focus and materials, engaging for participants, and reflective of my understanding of the importance of active learning. I constantly revise my courses, learn new technologies, and spend time developing new approaches to content and learning strategies. Every class that I have taught has included an evening at my home, during which my husband and I serve dinner and create an environment that fosters collegial and personal conversation.

As an advisor, I subscribe to what I call "full-service advising"; that is, I am willing to talk with students about whatever issues they believe may relate to their learning, including those in the domain of their broader lives. This means I make time for students even, when needed, in the evenings and on weekends; create relationships of openness and trust where my students and I come to know each other as people and colleagues with full and complex lives; and find ways to help students negotiate the many challenges that can interfere with the completion of their graduate work.

Is this comprehensive, time-intensive approach to teaching philanthropic? On one level, I believe the answer is yes because I am giving time to others that I could have used for myself or my family. I know that I voluntarily go beyond the explicit requirements of my appointment as a faculty member. Technically, while I am expected to teach and advise, the details are not specified, and more modest efforts than mine would be considered acceptable. However, I also think that I am fulfilling what I believe is the heart of what a "good faculty member" does, each in his or her own way. That is, many of us who teach with passion and deep commitment probably believe that the definition of a teacher is someone who connects with their students with the fullness of their "identity and integrity" as a person (Palmer, 1998, p. 10) and who uses their disciplinary or field expertise to help students connect with that field in ways that open new ideas and avenues of thinking.

The rewards I experience are intrinsic—the satisfaction of seeing students get excited about the ideas we are encountering, the joy of knowing that, after years of hard work and sacrifice, a student and his or her family are celebrating the accomplishment of the doctorate that will lead to new career possibilities, the meaningful letter from a student in an underrepresented group who was my master's advisee in years past to tell me that she just graduated with her doctorate and that my consistent encouragement and confidence in her ability when she was a young person is what had enabled her to even consider that she might have the potential to do advanced graduate work.

Another aspect of my work that could be considered philanthropic involves reviewing, evaluating, and giving feedback to others. I spend many hours each week reviewing manuscripts sent to me by journals, assessing proposals for conferences or for funding agencies considering whether to award a grant, and reading the manuscripts of colleagues earlier in their careers who seek my advice. This work is time-consuming, sometimes requiring up to 20 hours a week above my regular responsibilities of teaching, leading research grants, and handling responsibilities as an institutional citizen. Why do I do this work, which is not explicitly required in my contract?

To my thinking, part of being a faculty member is being a colleague and citizen of my department, college, university, and scholarly profession. While the responsibilities of "colleague" are typically not specified, to me they mean contributing to the many tasks that are required to run a department and university, such as serving on admissions and scholarship committees and participating in institutional governance. Being a colleague and citizen also means contributing to the well-being and success of other colleagues—both those in my institution and others whom I may not know personally but who are part of the scholarly community in which I work. Being a thoughtful and "good" colleague is, from one perspective, a "gift" to others, and it is not always explicitly rewarded. Nevertheless, the rewards are rich and full, if intrinsic—the reciprocity one receives when others offer their ideas or encouragement, the satisfaction from the generativity of guiding those earlier in their career, and the knowledge that one is contributing to the broader good of the field in which one is invested and from which one has gained many rewards and experiences.

Beyond consideration of rewards, contributing to the good of the academic community of which one is a member is an implicit responsibility of a faculty member; a corollary point, in my mind at least, is that members of a family, a civic organization, or a community should feel some responsibility for contributing their part to the good of the whole. In my university, we require faculty members preparing dossiers for tenure or promotion to provide information, evidence, and discussion about the aspects of their work that can be considered institutional service (institutional citizenship, to enlist the language I am using here), and this information is part of the overall materials considered in the review process.

For those faculty members in fixed term, non-tenure-track, and part-time positions, institutional citizenship may not be part of their assigned or implicitly understood duties. Thus, with the increasing proportion of faculty employed in such positions, some observers of academic work are concerned that the full-time and permanent faculty may find that they are shouldering an increasing—and perhaps worrisome—amount of the day-to-day institutional citizenship work needed to run the organization. In such situations, high levels of institutional citizenship work might indeed be philanthropic in terms of being work for the public good, but such work might be even more extensive than has been the case (and, therefore, far from "voluntary") if there are relatively few others available with whom to share this work in a collegial way. From my perspective, this issue of who handles the full array of responsibilities within a higher education institution is one of a number of serious concerns as the academic labor market experiences a shift away from permanent faculty appointments toward a more temporary workforce.

The third component of my work that I highlight in this discussion of philanthropy is my international involvement. In 1998, I spent a year as a Fulbright Scholar in South Africa; at the time, the country had recently overthrown the apartheid system, and I had the privilege of working with colleagues in South Africa committed to building a university that served the full population and the many needs of the immediate community and country. Over the past 15 years, I have continued to work regularly in South Africa, facilitating groups of graduate students and faculty from my university who collaborate with colleagues there on issues around faculty professional development, curriculum design and teaching improvement, and out-of-class learning.

This work is not specifically required in my academic assignments, but it has become very important to those with whom we work in South Africa, who cite many outcomes from this collaboration, and also to the graduate program where I teach, since these relationships offer significant opportunities for graduate students. It could be considered philanthropic as voluntary work for the greater good of students and of higher education in South Africa. The weeks I spend away from home, the many hours dedicated to preparing graduate students for their work in South Africa, the time on the ground in South Africa to assure details work smoothly and relationships are well-tended, the attention given to students who are traveling internationally for the first time, the thought and efforts to ensure that everyone is safe—these are responsibilities that I take on as part of this work, and that constitute voluntary activities well beyond my explicit assignments. In the words of philanthropy, the investment I make in this work could also be considered a "gift."

However, at the same time, the work has resulted in immense personal benefits, including research and writing opportunities, insights into my areas of professional expertise, international travel experiences, and personal and professional relationships that bring much satisfaction and friendship. Beyond these many benefits, my time working in South Africa, contributing to faculty and students there, and introducing my students to the many dimensions of the country, gives me a deep sense of happiness and meaning. My experiences enhance my belief in the possibilities for humankind even amid many struggles, bring forth the inspiration one receives when interacting with people who have overcome many challenges, and instill in me the deep sense of joy from doing work that may "make a difference" even in a small way. So, for all these many reasons, I lead trips to South Africa even though these specific activities are not required of me. I am both giving and receiving a "gift" in this work, and, at the same time, I see this work as an essential element of the full package of my roles and responsibilities as an academic.

Early in my career, I had the benefit and privilege of being guided by several excellent mentors, all of whom approached their work, each in a unique way, with enthusiasm, commitment, passion, and responsibility. Watching and interacting with them helped me see that a career as an academic involves, at its best, a commitment to bringing one's whole self into the work, including a willingness to go beyond fulfilling only narrowly defined expectations, toward, rather, a life of using one's talents, energy, and abilities in deep service to humanity.

As a professional, I now also recognize my responsibility to go well beyond narrow and explicit definitions and to bring my identity and values into my daily efforts to fulfill the multiple dimensions of academic work, just as my mentors did. The rewards indeed are not always extrinsic for these efforts, in terms of additional salary, for example. However, while the rewards are intrinsic, they are indeed real, meaningful, and important in shaping my career. Like a philanthropist, I am seeking to use my resources to make as significant an impact as possible. I also have the autonomy as a faculty member to decide how I use my time and resources; choice is related to the notion of "voluntary." However, perhaps different from a philanthropist, I see this commitment to giving and making an impact as essential, not as a voluntary component of my work, but rather as core to what I understand to be the long-established essence of being a member of the academic profession.

LENS TWO: THE LITERATURE ON ACADEMIC WORK

As a scholar who studies the academic profession and academic work, I turn now to the scholarly literature to ask what insights can be gained about how to consider "philanthropy" as a description or metaphor for understanding academic work. To do so, I look at two aspects of academic work—the components of faculty work and the reward system.

The Components of Academic Work

Over the past decade or so, graduate deans, faculty members, and researchers have engaged in a national dialogue about doctoral education and its purposes, including the roles and responsibilities future faculty will assume. In an essay on doctoral education and the socialization of future faculty, Ann Austin and Melissa McDaniels (2006) outlined a comprehensive set of skills and abilities important for future faculty to develop. The set includes *conceptual understandings* (e.g., understanding and appreciation of the purposes and history of higher education, understanding of the types of higher education institutions and their missions, knowledge of the discipline, and understanding of one's professional identity as a professor and scholar); *knowledge and skills in areas of faculty work* (e.g., teaching and learning processes, research processes, engagement and service, and institutional citizenship); *interpersonal skills* (e.g., communication skills, teamwork and collaboration skills, and appreciation of diversity); and *professional attitudes and habits* (e.g., ethics and integrity, motivation for lifelong learning, cultivating professional networks, and nurturing one's passion while maintaining balance). Several of these areas of needed competency are relevant to the consideration of philanthropy and academic work.

Faculty members need knowledge and skills in the specified domains of teaching, research, service, and institutional citizenship. Within teaching, future faculty are expected today to develop an array of abilities and skills, including "pedagogical content knowledge" (defined by Hutchings & Shulman, 1999, as the pedagogical strategies relevant to teaching specific disciplinary issues), ability to help students see the links between disciplinary knowledge and societal issues (Austin & Barnes, 2005; Schneider, 2004), and ways to use technology to facilitate learning. The extensive literature on how to improve teaching and learning processes assumes and encourages faculty members to see themselves as far more than dispensers of knowledge; rather, they are facilitators of learning environments in ways that require constant updating, innovative thought, and efforts to help students make connections between traditional learning and the broader society. This comprehensive set of responsibilities is part of academic work; that is, the role of teacher requires far more than simply meeting with classes.

In regard to research, future faculty must be able to frame questions, design studies, collect and analyze data, present results, and give feedback (Austin & McDaniels, 2006). Doing research involves not only conducting research but also sharing it with multiple communities and providing feedback to others. Furthermore, for almost 25 years, the work of Ernest Boyer (1990) has informed the definitions of scholarly work, reminding academics and their universities that scholarship involves not only the scholarship of discovery but also the scholarships of teaching and learning, integration, and application. Embedded within these several approaches to scholarship is the recognition that academic work involves a commitment to conducting research that addresses problems in society, and disseminating, translating, and applying research findings in ways that directly contribute to the public good and societal improvement. While academics are not told how to do their scholarship, the expectation that they will contribute to the public good is embedded in the very definition of scholarship.

Thus, learning how to link theory and practice (Austin & Barnes, 2005; Austin & McDaniels, 2006; Lynton & Elman, 1987), how to apply one's disciplinary expertise to societal problems, and how to talk with multiple and diverse audiences is all part of academic work. Recognizing the importance of preparing doctoral students for this aspect of their future work, Michigan State University (MSU) offers a graduate certificate in engagement, through which doctoral students explore the responsibility of engagement with society and the possible ways in which this responsibility can be enacted. These forms of work that contribute to the public good might include writing reports for community organizations and government agencies, engaging with community members in action research projects, or writing about the results and implications of research for the popular press (Austin & Barnes, 2005; Austin & McDaniels, 2006). MSU highlights the centrality of contributing to the broader public good through its use of a popular motto: "Advancing knowledge, transforming lives." As a land grant institution, its historical mission to translate research into applied knowledge is particularly strong, but throughout institutional types, higher education institutions recognize that faculty members have a role in bringing knowledge to bear on societal issues through their daily work—doing research, teaching, or directly engaging with the community.

Another key area of competence required of a faculty member pertains to understanding one's professional identity as a professor and scholar. Joan Stark, Malcolm Lowther, and Bonnie Hagerty (1986) argued that professional education should emphasize professional identity, defined as "the degree to which graduates integrate the profession's norms, competencies, and values into a conception of role" (p. 53). What are key aspects of such professional identity? According to James Bess (1978), future faculty should "understand fully the symbolic meaning of the activities in which a 'professor' engages" (p. 293). Stark et al. (1986) specifically noted that a well-prepared professional should have "scholarly concern for improvement" (p. 65), which would include contributing to the expansion of the knowledge base of the field and, presumably, contributing time to ensure that new research is carefully reviewed and assessed. Another component of responsibility to the relevant professional community involves being willing to participate in the community by interacting with others, such as in a mentoring role or as a collegial peer reviewer, and participating as an institutional citizen within one's institution. Overall, recognizing one's professional identity means including in one's work various contributions to others and to the scholarly community.

   This discussion of the components of academic work is intended to show that the work of a professor is complex and multifaceted. While formal contracts may state that faculty members will engage in teaching, research, and service, and may even specify the number of courses or hours spent on teaching, the actual meaning of the role of professor—and the related expectations—go beyond any explicit listing of duties. Some state legislatures have been interested in legislating the number of hours a faculty member must be in class or the number of student credit hours to be produced. The irony is that when a faculty member truly understands the profession, he or she is likely to go far beyond the specific duties noted in a legislated set of expectations—and, I fear, such efforts to specify expectations in the form of narrow definitions may actually undermine the very commitment and sense of responsibility that I am arguing is at the heart of the academic profession.

   Being a faculty member involves a professional identity that includes commitment to the importance of advancing knowledge, sharing knowledge through teaching, applying knowledge to the challenges and issues confronting society, and participating in the universities and colleges that are the organizational structures through which academic work is done. Individual faculty members, by virtue of the institutions where they are located and the appointment types in which they are situated, have different configurations of attention to these components of academic work. But the overall commitment to knowledge, teaching, and application of knowledge to societal problems is, I argue, at the heart of academic work. Thus, the work of a professor is philanthropic in the sense of being a contribution to the public good, and it is voluntary in the sense that some degree of autonomy is associated with most academic positions (even part-time non-tenure-track faculty often, although not always, have some choices about how they teach). However, academic work is far more than a narrow list of assignments. Thus, while giving to the public good is at the heart of academic work, the notion that contributing to the public good is a "gift"—that is, something beyond what a faculty member should do—is not compatible with my understanding of academic work. Calling academic work "philanthropy" highlights the centrality of the contributions made through academic work to the public good; but the use of the term can inadvertently diminish the recognition that contributing to the good of others is central to academic work, not a choice made above and beyond what defines academic work.

   Having argued here that the professional identity and responsibility of being a professor involves, at its core, contributing to the public good, I nevertheless recognize that the shifts in the academic labor market toward an alarming increase in the number and proportion of faculty members employed in temporary (sometimes called "contingent") positions have the potential to threaten the longstanding assumptions that I have argued are at the core of academic work. If many faculty members find themselves in positions defined by a narrow list of work requirements and little time, autonomy, or support for the array of activities and roles I have described here as characterizing academic work, or the autonomy to define their engagement, opportunities for contributing to the public good may become a more modest dimension of academic work.

The Reward System in Academic Work

When one engages in philanthropy, one is typically not receiving tangible rewards. Thus, an element in the argument advanced in the premise that academic work might be considered philanthropy is that academics are not tangibly rewarded for the contributions they make to the good of others and the broader society. In regard to tangible academic rewards, salaries for those who have full-time academic positions vary by institutional type and discipline but arguably are generally considered adequate for middle-class life. I acknowledge, however, that for faculty in non-tenure-track positions or part-time positions financial remuneration is often low in comparison with that of tenure-track and full-time faculty and is a major source of concern (Kezar, 2012; Kezar & Sam, 2010). Research shows that time spent on teaching actually correlates with lower pay as compared with time spent on research (Fairweather, 2005). Traditional thinking about academic work is that faculty value most highly the intrinsic rewards of their work, but that some attention needs to be directed to the extrinsic rewards, since satisfaction with salary is related to overall job satisfaction (Hult, Callister, & Sullivan, 2005), and perceived inequities in salary negatively influence satisfaction (Hagedorn, 1996).

Overall, however, while extrinsic rewards need to be adequate, faculty members derive considerable satisfaction from what are often considered intrinsic rewards. They value equity in pay (Hagedorn, 1996), access to resources, and fair treatment (Hagedorn, 2001; Hult et al., 2005; Johnsrud & Rosser, 2002; Rosser, 2004; Witt & Nye, 1992). Analyzing research on faculty satisfaction, Judith Gappa, Ann Austin, and Andrea Trice (2007) highlighted the importance of a sense of positive collegiality in the workplace, opportunities to grow professionally, feeling secure in one's position, and being recognized for one's contributions as important intrinsic rewards and contributing factors to satisfaction. Their research led them to offer a framework of essential elements of academic work that relate to faculty satisfaction, productivity, and commitment. The essential elements in the framework are respect, equity, academic freedom and autonomy, flexibility, professional growth, and collegiality.

Gappa et al. (2007) argued that institutional leaders and faculty members share a joint responsibility for the health of the academic workplace and for fulfilling the multiple missions of a university or college. In this reciprocal relationship between faculty as employee and the institution as the employer, faculty members contribute to meeting the responsibilities of the institution for teaching, research, and service or engagement, and the institution in return ensures that faculty members enjoy work characterized by equity, academic freedom and autonomy, flexibility, professional growth, and collegiality.

How does this conceptualization of academic work relate to faculty work as philanthropy? Philanthropic work is done without regard to reward, and particularly with no expectation of extrinsic rewards (although admittedly not typically without regard for recognition). In comparing academic work to philanthropic work, one commonality is that extrinsic rewards in the form of remuneration are not central. However, the reward system in academic work, I argue, differs from philanthropy in an important way. The definition of academic work implies a greater contribution to the greater good as part of the defined meaning of being an academic. Contributing to the greater good is not a "gift" faculty can choose to give or not; it is the very essence of academic work, and, as such, it is part of what the reward system values. That is, in academic work, an exchange is occurring in which faculty members are expected to engage in work that, by its definition, involves giving to students, the institution, and society.

As discussed earlier, academic work is more than simply fulfilling specific allocations of class assignments or research assignments. Faculty members have the responsibility of helping their institutions fulfill their missions. The shared responsibility that professors and institutional leaders have for fulfilling their institution's missions is part of that implicit but very real set of responsibilities. The reciprocal relationship between faculty members and institutions means that academics engage in a full set of responsibilities for their colleagues, institutions, and society in return for a set of rewards and benefits that are both tangible and intangible.

Opportunities for professional growth, for example, take shape in funds to travel to conferences as well as in the intangible awareness that one is supported professionally. Flexibility is both an intrinsic reward (e.g., the knowledge that one can make adjustments in one's schedule) and an extrinsic benefit (e.g., access to policies and programs to support child care or elder care). Equity is a benefit in an appropriate exchange between faculty members and their institutions; an environment characterized by equitable policies has the intrinsic reward of being a pleasant place in which to work and the extrinsic element of providing appropriate salary compensation regardless of one's employment type. Thus, when higher education institutions take seriously the implications of the reciprocal relationship that exists between faculty member and institution, then faculty members are both expected to engage in work that involves contributing to the good of the institution and the greater society and are rewarded with a workplace offering intrinsic and extrinsic rewards.

This reciprocal relationship implies that faculty members, especially those who enjoy the privilege of tenure, recognize and fulfill their responsibilities to their institutions and the broader society. On the other end, I believe that higher education institutions should give explicit attention to creating organizational cultures that highlight the centrality of professional duty toward the institution, profession, and broader society. Two examples of institutional efforts are clear articulations from institutional leaders about the role and responsibility of higher education institutions in society, and professional development opportunities for doctoral students and faculty members to explore the ways in which their scholarly talents can make a broad and deep impact within academe and beyond.

In summary, academic work and philanthropy share some similarities in regard to the reward system. But overall, the reward system in the academy may be more complex. It includes within it an expectation that academic work involves more than fulfilling explicitly listed job duties; rather, academic work includes responsibility for contributing to the broader institutional mission. Contributing to the public good is not a "gift" that faculty members give beyond their required roles; it is embedded within their required responsibilities. The relationship between faculty member and employing institution may not always work effectively, particularly when non-tenure-track or part-time faculty are not adequately rewarded or supported. However, when the relationship works well, the reward system also provides both intrinsic and extrinsic rewards. This analysis suggests that philanthropy as a perspective for understanding academic work is somewhat useful but also has limitations in understanding the reward system within academe.

LENS THREE: BENEFITS, DRAWBACKS, AND QUESTIONS ABOUT PHILANTHROPY AS A PERSPECTIVE ON ACADEMIC WORK

One benefit of the concept of philanthropy in regard to academic work is that it highlights the ways in which faculty members are serving society as they fulfill their responsibilities. The term calls out what are often invisible aspects of the daily work of academics and makes those many facets of their work—in regard to their teaching, research, service, and institutional citizenship—more visible. Given the increasing skepticism among the public in recent years about what faculty do and whether they merit the costs of their salaries, language and framing that bring out the roles and responsibilities of professors as contributors to society may help the public more fully understand academic work. At present, faculty members have few options within academic language to discuss service to society as part of their work; perhaps the most useful and used term at present is *scholarship of engagement*. Enlarging the available vocabulary, such as through the use of the term *philanthropy*, could deepen and refocus discussions of academic work among academics and others in the society.

Connecting the notion of philanthropy to academic work may also be useful in attracting excellent young scholars to the academy. One concern in recent years has been the growing skepticism among young scholars about whether a faculty career is sufficiently attractive in regard to time pressures, ability to balance work and personal life, and flexibility in pursuing one's interests (Rice, Sorcinelli, & Austin, 2000; Trower, 2012). Highlighting the many ways in which academic work involves serving others and contributing to a better society, as well as providing opportunities for faculty members to exercise their autonomy in deciding how to serve the greater good, may help some graduate students see reasons for entering academe over other employment sectors.

While the concept of philanthropy has benefits when applied to academic work, it also raises some concerns. Discussions of philanthropy that suggest that the many aspects of academic work that involve going beyond meeting basic expectations are "voluntary" could diminish public understanding of the meaning of academic work. Inadvertently, such discussions could suggest that time spent on student conversations, integrating new teaching methods into one's planning, talking with community groups, or sharing research findings are discretionary. One implication could therefore be that only perceived core activities of academic work are necessary, with all other parts (the "voluntary" parts) being superfluous; if perceived as "extra" or superfluous, such components of faculty work might not be counted when faculty are evaluated or faculty members might be encouraged to omit these activities in the context of fiscal constraint.

Of course, the increased frequency of hiring faculty members into part-time or nonpermanent positions is already accompanied by a disregard for the importance of these kinds of contributions. Similarly, faculty members themselves might conclude that their primary responsibilities do not include such "voluntary" activities, and, as some faculty members sometimes comment, "just say no" could become an acceptable response. Because I believe that the work being called "philanthropic" is at the heart of the academic profession, I would find any conclusions of the kind just described as an unfortunate outcome of applying the concept of philanthropy to academic work.

The term *philanthropy* should be used to foster conversation, but also be handled with care. Use of the notion might be accompanied by ongoing research concerning related questions. How do faculty members and administrators differ in the ways they understand academic work as "philanthropic"? In what ways does the public respond to efforts to frame academic work as philanthropic? How do faculty members differ across institutional types, career stages, and appointment types in how they express their work in philanthropic ways and in how they view this concept? In what ways can doctoral students who aspire to be faculty members be introduced to the notion of academic work in service to the public good, and to the choices and responsibilities for allocating their time and talents that they will face in their careers? In what ways can faculty not serving in traditional tenure-track roles—for example, non-tenure-track faculty and those in part-time positions—also be assured that their work includes opportunities to exercise choice and autonomy in selecting philanthropic dimensions? Faculty work is complex and multidimensional. The concept of philanthropy opens avenues for pursuing productive discussions and questions, if explored with care.

REFERENCES

Austin, A. E., & Barnes, B. J. (2005). Preparing doctoral students for faculty careers that contribute to the public good. In T. Chambers, A. Kezar, & J. C. Burkhardt (Eds.), *Higher education for the public good: Emerging voices from a national movement* (pp. 272–292). San Francisco, CA: Jossey-Bass.

Austin, A. E., & McDaniels, M. (2006). Preparing the professoriate of the future: Graduate student socialization for faculty roles. In J. C. Smart (Ed.), *Higher education: Handbook of theory and research* (Vol. 21, pp. 397–456). Amsterdam, Netherlands: Springer.

Bess, J. L. (1978). Anticipatory socialization of graduate students. *Research in Higher Education, 8*(4), 289–317.

Boyer, E. L. (1990). *Scholarship reconsidered: Priorities of the professoriate*. New York, NY: The Carnegie Foundation for the Advancement of Teaching.

Fairweather, J. S. (2005). Beyond the rhetoric: Trends in the relative value of teaching and research in faculty salaries. *Journal of Higher Education, 76*(4), 401–422.

Gappa, J. M., Austin, A. E., & Trice, A. G. (2007). *Rethinking faculty work: Higher education's strategic imperative*. San Francisco, CA: Jossey-Bass.

Hagedorn, L. S. (1996). Wage equity and female faculty job satisfaction: The role of wage differentials in a job satisfaction causal model. *Research in Higher Education, 37*(5), 569–598.

Hagedorn, L. S. (2001). Gender differences in faculty productivity, satisfaction, and salary: What really separates us? ERIC Document 464 548.

Hult, C., Callister, R., & Sullivan, K. (2005). Is there a global warming toward women in academe? *Liberal Education*. Available at http://www/aacu-edu.org/liberaleducation/le-sufa05/le-sufa05perspective.cfm

Hutchings, P., & Shulman, L. S. (1999). The scholarship of teaching: New elaborations, new developments. *Change, 31*(5), 10–15.

Johnsrud, L. K., & Rosser, V. J. (2002). Faculty members' morale and their intentions to leave: A multilevel explanation. *The Journal of Higher Education, 73*(4), 518–542.

Kezar, A. (2012). Needed policies, priorities, and values: Creating a culture to support and professionalize non-tenure track faculty. In A. Kezar (Ed.), *Embracing non-tenure track faculty: Changing campuses for the new faculty majority* (pp. 2–27). New York, NY: Routledge.

Kezar, A., & Sam, C. (2010). Understanding the new majority of non-tenure-track faculty in higher education: Demographics, experiences, and plans of action. ASHE-ERIC Higher Education report, Vol. 36, No. 4. San Francisco, CA: Jossey-Bass.

Lynton, E. A., & Elman, S. E. (1987). *New priorities for the university: Meeting society's needs for applied knowledge and competent individuals*. San Francisco, CA: Jossey-Bass.

Palmer, P. (1998). *The courage to teach: Exploring the inner landscape of a teacher's life*. San Francisco, CA: Jossey-Bass.

Payton, R. (1988). *Philanthropy: Voluntary action for the public good*. New York, NY: American Council on Education/Macmillan.

Rice, R. E., Sorcinelli, M. D., & Austin, A. E. (2000). *Heeding new voices: Academic careers for a new generation*. Washington, DC: American Association of Higher Education.

Rosser, V. J. (2004). Faculty members' intentions to leave: A national study on their worklife and satisfaction. *Research in Higher Education, 45*(3), 285–309.

Schneider, C. G. (2004). Changes in undergraduate education: What future faculty need to know. *Peer Review, 6*(3), 4–7.

Stark, J. S., Lowther, M. A., & Hagerty, B. M. K. (1986). *Responsive professional education: Balancing outcomes and opportunities* (ASHE-ERIC Higher Education Report No. 3). Washington, DC: Association for the Study of Higher Education.

Trower, C. A. (2012). *Success on the tenure track: Five keys to faculty job satisfaction*. Baltimore, MD: The Johns Hopkins University Press.

Witt, L. A., & Nye, L. G. (1992). Gender and the relationship between perceived fairness of pay or promotion and job satisfaction. *Journal of Applied Psychology, 77*(6), 910–917.

CHAPTER 5

Gifting Time

Faculty Activities with a Philanthropic Orientation

Thomas F. Nelson Laird

Building from the notion that faculty members give the gift of their time and expertise in many situations as a part of their roles at colleges and universities, this chapter examines the amount of time faculty members dedicate to activities that are, at least in part, philanthropic. Because of their relative autonomy, faculty members can decide whether to devote time to instructional improvement, social time with students, co-curricular activity, community engagement, and other types of activities, such as committee service or advising student groups. Moreover, for most faculty members, their participation in these activities will take time and effort but typically will not substantively influence continued employment, institutional compensation, or advancement—even when they are considered in performance discussions. Faculty, however, still make the choice to engage in these activities as a part of their professorial practice.

Although faculty members have considerable autonomy, time is not a limitless resource. There are only 24 hours in a day and all faculty careers come to an end. Since time is a zero-sum resource, faculty members then face difficult choices about parsing time, especially when time is measured in such defined ways within the academy: semesters or quarters with rigid beginning and ending dates, periods reserved for final examinations, tenure clocks, time-determined contracts, or research grants with expiration dates. Time is as important a commodity as money or recognition. Time spent on research or teaching or community engagement inevitably comes at the expense of time spent somewhere else.

We know enough about the profile, productivity, and work life of the professoriate to know that faculty members feel pinched in terms of their time (Gappa, Austin, & Trice, 2007; Schuster & Finkelstein, 2006). We also know that the pressures faculty members face do not all push them toward "gifting" their time. For faculty whose role is defined largely by teaching (e.g., non-tenure-track faculty), the constraints of their roles and contexts and the increased demands of teaching push for a greater investment of time, even when doing so will not result in additional benefit (Gappa et al., 2007). For faculty who do research, personal motivation, reward structures within institutions and disciplines/departments (including promotion and tenure), and academic culture can push them to "ratchet up" their research and scholarly efforts, to spend more of their discretionary time away from other activities (Massy & Zemsky, 1994). This ratcheting up of research is evident in several areas, including the increased amount of time faculty members have been spending on research and scholarly activities (Massy & Zemsky, 1994; Milem, Berger, & Dey, 2000; Schuster & Finkelstein, 2006). However, as Milem et al. point out, so far the ratcheting up of research is not coming at the expense of time on teaching. Rather, while research time is ratcheting up, so too is teaching time. Thus, overall work time is increasing (Milem et al., 2000; Schuster & Finkelstein, 2006), presumably at the expense of what might euphemistically be called "personal time."

From 1972 to 1998, the average number of hours worked per week by faculty members at 4-year universities rose from 44 to 51 hours (an increase of 16%), with average hours spent working slightly lower at other types of institutions (Schuster & Finkelstein, 2006). Estimates from faculty at research universities show that faculty worked about 54 hours in a typical week in 2004 and 2005 (Link, Swann, & Bozeman, 2008), continuing the upward climb (up over 23% from the 1970s). The clear trend is that faculty members are working more and more each year and there is no evidence that this trend will end in the near term. Since total time at work is increasing (largely because of more time on teaching and research), the trade-offs must be coming in areas like time on service or non-work-related activities (e.g., personal or family time).

At work, when time is divided between teaching, research, and service, faculty members generally spend between 50% and 80% of their time on teaching; between 15% and 30% of their time on research; and the remainder of their time on service with the exact proportion depending on many factors, including type of institution, disciplinary area, and gender (Link et al., 2008; Schuster & Finkelstein, 2006).

Interestingly, behind much of the research on how faculty spend their time is a workforce or productivity orientation, where time on a task should result in a product and some affiliated reward (e.g., Bellas & Toutkoushian, 1999; also, Rhoades, Chapter 8, this volume, addresses implications of increased expectations for faculty productivity in more depth). So, for example, studying the amount of time one spends on research and scholarly activities or teaching is built on the relatively safe assumption that scholarly and research products (e.g., publications) or educational products (e.g., credits taught and, maybe, quantified learning outcomes) follow from time dedicated to those activities. And, through things like salary, promotion and tenure, and recognition, faculty receive rewards for that work. However, this is not the entire story of faculty work. It is difficult to fit committing extra time to a student, chairing a committee to better one's department or institution, or thinking about ways to improve a course assignment into the product/reward orientation. Further, since time is a zero-sum resource, time spent on these activities is a gift of sorts because faculty members have the potential to spend those minutes or hours on other activities with more direct personal gains attached. Certain types of faculty activities, I am arguing, have a philanthropic orientation.

This chapter supports the idea that we can build a greater understanding of the professoriate if we examine a wider range of academic activities and use different assumptions to explore faculty work. Specifically, this chapter examines how much time faculty devoted to the following activities in a typical week during the 2010–2011 academic year, while acknowledging that there are a number of other faculty-conducted activities that can also be considered as discretionary and, potentially, philanthropic. This list focuses on the most widely shared faculty activity—engagement with students.

- Reflecting on ways to improve one's teaching
- Working with undergraduates on research
- Supervising internships or field experiences
- Working with students on activities other than coursework (committees, orientation, student life activities, etc.)
- Other interactions with students outside the classroom

The orientation here is not about what is produced but what is being *given* by faculty members to their students, institutions, and fields. There is some altruism—because they include a concern for student success, development, and growth—built into all these activities and most faculty members are not *required* to do any of them.

To conceptualize time devoted to teaching improvement, the first item on our list, think of a professor trying to improve an assignment so that students can better learn the material or imagine an instructor experimenting with a new way to get students to collaborate. Because of the accelerating changes in technology, for example, many faculty devote extensive amounts of time to learning new techniques and applications—for the benefit of students—without expectation of reward. The incentives for doing this type of work are generally intrinsic—to become a better instructor or to gain the satisfaction of seeing students learn material or master some skill (McKeachie, 1997). Although some faculty will be rewarded by their colleagues or institutions for these endeavors (e.g., with recognition or awards), it is much more common for this type of work to go unnoticed by anyone other than the faculty member (even students do not often realize what goes into these efforts).

For undergraduate research, think of faculty members and their own research. For some, not all research is done to produce a product and some of it (even when there is a product) is done with a philanthropic orientation, such as building a base of knowledge for others to use. Many faculty members involve themselves in research with undergraduates, not because it is the most efficient route to research products or the path to the most profound discoveries, but because it serves an educational function and contributes to a greater good (e.g., it potentially develops students into future researchers for the field).

The item about supervising internships or field experiences is right on the border between an expected work task and philanthropy. Certainly, some faculty members in education, social work, and nursing, for example, do this type of supervision as a part of their teaching loads, or adjunct/part-time faculty are employed specifically to do this work. There are, however, plenty of examples of faculty who accept these "extra" activities for which no credit is given. In either case, I would argue that many or most faculty are guided by a sense of contribution to their students, the community, or their fields. It is difficult to argue, even when faculty are paid for these activities, that their compensation is commensurate with their efforts.

For the last two items, working with students on activities other than coursework (committees, orientation, student life activities, etc.) and other interactions with students outside the classroom, the argument for a philanthropic orientation is fairly simple. Many faculty members do not participate in these activities because they are not required (see results below). A faculty member can proceed through her or his career without connecting with students in these ways. Thus, to do so is a way to give back to one's community, to help a rising generation, and to make a difference in people's lives—all philanthropic orientations.

FACULTY TIME IN PHILANTHROPIC ACTIVITY

This study sought to answer two questions: First, how much time do faculty members spend on the aforementioned activities? Second, which groups of faculty members tend to spend more time on each of the activities and which groups spend less?

To answer these questions, I used data from the 2011 administration of the Faculty Survey of Student Engagement (FSSE), a national survey of college and university faculty at bachelor's-granting institutions that complements the National Survey of Student Engagement (NSSE). I used responses from 13,699 faculty members from 152 colleges and universities in the United States. The 152 institutions represent a wide cross-section of higher education institutions. In fact, the institutions look very similar to the U.S. population of bachelor's-granting colleges and universities in terms of Carnegie Classification, control (public vs. private), undergraduate enrollment, and region (FSSE, 2011).

The faculty respondents also mirror the U.S. population of faculty members in many ways, although a higher proportion were women (which is common for surveys) and worked on a full-time basis (FSSE, 2011). Of the respondents, 47% were women and most were White (75%), while 6% were Black or African American, 5% were Asian or Pacific Islander, 3% were Hispanic or Latino, 3% were of another race/ethnicity (including American Indian/Native American, multiracial, and other races/ethnicities), and 8% indicated a preference not to identify their race/ethnicity. Of the sample, 6% were non–U.S. citizens and 70% held doctorates. Combining rank and employment status, the sample had 12% part-time lecturers and instructors, 10% full-time lecturers and instructors, 26% assistant professors, 25% associate professors, and 27% professors. The sample included faculty members from many different fields. When clustered into disciplinary areas, 26% came from the arts and humanities, 6% from the biological sciences, 10% from business, 9% from education, 4% from engineering, 11% from the physical sciences, 9% from other professional fields (e.g., health fields), 13% from the social sciences, and 12% were in other fields. The average teaching load was six courses per year.

The findings described in the next section come from a mixture of analyses. I report the frequencies of faculty members' responses in some cases and then produce estimates of the average amount of time faculty members spent on each activity and the sum of the activities.[1]

How Faculty Use Their Time

The results show that the majority of faculty members spent 0 or 1–4 hours on each of the five activities (see Table 5.1). Nearly all faculty members reflected on ways to improve their teaching, while fewer than half of the faculty spent any time supervising internships or other field experiences in a typical week.

The average faculty member spent about 5 hours in a typical week reflecting on ways to improve instruction and 2 to 3.5 hours on each of the other activities (see Table 5.2)—as a reminder, a typical faculty member spends 50 or more hours per week on work. Combined, the average faculty

Table 5.1. Distribution of Faculty Members' Reported Hours Spent in a Typical 7-Day Week on Five Philanthropically Oriented Activities

Activity	0 hours	1–4 hours	5–8 hours	9 or more hours
Reflecting on ways to improve one's teaching	2%	66%	22%	11%
Other interactions with students outside the classroom	18%	61%	14%	7%
Working with students on activities other than coursework	40%	49%	8%	3%
Working with undergraduates on research	42%	41%	11%	6%
Supervising internships or other field experiences	61%	26%	7%	6%

Table 5.2. Average Hours Spent in a Typical 7-Day Week on Five Philanthropically Oriented Activities

Activity	Average hours
Reflecting on ways to improve one's teaching	4.7
Other interactions with students outside the classroom	3.5
Working with undergraduates on research	2.6
Working with students on activities other than coursework	2.3
Supervising internships or other field experiences	2.0
All activities combined	15.2

member reported spending about 15 hours per week on these activities in total—or about 30% of a 50-hour work week. The amount of time spent on these activities varied depending on certain faculty characteristics, though the effects of these characteristics were not consistent from activity to activity. To illustrate, Tables 5.3 through 5.5 show differences for three faculty characteristics: race/ethnicity, rank and employment status, and disciplinary area. The differences reported in these tables come from regression models that included gender, race/ethnicity, citizenship status, highest degree earned, rank and employment status, course load, and disciplinary area. Thus the mean differences reported in Tables 5.3 through 5.5 were adjusted to account for differences in the other characteristics.

Differences by Race/Ethnicity

Table 5.3 shows that, in general, faculty of color and those faculty who chose not to indicate a race/ethnicity reported spending more time in a typical week on the various philanthropically oriented activities than their White colleagues, even after controlling for other faculty characteristics. Black/African American faculty, on average, spent the most time in a typical week on four out of the five activities. (See Chapter 7 by Emily L. Moore and J. Herman Blake for a description of Black/African American faculty commitment of time to student success.) It was faculty who indicated a race/ethnicity other than Asian/Asian American, Black/African American, Hispanic, or White who reported the most time on supervising internships or other field experiences. On average, Black/African American faculty reported spending 8 hours per week more than their White colleagues on these activities combined. The analogous difference was just over 4 hours for Asian/Asian American faculty and about 3 hours for Hispanic faculty and those faculty members in the "Other" category.

Differences in this study mirror those in other work that examined hours on general service activities (Bellas & Toutkoushian, 1999). However, quantitative findings regarding racial/ethnic differences in service participation are not consistent (Porter, 2007). Interestingly, qualitative findings in this area resoundingly support the notion that faculty of color spend more time on service and are pressured into doing so by institutional needs for diversity and a sense of personal obligation. The mismatch between quantitative (mixed) and qualitative (all showing clear differences) findings is a concern. I wonder, however, if the key to sorting out the difference lies in separating activities by that sense of obligation or, as I talk about it in this study, the philanthropic orientation. If we sorted service activities in this way, the differences by race might be clearer.

Differences by Rank and Employment Status

Perhaps unsurprisingly, Table 5.4 shows that, on average, full-time non-tenure-track faculty (full-time lecturers and instructors) and tenure-track faculty (assistant, associate, and full professors) reported spending 5.1 to 5.7 hours more on the philanthropically oriented activities than part-time lecturers and instructors, even after controlling for other characteristics, including course load. Full-time lecturers and instructors had the highest average on reflecting on ways to improve their teaching (tenure-track faculty reported about the same average amount of time on this activity as their part-time lecturer/instructor colleagues), while tenure-track faculty averaged the most time on research with undergraduates (full- and

Table 5.3. Racial/Ethnic Differences in Hours Spent in a Typical 7-Day Week on Philanthropically Oriented Activities

Activity	DIFFERENCE FROM WHITE FACULTY IN HOURS SPENT				
	Asian/ Asian American	Black/ African American	Hispanic	Other race/ ethnicity	Chose not to report race/ ethnicity
Reflecting on ways to improve one's teaching	1.8	2.9	1.8	0.4[b]	1.1
Other interactions with students outside the classroom	0.4[b]	1.6	0.1[c]	0.7	0.2[c]
Working with students on activities other than coursework	0.7	1.7	0.3[c]	1.0	0.2[c]
Working with undergraduates on research	1.0	1.4	0.7	−0.6	0.4
Supervising internships or other field experiences	0.5[a]	0.8	0.0[c]	1.2	0.1[c]
All activities combined	4.3	8.3	2.8	2.8	2.0

Note: Differences in this table control for the effects of gender, citizenship status, highest degree earned, rank and employment status, course load, and disciplinary area. All differences significant at $p < 0.001$ except where noted.
[a] $p < 0.01$; [b] $p < 0.05$; [c] $p > 0.05$

part-time lecturers/instructors averaged very similar amounts of time on this activity). The average full-time non-tenure-track and tenure-track faculty members spent similar amounts of time on other interactions with students outside the classroom, working with students on activities other than coursework, and supervising internships or field experiences. However, on those three activities, the part-time lecturers and instructors

Table 5.4. Rank and Employment Status Differences in Hours Spent in a Typical 7-Day Week on Philanthropically Oriented Activities

Activity	DIFFERENCE FROM PART-TIME LECTURERS/ INSTRUCTORS IN HOURS SPENT			
	Full-time lecturers/ instructors	Assistant professors	Associate professors	Full professors
Reflecting on ways to improve one's teaching	0.8	0.3[b]	0.1[c]	0.0[c]
Other interactions with students outside the classroom	1.9	1.7	1.7	1.8
Working with students on activities other than coursework	1.4	1.4	1.4	1.4
Working with undergraduates on research	−0.1[c]	0.9	1.0	0.9
Supervising internships or other field experiences	1.2	1.3	1.2	1.1
All activities combined	5.2	5.7	5.4	5.1

Note: Differences in this table control for the effects of gender, race/ethnicity, citizenship status, highest degree earned, course load, and disciplinary area. All differences significant at $p < 0.001$ except where noted.

[a] $p < 0.01$; [b] $p < 0.05$; [c] $p > 0.05$

averaged over an hour less than their colleagues even after adjustments by course load and other measures.

The findings by rank and employment status support conclusions by Schuster and Finkelstein (2006). When they examined tenure-track and non-tenure-track faculty, they concluded, at least in the area of teaching, full-time non-tenure-track faculty looked very similar to their tenure-track colleagues. As in this study (for working with undergraduates on research), it was in areas related to research where Jack Schuster and

Martin Finkelstein saw that full-time non-tenure-track faculty differed from their tenure-track colleagues. The differences seem connected to the parameters of faculty roles and expectations (e.g., non-tenure-track faculty are often employed only to teach and have no research expectation). However, the differences for part-time faculty are also likely connected to trade-offs between their part-time work and other parts of their lives as well as access to resources, like work space outside the classroom and time for informal connections that lead to interacting with students outside of class (see Kezar, 2012).

Differences by Disciplinary Area

Table 5.5 shows disciplinary differences in time spent in a typical week on the philanthropically oriented activities after adjusting for the effects of other faculty characteristics. For the specific activities, most differences among faculty between the listed groups and the physical sciences were less than an hour. Education faculty averaged the most time on four out of the five activities, with biological sciences faculty averaging the most time on research with undergraduates (it is worth noting that education faculty averaged the least time on this activity). Not surprisingly, faculty in education and other professional fields (mostly health-related fields) reported significantly more time spent (3.5 hours) in a typical week on supervising internships and other field experiences. Those differences drove the largest differences seen on the combined measure of time spent on the five activities. Other differences on the combined measure were less than 2 hours except for biological sciences faculty, who averaged 3 hours per week more on the five activities when compared with their physical sciences colleagues.

Although most of the disciplinary differences are not large in size, the pattern of differences for each item is revealing. For reflecting on teaching and time spent working with undergraduates on research, there is a clear split between hard fields (e.g., biological sciences, engineering, and physical sciences) and soft fields (e.g., arts and humanities and social sciences) (Biglan, 1973; Braxton & Hargens, 1996). Faculty members in soft fields tend to reflect on their teaching more, while faculty in hard fields tend to spend more time on undergraduate research. This is hardly surprising given that soft fields tend to see teaching spaces as places in which to engage challenging problems (which needs preparation and reflection) and those in hard fields tend to agree on the accepted modes of teaching—so reflection may not be viewed as necessary.

Continuing to use Anthony Biglan's (1973) categorization, faculty in applied fields (education, engineering, and other professions)—fields concerned with the application of knowledge—tended to work with students

Table 5.5. Disciplinary Area Differences in Hours Spent in a Typical 7-Day Week on Philanthropically Oriented Activities

Activity	DIFFERENCE FROM PHYSICAL SCIENCES FACULTY IN HOURS SPENT						
	Arts	Bio	Bus	Educ	Engin	Other prof	Social sci
Reflecting on ways to improve one's teaching	0.8	0.0[c]	0.4[b]	1.7	–0.3[c]	0.8	0.3[b]
Other interactions with students outside the classroom	0.4[a]	0.3[c]	0.0[c]	0.8	0.2[c]	0.1[c]	0.2[c]
Working with students on activities other than coursework	0.5	0.5[a]	0.5	1.1	0.7	0.6	0.5
Working with undergraduates on research	–0.3[b]	1.4	–1.4	–1.4	0.4[c]	–1.1	0.0[c]
Supervising internships or other field experiences	0.2[c]	0.8	0.6	3.5	0.5[a]	3.5	0.9
All activities combined	1.7	3.0	0.1[c]	5.7	1.5[b]	3.9	1.9

Note: Differences in this table control for the effects of gender, race/ethnicity, citizenship status, highest degree earned, rank and employment status, and course load. All differences significant at p < 0.001 except where noted. Arts = arts and humanities, Bio = biological sciences, Bus = business, Educ = education, Engin = engineering, Other prof = other professional fields, and Social sci = social sciences.

[a] p < 0.01; [b] p < 0.05; [c] p > 0.05

on activities other than coursework more than their colleagues in pure fields (arts and humanities and the sciences). It seems likely that activities other than coursework are seen as an avenue for knowledge application and of particular use for students.

For the other two activities, other interactions with students outside class and supervising internships and field experiences, the split is largely between life fields (biological sciences, education, and social sciences)—those fields dealing with life systems (Biglan, 1973)—and nonlife fields (arts and humanities, engineering, and physical sciences). Life fields tend to score higher on both measures. This makes sense for the supervision measure, since internships and field experiences are required in many life fields. The life/nonlife split on the other interactions outside class measure is less clearly explained by Biglan's categories. However, there is a strong overlap between life fields and what John Holland (1997) calls social environments—environments that attract people who like to cooperate and interact with one another. That people in social environments enjoy interaction with one another would certainly explain why faculty in those fields tend to interact with their students more than faculty in other disciplines.

The overall pattern, then, is that faculty members tend to align the gifting of some of their time with activities inherent to their fields. This is not surprising given that faculty members tend toward this kind of alignment across their work activities (Finkelstein, 1984) and such alignment is well documented for the choices faculty make in terms of teaching (Braxton & Hargens, 1996; Smart, Feldman, & Ethington, 2000).

RETHINKING OUR LENS ON FACULTY TIME

Using a productivity lens to examine how faculty members spend their time ends with some predictable outcomes. For example, time spent on teaching and service, especially above the average, is seen as a distraction from research productivity and the rewards that go with it, including monetary and other tangible resources as well as less tangible resources like cultural capital. Since "research and publishing tend to be more heavily rewarded than teaching and service, faculty who devote more time to research and less to other activities will have a greater likelihood of success" (Bellas & Toutkoushian, 1999, p. 383).

The zero-sum nature of time has led some (Hirshfield & Joseph, 2012; Padilla, 1994) to label the extra time faculty of color spend on certain service activities as a cultural or an identity "tax." As asserted, with some empirical support, that tax comes at the expense of research productivity. There is something a bit unsettling, however, about labeling certain activities (e.g., advising or working with students outside class) as a tax. That language undermines faculty members' agency in working on such activities. Further, while that language works to some degree in the context of racial/ethnic differences and the institutional racism faced by faculty of color, it might work less well in the context of other differences, like rank and employment status differences and disciplinary differences. Do part-time faculty or faculty members in education face similar cultural or identity taxes?

The results of this study illustrate some problems with the productivity and taxation orientations to faculty work. Yes, faculty members of color, particularly Black/African American faculty, reported spending more time on the five activities. However, the activities examined in this study cut across the teaching–research–service spectrum. By expanding the set of activities, we complicate assertions about time on service, for example, necessarily taking time away from research or teaching. It might be that faculty of color, for a host of reasons, are more attuned to the quality with which they do their work or the impact of their work, which in turn disposes them to spend more time on teaching, research, *and* service activities that foster good for others. Is such effort a *tax* of some sort or is it more rightly viewed as a *gift*? A philanthropic view would argue for the latter but not necessarily discount the factors contributing to the tax orientation.

The case of part-time faculty is illustrative because they are also not a part of the dominant culture within institutions. The effect of that lack of connection is quite different, however. Full-time non-tenure-track and tenure-track faculty spent similar amounts of time per week on the five activities in this study but about 5 hours more per week than their part-time colleagues. While this is not too surprising, a philanthropic orientation offers a modified insight. The results suggest that the full-time faculty at an institution (tenure-track faculty are overwhelmingly full time) all give about the same amount of time. It has been noted that part-time faculty likely lack integration into the culture of an institution (Gappa et al., 2007). The results of this study may reflect this lack of cultural connection. Still, thinking about this work as giving may lead administrators and faculty leaders to different questions and approaches for encouraging involvement by part-time faculty members. Knowing that most people need to be asked to give (Toppe, Kirsch, & Michel, 2002) should lead academic leaders to ponder whether and how part-timers have been asked to give in these ways. It is also imperative to ask whether it is just or appropriate to invite part-timers to give in these ways without first creating a respectful culture, as described by Gappa et al. (2007). Collectively, this leads to important questions for institutions of higher education: Under what conditions is it appropriate to ask all faculty members or particular subgroups of faculty members for the gifting of their time? Further, which groups of faculty should be expected to give more and which less? Should institutions be asking at all, and what would happen if faculty did not choose to do these things for their students and others?

Unlike studies of research productivity and effective teaching practice, which largely produce predictable and stable disciplinary differences, this study shows that examining how faculty give to their students, institutions, and fields can yield interesting and less predictable patterns. In particular, there are some places where there is little difference (e.g., other interactions with students outside the classroom and working with students on activities other than coursework) and, when there were differences, the pattern of those differences was not consistent from activity to activity, though they seemed connected to the values within particular fields.

Finally, this study looked at only a few ways that faculty members gift their time. It was limited by the set of questions on FSSE that ask faculty members about the ways they spend their time on professorial activities. What would the patterns look like if we asked about a full range of ways faculty spend their time giving to their students, institutions, and fields? What about time spent on certain kinds of advising (e.g., dealing with career or personal issues), colleagueship (e.g., mentoring colleagues), community building (e.g., giving or attending a research talk over lunch), administration (e.g., personally driving a job candidate to or from the airport), service to your field (e.g., being a member of an advisory board for a professional organization), teaching (e.g., helping students who are struggling with a project), and community engagement (e.g., serving as a board member for a discipline-related nonprofit or using service learning to conduct research on a community issue)?

It would also be worth asking where the trade-offs in time are really coming from, since time is finite—whether in a day, a semester, or a probationary period before a tenure decision. Time on work activities seems to be increasing (Schuster & Finkelstein, 2006). Therefore, many of those questions would have to be about things like time with family, sleep, and other uses of personal time. Inquiries into the changing patterns of time allocations might lead to productive policy discussions of matters such as the length of probationary periods, intervals for performance reviews, duration of contracts for part-time faculty, or the nature of incentive programs. Should institutions of higher education be workplaces that are encouraging or asking for certain types of time expenditures or gifts that come at real costs to someone's family or health?

CONCLUSION

In this chapter, a philanthropic orientation to the way faculty members spend their time was used to illustrate how a different lens on faculty work offers alternate lessons and promotes the asking of new questions. From the investigation detailed here, it appears that faculty members of color and full-time faculty (tenure track and non–tenure track) tend to gift more of their time. The patterns by disciplinary area point to patterns that vary by activity, though some fields (education and biological sciences) seem to gift more time than others overall. Above all else, this work illustrates the value of, at least sometimes, moving away from or adding to the productivity orientation to faculty work. It also raises important policy questions about how to promote fair giving by all groups of faculty and, perhaps, how to ensure that the American professoriate remains healthy and vital at a time of growing global competitiveness.

NOTE

1. While the FSSE is the resource for this chapter, there are other data sources for considering faculty engagement in "voluntary action for the public good," such as the Higher Education Research Institute's faculty survey housed at UCLA (see Gary Rhoades, Chapter 8, this volume).

REFERENCES

Bellas, M. L., & Toutkoushian, R. K. (1999). Faculty time allocations and research productivity: Gender, race, and family effects. *Review of Higher Education, 22*(4), 367–390.

Biglan, A. (1973). The characteristics of subject matter in different academic areas. *Journal of Applied Psychology, 57*(3), 195–203.

Braxton, J. M., & Hargens, L. L. (1996). Variation among academic disciplines: Analytical frameworks and research. In J. Smart & W. J. Tierney (Eds.), *Higher education: Handbook of research and theory*, (Vol. 11, pp. 1–46). New York, NY: Agathon Press.

Faculty Survey of Student Engagement. (2011). *FSSE 2011 overview*. Bloomington, IN: Center for Postsecondary Research.

Finkelstein, M. J. (1984). *The American academic profession: A synthesis of social scientific inquiry since World War II*. Columbus, OH: Ohio State University Press.

Gappa, J. M., Austin, A. E., & Trice, A. G. (2007). *Rethinking faculty work: Higher education's strategic imperative*. San Francisco, CA: Jossey-Bass.

Hirshfield, L. E., & Joseph, T. D. (2012). 'We need a woman, we need a Black woman': Gender, race, and identity taxation in the academy. *Gender and Education, 24*(2), 213–227.

Holland, J. L. (1997). *Making vocational choices: A theory of vocational personalities and work environments* (3rd ed.). Lutz, FL: Psychological Assessment Resources.

Kezar, A. (Ed.). (2012). *Embracing non-tenure-track faculty: Changing campuses for the new faculty majority*. New York, NY: Routledge.

Link, A. N., Swann, C. A., & Bozeman, B. (2008). A time allocation study of university faculty. *Economics of Education Review, 27*(4), 363–374.

Massy, W. F., & Zemsky, R. (1994). Faculty discretionary time: Departments and the "academic ratchet." *The Journal of Higher Education, 65*(1), 1–22.

McKeachie, W. J. (1997). Wanting to be a good teacher: What have we learned to date? In J. L. Bess (Ed.), *Teaching well and liking it: Motivating faculty to teach effectively*. Baltimore, MD: The Johns Hopkins University Press.

Milem, J. F., Berger, J. B., & Dey, E. L. (2000). Faculty time allocation: A study of change over twenty years. *Journal of Higher Education, 71*(4), 454–475.

Padilla, A. M. (1994). Ethnic minority scholars, research, and mentoring: Current and future issues. *Educational Researcher, 23*(4), 24–27.

Porter, S. R. (2007). A closer look at faculty service: What affects participation on committees? *The Journal of Higher Education, 78*(5), 523–541.

Schuster, J. H., & Finkelstein, M. J. (2006). *The American faculty: The restructuring of academic work and careers*. Baltimore, MD: The Johns Hopkins University Press.

Smart, J. C., Feldman, K. A., & Ethington, C. A. (2000). *Academic disciplines: Holland's theory and the study of college students and faculty*. Nashville, TN: Vanderbilt University Press.

Toppe, C. M., Kirsch, A. D., & Michel, J. (2002). *Giving and volunteering in the United States 2001: Findings from a national survey*. Washington, DC: Independent Sector.

CHAPTER 6

Philanthropy Without Tenure

Genevieve G. Shaker

There are a few things I love the most about teaching, but what keeps me coming back is that it feels like I'm doing something valuable for the world.

—Part-time faculty member (Warner, 2012b)

Concerns about American higher education are far-reaching. Worries include several directly related to faculty, for example, documenting instructional quality, increasing student success through tracking learning outcomes, maintaining academic freedom, operating in a more transparent and accountable environment, understanding the implications of higher tuition costs, and maximizing faculty productivity and institutional commitment. Not inconsequential is the rapid erosion of faculty's discretion over their own time, which provides them with the professional autonomy necessary to fulfill their increasingly complex and demanding job responsibilities—and to go beyond those explicit responsibilities to ensure student, institutional, and societal success.

The conversion of America's academic workforce to a majority non-tenure-track faculty[1] is thought to be at least partially to blame for many postsecondary difficulties and challenges (Bland, Center, Finstad, Risbey, & Staples, 2006; Cross & Goldenberg, 2009; Jaeger & Eagan, 2010; Umbach, 2007). Such claims are not abstract. Instead, they reflect on the individuals in these contingent roles—well-meaning people who may face misguided, even virulent, critique as the source of much that is wrong in the academy. In a system that relies on their labor (and perpetuates their roles), contingent faculty might be characterized as "pawns" who meet functional needs and are simultaneously diminished—if not demonized—for their very existence. In reality, these faculty have relatively little control over their time within their formal or contractual duties, yet many elect to devote—arguably, donate—their personal time to aid in the progress or goal-attainment of those whom they are teaching or otherwise serving.

Within such a context of negativity and blame, what causes non-tenure-track faculty to remain in their positions any longer than necessary? This question addresses how a desire to do good for others may be a force in the motivation and retention of individual contingent faculty, particularly those who are primarily engaged in teaching. Is it possible that contingent faculty begin in the profession and stay in academia due *in part* to philanthropic values, such as concern for the public good and care for society, especially in relation to the welfare and success of students? The lack of research on the motivations of contingent faculty indicates a need for a comprehensive examination of all aspects of this workforce, since so much of higher education rests in their hands (Baldwin & Chronister, 2001; Kezar & Sam, 2010, 2011; Schuster & Finkelstein, 2006). At the same time, the lack of a convincing and coherent analysis invites exploration of many perspectives. The lens provided by philanthropy is a speculative approach both to examine what is at risk and to highlight one of the hidden values of the contingent workforce in the absence of a more compelling explanation. Specifically, I hope to stimulate further discussion about how philanthropic ideals may help us understand contingent faculty motivations and how this approach is relevant to the changing environment of higher education.

CONTINGENT FACULTY AND THE ACADEMY

Non-tenure-track faculty work in academic positions without an opportunity for long-term economic security or for significant institutional investment. (Today, due process—the third pillar of tenure—is essentially required by law.) Contingent faculty appear in a variety of guises—as clinical faculty, lecturers, adjuncts, visitors, and instructors, to name a few titles—at all manner of institutions from the largest research universities to the smallest community colleges and from selective schools to those with open admissions (Kezar & Sam, 2010). They teach the majority of undergraduate credit hours and are the faculty majority in the United States, composing 75% of the faculty population (Curtis & Thornton, 2013; JBL Associates, 2008; Knapp, Kelly-Reid, & Ginder, 2010). They are not only focused on teaching; particularly the full-time cohort also conducts research, engages in service, and administers programs (Bergom & Waltman, 2009; Bergom, Waltman, August, & Hollenshead, 2010; Kezar & Sam, 2010; Schuster & Finkelstein, 2006). Women are disproportionately represented in the non-tenure-track ranks in comparison with the tenure-eligible population (Bergom & Waltman, 2009; Schuster & Finkelstein, 2006).

While a smaller proportion of contingent faculty has a terminal degree than do the tenure-line faculty, the number of those with this credential is not insignificant. For example, one national survey found 57% of part-time faculty to have a doctorate, professional, or terminal degree (Coalition on the Academic Workforce, 2012). In the same survey, an additional 7% had finished their doctoral coursework except for the dissertation. Non-tenure-track faculty have been divided into willing and unwilling entrants to the profession—some prefer these roles to others in academe, while some perceive these positions, rightly or wrongly, as stepping-stones toward future tenure-track opportunities (Maynard & Joseph, 2008). Not surprisingly, these initial distinctions have often been found to affect the faculty's responses to their positions in the longer term (Baldwin & Chronister, 2001; Gappa, Austin, & Trice, 2007; Maynard & Joseph, 2008; Shaker, 2008).

The practice of protecting academic employment (and freedom) with tenure is a phenomenon that began early in the 20th century. By the end of that century, however, part-time faculty appointments outpaced tenure-eligible positions and full-time non-tenure-track appointments played an increasingly important role. Initially, part-time faculty were employed to make use of their expert knowledge and then most prominently for cost savings, and full-time non-tenure-track faculty came to be seen as a positive option to the overreliance on part-time faculty and as more flexible, fiscally and otherwise, than tenure-line appointments (Levin, Shaker, & Wagoner, 2011). Most (but not all) contingent faculty receive compensation that is far from equivalent to that of their tenure-track colleagues, and part-time faculty are short-changed not only in salary but also with respect to health and retirement benefits; professional development opportunities; and functional support, such as office space (Cross & Goldenberg, 2009; Curtis & Thornton, 2013; Gappa et al., 2007; Kezar & Sam, 2010; Knapp, Kelly-Reid, & Ginder, 2011; Levin et al., 2011). A 2011 crowd-sourced study found the average wage per class for part-time teaching was $2,700; national data about full-time contingent employment points to salaries, regardless of seniority, that are thousands of dollars below tenure-line faculty at the assistant professor level (Coalition on the Academic Workforce, 2012; Knapp et al., 2011). The financial situation can be so bad that some part-time faculty receive food stamps and governmental assistance to supplement their incomes (Patton, 2012).

Contingent faculty experience low status in policy and practice, limited opportunity for advancement and recognition, and a diminished sense of professionalism (Baldwin & Chronister, 2001; Gappa et al., 2007; Kezar & Sam, 2010; Levin & Shaker, 2011; Shaker, 2008). Often, contingent faculty do not receive an orientation, are excluded from faculty governance, do not participate in curriculum design, and do not receive ample notice for their teaching assignments, conditions which arguably affect student learning and success (Kezar, Longanecker, & Maxey, 2013). Yet they are a heterogeneous group whose reactions to their job conditions cannot be easily or broadly predicted. Their experiences vary based on a range of factors as diverse as departmental environments and leadership, disciplinary traditions, credentials, life and career phase, career paths, newness to teaching, peer comparison group, perceptions of marginalization and inclusion, professional relationships, and primary job responsibilities (Bergom & Waltman, 2009; Bergom et al., 2010; Shaker, 2008).

Generally speaking, however, the discrepancy of work and reward for contingent faculty can be so large as to raise the question of why these academic workers persist when other opportunities would be more remunerative and possibly less discouraging. With such challenging working conditions, contingent faculty are left to construct alternative rationales for remaining in an environment with limited personal recognition, professional security (or financial remuneration), and opportunity for advancement.

PHILANTHROPY AND ACADEMIC WORK

Tenure is not required for faculty to be philanthropic and, indeed, because the shared responsibilities that accompany tenure are lost to many tenure-stream faculty (Kennedy, 1997; Plater, 1998), the tenure label is not in itself the determining factor of whether (and why) faculty contribute to their institutions and communities in extraordinary ways. Contingent faculty members do not enjoy tenure's rights and benefits, such as guaranteed employment, job security, prestige, and the specialized protection of academic freedom, nor do they share in tenure's set of inherent responsibilities to institutions, disciplines, colleagues, students, and society (American Association of University Professors [AAUP], 1940; Kennedy, 1997).

It is true that some contingent faculty may choose to do less than they must: "There is no incentive to give 100 percent. . . . Mediocrity is built into the system," said one non-tenure-eligible individual in a *Chronicle of Higher Education* article (Wilson, 2009). Conversely, other contingent faculty do more than they must and for reasons that are outside personal benefit or obvious incentives (Hollenshead et al., 2007; Shaker, 2008). In this case—when contingent faculty do more than necessary and are not "blessed with" the institutional investment of tenure—perhaps they are exhibiting greater philanthropic tendencies than their tenure-line colleagues. Moreover, in earning salaries that are less than generous and less stable than those provided on the tenure track, do contingent faculty "give" their work for less than it may be worth in another employment arena from a desire to contribute to society (principally in the form of helping ensure students' success), especially where they have other, even marginally, more financially rewarding options?

The idea that faculty work may be philanthropic—in some sense and to some degree—hinges on the definition of philanthropy as "voluntary action for the public good" (Payton, 1988, p. 3). Philanthropy is often mistaken for being correlated to financial wealth or financial gifts. In truth, money and tangible goods are only one kind of gift, and they have convenient and measureable, but limited, worth. Intangible contributions of intellectual resources are those that faculty are most often able to give to others (see Marty Sulek, Chapter 3, this volume), especially given their deep knowledge and expertise.

These kinds of gifts are priceless in the sense that their value is impossible to measure and their outcomes may be ongoing, stretching beyond our potential to document them over time. Moreover, we rely on our intellectual capacity to make fiscal gifts worthwhile and appropriate. (Consider the effects of great thinkers on society and civilization in comparison with a financial gift whose reach may be significant, but whose effectiveness is a direct result of those who conceived it and applied it to the problem at hand.) Money isn't everything, and what faculty have to offer may actually be a great deal more valuable in a philanthropic sense.

Turning from the esoteric to the more practical, the notion that faculty may behave philanthropically or be philanthropic by intention requires some attention to salary and the issue of whether receiving compensation removes the possibility of philanthropic intent. Employees doing work that includes some level of compensation, and individuals receiving intangible benefits from giving (such as good feelings), may also be acting philanthropically in part. Labor economists employ a "labor donation" hypothesis by which nonprofit workers, such as university employees, are willing to accept lower pay in return for working in a socially beneficial setting (Preston, 1989). Similarly, the identification model of philanthropic motivation (Schervish, 1992; Schervish & Havens, 1997) and the concept that both givers and receivers may benefit from philanthropy (Martin, 1994) also have relevance. Admittedly, these latter scholars did not intend their theories to extend understandings of workplace motivations, but they do provide examples of available tools for considering philanthropic acts or motives as not exclusive of an individual's own interests, such as the need to earn a living or desire to enjoy the satisfaction of doing good.

Framed in rational utilitarianism theory (Becker, 1976), which challenged the possibility of purely altruistic behavior, Schervish and Havens (1997) argue that philanthropic motivations cannot be explained exclusively as either altruistic or self-interested. They contend, rather, that "the type and degree of empathetic identification with the needs of others generates philanthropic commitment" (p. 238) and that people give as a part of a community of participation.

Faculty, who are part of academic communities, share common purposes and are witness to the needs of students, institutions, colleagues, and
society through their professional perspective. Faculty are also onetime students who received support and encouragement, as well as colleagues who
desire advice from their peers. As institutional insiders, they know better
than anyone what an institution requires to function. As participants in society and public life, they are aware of how to serve society with their specialized expertise. In brief, faculty have ample opportunity to develop empathy
that can lead to philanthropy, in this case, through extraordinary efforts in
the workplace.

"Organizational citizenship behavior," or OCB as it is frequently referenced, includes workers' actions beyond formal job expectations, which are
not formally rewarded, and may further their organizations, help their coworkers, or provide assistance beyond organizational boundaries (Lepine, Erez, &
Johnson, 2002). A substantial literature exists around this concept—too complex to be fully explained or incorporated here. Still, it is noteworthy that two
sources of such behavior—intrinsic satisfaction and conscientiousness—align
with the values expressed by contingent faculty, which are explored in the
next section. Dimensions of OCB—often operationalized as altruism, good
sportsmanship, civic virtue, and courtesy—may be overlapping and, as such,
support the notion of OCB as an overall individual tendency toward a particular kind of behavior. It is this tendency, by whatever name or theoretical
construct, which can also be explored through the lens of philanthropy, as in
this discussion of faculty work.

THE VALUE OF THE PHILANTHROPIC LENS

Given the range of possible approaches to understanding why non-tenure-
track faculty are drawn to this work—or remain in it—despite comparatively low compensation and poor conditions, even in light of ostensibly better
options, what value is added by using the unfamiliar framework of philanthropy? The argument for introducing a new perspective on a familiar if
unspoken issue is fundamentally one of advancing the public policy debate.
What is at stake is nothing less than the nature of faculty work in the coming
decades and the fate of an "industry"—or social good—that has been nearly
uniformly labeled as key to this nation's economic, social, political, and scientific place in the world. Higher education develops the talent pipeline
that will provide both an adequately prepared citizenry capable of making
decisions to ensure an equitable and sustainable future and a talent pool
capable of innovating faster than adverse conditions. Regardless of whether
the value of higher education is ascribed more to vocationally oriented associate degrees and certificates or to liberal education and postbaccalaureate

advanced degrees, the academic workforce remains vulnerable to the changed conditions that began this chapter. While the concerns about faculty apply to tenure track and non-tenure track alike, the policy considerations must take note that some three-fourths of the academic workforce is contingent to significantly different from the public perception of who compose the faculty (Curtis & Thornton, 2013).

If higher education is so singularly important as an economic sector—leaving aside its social value to the public good—what other essential service industry would knowingly and willingly allow 75% of the professionals responsible for its success to serve their respective institutions with such tenuous linkages? Imagine, for a moment, hospitals, police departments, or judicial systems where more than half the professional employees—the people responsible for results (learning outcomes in this instance) are contingent, comparatively poorly paid, lacking autonomy, and deprived of some aspects of the basic work conditions widely considered necessary for minimally acceptable results. Indeed to be a professional means to be self-governing to some degree, to have control over preparation for one's career, and to have a high level of autonomy—in exchange for some attention to the public good—but non-tenure-track employees have few of these characteristics and often feel uncomfortable in their professional identity (Levin & Shaker, 2011; Sullivan, 2007). Yet we expect high-quality teaching, commitment to students, and dedication to university (and universal) ideals from all of the academic workforce.

The question again: Why is philanthropy a useful lens for examining this growing public policy issue? And is it a public policy issue or merely a series of business decisions by different institutions—public, nonprofit, for-profit, or the indeterminate (as is the case for many of the emerging online programs)? One answer is basic and simple. Higher education is unquestionably a public good (Kezar, Chambers, Burkhardt, & Associates, 2005). Only a tiny handful of postsecondary institutions decline the federal or state financial aid that students bring to them—and all are dependent on that aid for their existence. We can find not one public or private institution that does not at least depend on philanthropic dollars for its support directly or indirectly (including the benefit of a tax-exempt status for most, a highly valuable good that the public provides these institutions because of their social return). Moreover, many institutions depend on public funds for research, and a growing portion of the contingent workforce is assigned tasks directly related to research (Bergom et al., 2010). On economic grounds alone, the future employment condition of the academic workforce is without question a public policy issue.

And philanthropy is, fundamentally, a matter of economic choice, whether the medium for the transaction is money, talent, time, goods, reputation, or something else of value. Institutions are investing public funds

from multiple sources in decisions that profoundly affect the learning outcomes imputed to graduates by their alma maters and by the agencies that
accredit them. And what are they investing in when it comes to faculty? The
answer, of course, is many things, including talent, preparation, credentials,
reputation, and the like—but what is common to all faculty hires across all
classifications and all distinctions of tenure? It is, of course, the time and
commitment of the faculty. Tenured and tenure-track faculty have an inherent and explicit commitment based on the reciprocal responsibilities of
tenure: the tenure-track faculty will give 100% their time *and* their commitment to the institution in return for the protections of tenure (AAUP, 1940).
Many institutions allow faculty to devote part of their time to work outside
the university for consulting or other activities, both remunerated and un-
remunerated, but always subject to the policies—and typically the explicit
approval—of the institution, and often permitted as an act of contributing
to the public good. They will not engage in work—compensated work—outside their tenure-granting workplace without its consent. But what of the
vast majority of faculty who have no such reciprocal agreement?

At the heart of the public policy debate is the discretionary uses of faculty time. For tenure-stream faculty, this is a highly valued aspect of professional status. The implicit bargain goes something like this: As long as
you meet your classes and keep defined appointments with students, you are
free to use your time in whatever way you choose as individual professionals to achieve results in teaching, research, and service for which you will be
held accountable based on some real or imputed proportion of commitment.
Thus freed, these fortunate few invest their time where they find the greatest
rewards—intrinsic as well as compensated. For them, time is fungible. Contingent faculty are not so lucky. The allocation of their time is zero-sum accounting. Time spent on activities not required by their position description
or contract is inherently voluntary, and in almost all instances, these contributions add to the bottom line of the public good: philanthropy. Tenured or
tenure-track faculty may also make contributions that exceed the proportion-
ate expectations of their positions, so they, too, may donate their time—but
the very fact of tenure makes a difference in that the contingent faculty are
by their very definition without the same sort of reciprocal relationship.

What constitutes the discretionary and voluntary investment of faculty
time is open to legitimate question and debate. However, in the instance of
the part-time adjunct professor teaching one course, the further investment
of time comes in the form of coming to class early and staying late to meet
with students (since office hours usually aren't part of the formal duties);
beyond the class-specific advice, there is often general advising and even
mentoring, what one professor referred to as opportunities for students to
build "cultural and social capital" through professional introductions and

letters of recommendation (Flanders, 2013). Most contingent faculty invest hours each week in preparation, often reading research and pedagogical literature to keep current (something to be encouraged and valued, surely). A few contribute to curriculum development by offering feedback on what is working or not working in the classroom. These days it is impossible to escape technology, and part-time faculty in particular may have to learn different course management systems for different institutions; further, there is email—when it comes to students whose success may depend on the timeliness of a teacher's response, the demands for responsiveness can be high. And then there is professional development in all its dimensions—the constant challenge to remain a professional by advancing with the discipline, something built into the tenure obligation but absent from most contingent faculty job descriptions.

It remains to be determined what these—and other—voluntary contributions might add to a typical course either in the amount of time spent or the resulting student success, but it is safe to say the investment, that is, the discretionary, voluntary contribution, is substantial and valuable. The probable directions of contingent faculty labor as a policy issue are made stark by contrast through the voices of contingent faculty when they speak for themselves about why they do what they do.

VOICES OF NON-TENURE-TRACK FACULTY

As a part of a rising wave of attention to contingent faculty matters, a series, "Adjunct Heroes" on the *Inside Higher Ed* news website asked select part-time faculty what was rewarding about teaching and what kept them coming back to the classroom. Their comments were typically multidimensional, encompassing both the struggle of difficult and often disappointing employment circumstances and then, more prominently, the fulfillment that comes from witnessing students' development. Philanthropy has a multitude of purposes, and several of these are evident in the statements of the faculty, specifically the enhancement of human potential, promotion of equity and justice, and contribution to human fulfillment (Tempel, 2003). What these faculty give to their students is significant: knowledge, skills, experience, caring, and compassion, with the aim of preparing them for life, whether through the development of specific knowledge or through the life skills defined by the liberal arts. Excerpts from five of the interviews follow and illustrate the way philanthropy informs faculty self-conceptualizations:

1.   There's [*sic*] a couple of reasons, one cynically stubborn, and one idealistic. The cynical reason is that I am hanging on by my

fingernails in academia, because I know just how hard it is to get back in if I was [*sic*] to leave . . . but really, it's because I truly do feel a great sense of purpose, of accomplishment, when a student's eyes light up—when someone "gets" it, gets interested, gets excited about learning (Warner, 2012e).

2. I did the math recently and found that I've taught about 400 students in my time as an adjunct. . . . I remember most of them, and some of them (enough to keep me going, anyway) have expressed their thanks to me either for being understanding or helpful or for being a good teacher. . . . It's nice to know that you've done something even remotely meaningful. It helps in those dark moments when you're asking yourself what in the world you're doing and if it's worth the effort (Warner, 2012a).

3. It's easily the students. . . . There's nothing better than watching people grow right before your eyes and being the person who facilitates that. One of the best things about teaching writing . . . is that you don't just deal in writing, you deal in thinking and in thinking, particularly, about complex and often disturbing issues in our culture. . . . I really enjoy the autonomy of teaching. There's a freedom in that that I'm not sure exists in most other professions (Warner, 2012d).

4. What keeps me coming back each semester are the days when I am on campus, teaching, working with students, etc. and it feels like this is my full time job, my life. If I forget about my salary and money problems associated with my job, it's so easy to fall in love with my work (Warner, 2012c).

5. There are a few things I love the most about teaching, but what keeps me coming back is that it feels like I'm doing something valuable for the world. Not all of the time. Much of the time it feels like I'm running on a treadmill. But the little moments, like when students say "I can't go see X any more without thinking of Y, since I took your class," go a long way (Warner, 2012a).

The ability to give to students (and inherently contribute to philanthropic purposes) provides faculty with both professional motivation and personal meaning. Those who know (or are) contingent faculty can likely vouch for the accuracy of this sampling of non-tenure-track perspectives. This is further highlighted by the few contingent faculty who speak openly about not being as "giving" to students as they would be in full-time roles. As one faculty member—tenured at one institution and adjunct at another—wrote about the latter case, "These students are a pleasure to teach, and I want to see them succeed, but there is no reward beyond personal satisfaction for me in doing unpaid service beyond the terms of my contract" (Flanders, 2013). The author goes on to contrast this attitude to his willingness to support students at his primary institution. By unbundling faculty roles and paying contingent faculty per course, service is underscored as personal philanthropy as well as an economic choice.

The motivation to teach out of a sense of contributing to the greater good, which is expressed by these part-time faculty comments, is affirmed by empirical research conducted with a group of full-time contingent faculty in English (Shaker, 2008, 2013). I interviewed 18 full-time, non-tenure-track teaching faculty from three large public institutions and completed a phenomenological analysis (van Manen, 1990), following the methods of Carspecken (1996), Creswell (2003), and Moustakas (1994). The faculty in the study thought of themselves as people who helped and served by doing well at what they loved most—teaching and helping students. "We help people," said one person simply. Others said they wanted "to make a difference" in students' lives:

> People who teach at the [contingent] level, they're not trying to climb the ladder. . . . They're looking for an environment in which they can feel useful and content with what they do and feel like they're making a difference. (Shaker, 2008)

The call to teach at the college level was an avocation with deep meaning for which several had forgone more prestigious or less demanding careers.

For an overwhelming majority of my participants, helping students was at the heart of their work; this is what motivated them to continue teaching, to do their best and, at times, to go beyond any reasonable expectations (Shaker, 2008). Several said things like "I do give a lot of extra time to students, and I don't mind that. I love that." Another explained the great lengths she had gone for her students on her own time to navigate their personal problems and challenges. One person commented, "I see myself as equipping [students] to live in the modern world in a way that they can make decisions for themselves, so it goes really beyond the university." By preparing their students to be contributing members of their communities, these faculty also sought to make a contribution to society as a whole. An experienced contingent professor said, "Well, what motivates me? The fact that I'm doing something, contributing to people's well-being; that motivates me. . . . It's an intrinsic kind of motivation."

Although the motivations reported by the contingent faculty carried great weight, the faculty in the study were unhappy with other job characteristics, including the fiscal compensation (Shaker, 2008). A large majority of the participants was either critical or ambivalent about their salaries. One person said, "Of course, I don't think any of us are satisfied with our salary, but going in I knew that you don't do it really for the pay." These responses were tempered by the sense that contingent work is about something other than money and also focused on the social benefits of such work.

Teaching and contingent work, then, is not about money alone, as expressed in a *Chronicle of Higher Education* survey that concluded contingent faculty were rarely motivated only by financial concerns (June, 2009a). One contingent faculty member spoke for many in saying that teaching is "about giving back to the community and seeing the students excel." Another said in a related article, "Teaching writing is a way to show students they have a voice. . . . I think teaching at UIC [University of Illinois at Chicago] in this discipline allows me to enact my idea of social justice. I do feel like I'm making a difference" (June, 2009b).

The evidence is certainly not definitive, but it is possible that contingent faculty may work for less than they think they are due because they believe they are making a philanthropic contribution. By rationalizing their compensation as part of an arrangement they are party to, the participants accommodate for a harsh reality, perhaps using the goal of helping others as a device for maintaining self-respect. But there may be other consequences beyond just the individual.

IMPLICATIONS OF WORKING FOR THE PUBLIC GOOD

As the trend toward greater reliance on contingent faculty proceeds in response to diminished public resources (direct allocations for public institutions as well as diminished financial aid or research support for all institutions), the elasticity in pricing higher education may be reaching its end, thus putting even greater pressure on institutions to cut costs and increase efficiencies. Little room exists to expand the proportion of contingent to tenure-related faculty, so the drive for efficiency in the expectations for contingent faculty may make harsh conditions even harsher. Unless the voluntary contributions of faculty (again, all faculty but especially the contingent faculty) are recognized, measured, and valued, their contributions to the public good and benefits for American higher education may be lost. Indeed, not all contingent faculty are able to fulfill the needs of students and, without the philanthropic commitment of many part-time faculty, the overreliance on contingent faculty may affect students' academic experiences.

The presence of philanthropic attitudes and intent among contingent faculty is to be celebrated and recognized because such attention is the right thing to do and because this is a public policy, society has to recognize what is at stake in, first, increasing the nation's dependence on contingent faculty and, second, deciding how to value these professionals' discretionary investment of their time, talent, and more. The notion should also be approached with some caution, warn those who study contingent faculty in English composition. Institutions may take advantage of the "psychic income" or the "perceived personal, social, and cultural compensation that a job brings to an individual above and beyond wages" (Wills, 2004, p. 201) by promoting the intangible benefits of faculty work—whether selfish or selfless—to keep faculty coming back without paying a fair wage. "Women, especially, seem to be willing to work to satisfy abstract concepts of duty or service," Katherine Wills writes, "because part-time teaching falls within a discourse of philanthropy" (p. 202). In this line of thinking, the compensation contingent faculty receive (psychic or otherwise) may not be what they expect and need (Levin & Shaker, 2011), and thus encouraging contingent faculty to work for these reasons perpetuates a deeply flawed system of abuse. In order to maintain the momentum of overall efforts to gain appropriate compensation and recognition for non-tenure-track faculty, Wills argues, faculty must stop thinking in psychic terms and begin thinking about the bottom line: fiscal compensation. What is the actual value of these discretionary investments?

Contingent faculty should not "need" to be as philanthropic, as they already work for less than their tenured colleagues. Nevertheless, asking them to remove their care for others and dedication to students, which characterizes the majority of motivations in this chapter, will result in a loss of meaning that is emblematic of philanthropy—and is likely an impossible request. Asking faculty to think in purely financial terms about their work would be damaging for students, society, and institutions. If faculty let go of social purpose and institutions recognize only quantifiable markers of productivity, such as students in seats or research dollars in hand, higher education in the United States will become unrecognizable and dehumanized. The argument of the "psychic income" born of philanthropic purposes is legitimate, but it must be turned on its head and used to the advantage of the reputation, sincerity, and value of contingent faculty. That they do the work for something other than financial reward is to be recognized but not used as an excuse to perpetuate a flawed system. Moreover, some will argue that if these faculty want to do more than is necessary, then it is their choice to behave "philanthropically" so there is no need to reward such behavior through increased compensation—a perspective that could likewise be a handy method for perpetuating an unfortunate reality. The contention is not that contingent faculty should receive more compensation simply because they are philanthropic, rather, it is that fair compensation should equate to the level of their contributions. Undoubtedly, were they to be better compensated, they would continue to be motivated by a desire to help others.

This chapter is a marker on the path to better understanding contingent faculty by acknowledging why they may do what they do. It tells us that generosity cannot be thought of as the exclusive domain of the tenured "class." If the desire to do good for others is a driving force for contingent faculty, this sense of purpose may encourage faculty in these appointments to soldier on despite subpar salaries and low status, to their own detriment, but for the benefit of students and, perhaps through their self-sacrifice, a society that needs an educated population to thrive. If, on a larger scale, contingent faculty work for the common good and are philanthropically motivated, workforce changes do not necessarily signal the demise of faculty commitment—and excellence—and concerns about contingent faculty may be unfounded. Maintaining the current condition of contingent faculty and over-relying on their breadth of generosity and the motivation of care, however, would be unfair and unsustainable. And, in a changing landscape of professional expectations—where, for example, faculty may teach tens of thousands of students in massive open online courses—no institution, administrator, or faculty member can expect the status quo to persist or remain viable.

Further research is clearly required to actually quantify the value added by the discretionary allocation of time by contingent and tenure-track faculty alike. Specifically, institutions and researchers have to first recognize the investment of the time before they can measure, assess, and value it. Pending that research and observable results, the hypothesis put forward here is that without the philanthropic actions of faculty (all faculty but especially the majority who are contingent), both the overall quality of American higher education and its resulting learning outcomes are at risk.

NOTE

1. In this chapter, the term *non-tenure-track faculty* is used synonymously and interchangeably with the term *contingent faculty*—that is, all those full- and part-time faculty who are not eligible for tenure regardless of whether their duties are exclusively focused on one dimension of faculty work (teaching, research, or service) or a combination; their appointments may include academic administration, advising, community engagement, clinical duties, supervision, or others. These terms highlight the distinction of tenure and the uncertain working conditions of people without tenure—who undertake at least some of the same faculty work as tenured colleagues but without the full faculty reward structure.

REFERENCES

American Association of University Professors. (1940). Statement of principles on academic freedom and tenure. Available at http://www.aaup.org/AAUP/pubsres/policydocs/1940statement.htm

Baldwin, R. G., & Chronister, J. L. (2001). *Teaching without tenure: Policies and practices for a new era.* Baltimore, MD: The Johns Hopkins University Press.

Becker, G. S. (1976). *The economic approach to human behavior.* Chicago, IL: The University of Chicago Press.

Bergom, I., & Waltman, J. (2009). Satisfaction and discontent: Voices of non-tenure-track faculty. *On Campus with Women, 37*(3). Available at http://www.aacu.org/ocww/volume37_3/feature.cfm?section=2

Bergom, I., Waltman, J., August, L., & Hollenshead, C. (2010). Academic researchers speak. *Change, 42*(2), 45–49.

Bland, C. J., Center, B. A., Finstad, D. A., Risbey, K. R., & Staples, J. (2006). The impact of appointment type on the productivity and commitment of full-time faculty in research and doctoral institutions. *The Journal of Higher Education, 77*(1), 90–123.

Carspecken, P. F. (1996). *Critical ethnography in educational research: A theoretical and practical guide.* New York, NY: Routledge.

Coalition on the Academic Workforce. (2012). A portrait of part-time faculty members: A summary of findings on part-time respondents to the Coalition on the Academic Workforce survey of contingent faculty members and instructors. Available at http://www.academicworkforce.org/survey.html

Creswell, J. W. (2003). *Research design: Qualitative, quantitative, and mixed method approaches.* Thousand Oaks, CA: Sage.

Cross, J. G., & Goldenberg, E. N. (2009). *Off-track profs: Nontenured teachers in higher education.* Cambridge, MA: MIT Press.

Curtis, J. W., & Thornton, S. (2013). *The annual report of the economic status of the profession, 2012–2013.* Washington, DC: American Association of University Professors. Available at http://www.aaup.org/file/2012-13Economic-Status-Report.pdf

Flanders, S. (2013, June 24). I'm an adjunct, not a volunteer. *The Chronicle of Higher Education.* Available at http://chronicle.com/article/Im-an-Adjunct-Not-a/139969/

Gappa, J. M., Austin, A. E., & Trice, A. G. (2007). *Rethinking faculty work: Higher education's strategic imperative.* Hoboken, NJ: John Wiley & Sons.

Hollenshead, C., Waltman, J., August, L., Miller, J., Smith, G., & Bell, A. (2007). *Making the best of both worlds: Findings from a national institution-level survey on non-tenure track faculty.* Ann Arbor, MI: Center for the Education of Women. Available at http://www.cew.umich.edu/PDFs/CEW%20Final%20Report%20PP34.pdf

Jaeger, A. J., & Eagan, M. K. (2010). Examining retention and contingent faculty use in a state system of public higher education. *Educational Policy, 24*(4), 1–31.

JBL Associates. (2008). *Reversing course: The troubled state of academic staffing and a path forward*. Washington, DC: American Federation of Teachers.

June, A. W. (2009a, October 18). Love of teaching draws adjuncts to the classroom despite low pay. *The Chronicle of Higher Education*. Available at http://chronicle.com/article/Love-of-Teaching-Draws/48845/

June, A. W. (2009b, October 18). Full-time instructors shoulder the same burdens that part-timers do. *The Chronicle of Higher Education*. Available at http://chronicle.com/article/Full-Time-Instructors-Shoulder/48841/

Kennedy, D. (1997). *Academic duty*. Cambridge, MA: Harvard University Press.

Kezar, A., Chambers, T. C., Burkhardt, J. C., & Associates. (2005). *Higher education for the public good: Emerging voices from a national movement*. San Francisco, CA: John Wiley & Sons.

Kezar, A., Longanecker, D., & Maxey, D. (2013, March 26). Our dirty little secret. *Inside Higher Ed*. Available at http://www.insidehighered.com/views/2013/03/26/essay-calls-college-leaders-admit-they-treat-adjuncts-unethically

Kezar, A., & Sam, C. (2010). *Understanding the new majority of non-tenure-track faculty in higher education. Demographics, experiences, and plans of action.* (ASHE Higher Education Report, Vol. 36, No. 4). San Francisco, CA: Jossey-Bass.

Kezar, A., & Sam, C. (2011). *Non-tenure-track faculty in higher education #2.* (ASHE Higher Education Report, Vol. 36, No. 5). San Francisco, CA: Jossey-Bass.

Knapp, L. G., Kelly-Reid, J. E., & Ginder, S. A. (2010). *Employees in postsecondary institutions, fall 2009, and salaries of full-time instructional staff, 2009–10.* (NCES 2011-150). U.S. Department of Education. Washington, DC: National Center for Education Statistics. Available at http://nces.ed.gov/pubsearch

Knapp, L. G., Kelly-Reid, J. E., & Ginder, S. A. (2011). *Employees in postsecondary institutions, fall 2010, and salaries of full-time instructional staff, 2010–11* (NCES 2012-276). U.S. Department of Education. Washington, DC: National Center for Education Statistics. Available at http://nces.ed.gov/pubsearch

Lepine, J. A., Erez, A., & Johnson, D. E. (2002). The nature and dimensionality of organizational citizenship behavior: A critical review and meta-analysis. *Journal of Applied Psychology, 87*(1), 52–65.

Levin, J. S., & Shaker, G. G. (2011). The hybrid and dualistic identity of full-time nontenure-track faculty. *American Behavioral Scientist, 55*(11), 1461–1484.

Levin, J. S., Shaker, G. G., & Wagoner, R. (2011). Post neoliberalism: The professional identity of faculty off the tenure-track. In K. Kempner, S. Marginson, I. Ordorika, & B. Pusser (Eds.), *Universities and the public sphere: Knowledge creation and state building in the era of globalization* (pp. 197–217). New York, NY: Routledge.

Martin, M. W. (1994). *Virtuous giving: Philanthropy, voluntary service, and caring*. Bloomington, IN: Indiana University Press.

Maynard, D. C., & Joseph, T. A. (2008). Are all part-time faculty underemployed?

The influence of faculty status preference on satisfaction and commitment. *Higher Education, 55*(2), 139–154.

Moustakas, C. (1994). *Phenomenological research methods.* Thousand Oaks, CA: Sage.

Patton, S. (2012, May 6). The Ph.D. now comes with food stamps. *The Chronicle of Higher Education.* Available at http://chronicle.com/article/From-Graduate-School-to/131795/

Payton, R. (1988). *Philanthropy: Voluntary action for the public good.* New York, NY: American Council on Education/Macmillan.

Plater, W. M. (1998). Using tenure: Citizenship within the new academic workforce. *American Behavioral Scientist, 41*(5), 680–715.

Preston, A. (1989). The nonprofit worker in a for-profit world. *Journal of Labor Economics, 7*(4), 438–463.

Schervish, P. G. (1992). Adoption and altruism: Those with whom I want to share a dream. *Nonprofit and Voluntary Sector Quarterly, 21*(4), 327–350.

Schervish, P. G., & Havens, J. J. (1997). Social participation and charitable giving: A multivariate analysis. *Voluntas, 8*(3), 235–260.

Schuster, J. H., & Finkelstein, M. J. (2006). *The restructuring of academic work and careers.* Baltimore, MD: The Johns Hopkins University Press.

Shaker, G. G. (2008). Off the track: The experience of being full-time nontenure-track in English. Dissertation Abstracts International. (UMI No. 3387054).

Shaker, G. G. (2013). The road taken: A report on the career paths of a modern academic workforce for faculty developers. *The Journal of Faculty Development, 27*(3), 57–62.

Sullivan, W. M. (2007). *Work and integrity: The crisis and promise of professionalism in America.* San Francisco, CA: Jossey-Bass.

Tempel, E. R. (2003). Contemporary dynamics of philanthropy. In E. R. Tempel (Ed.), *Hank Rosso's achieving excellence in fundraising* (2nd ed., pp. 3–13). San Francisco, CA: Jossey-Bass.

Umbach, P. D. (2007). How effective are they? Exploring the impact of contingent faculty on undergraduate education. *The Review of Higher Education, 30*(2), 91–123.

van Manen, M. (1990). *Researching lived experience: Human science for an action sensitive pedagogy.* New York, NY: State University of New York Press.

Warner, J. (2012a, March 26). Introducing "adjunct heroes." *Inside Higher Ed.* Available at http://www.insidehighered.com/blogs/education-oronte-churm/introducing-adjunct-heroes

Warner, J. (2012b, April 2). Adjunct hero: Keverlee Burchett. *Inside Higher Ed.* Available at http://www.insidehighered.com/blogs/education-oronte-churm/dayofhighered-adjunct-hero-keverlee-burchett

Warner, J. (2012c, April 12). Adjunct hero: Justin Myer Staller. *Inside Higher Ed.* Available at https://www.insidehighered.com/blogs/education-oronte-churm/adjunct-hero-justin-myer-staller

Warner, J. (2012d, May 7). Adjunct hero: Andrew McFadyen-Ketchum. *Inside Higher Ed*. Available at https://www.insidehighered.com/blogs/education-oronte-churm/adjunct-hero-andrew-mcfadyen-ketchum

Warner, J. (2012e, June 12). Adjunct hero: Melissa Bruninga-Matteau. *Inside Higher Ed*. Available at https://www.insidehighered.com/blogs/education-oronte-churm/adjunct-hero-melissa-bruninga-matteau

Wills, K. V. (2004). The lure of 'easy' psychic income. In M. Bousquet, T. Scott, & L. Parascondola (Eds.), *Tenured bosses and disposable teachers: Writing instruction in the managed university* (pp. 201–208). Carbondale, IL: Southern Illinois University Press.

Wilson, R. (2009, October 18). At one 2-year college, adjuncts feel left out. *The Chronicle of Higher Education*. Available at http://chronicle.com/article/At-One-2-Year-College/48844/

CHAPTER 7

Inherent Philanthropy in Multicultural Faculty Work at a Research University

Emily L. Moore and J. Herman Blake

Our careers as faculty and administrators in a range of academic institutions convince us that our work as Black faculty is embedded in a comprehensive concept of the common good. When we think of philanthropy as "voluntary action for the public good" (Payton, 1988, p. 3), we acknowledge an inherent spirit of philanthropic action in our faculty lives. In this chapter, we describe examples of how our professional teaching and research automatically led to voluntary action for the public good. We also give accounts of student interviews of our colleagues from multiple racial and ethnic backgrounds that show the inherent nature of philanthropy in their professional work.

INHERENT PHILANTHROPY

Our emphasis in this chapter is on "inherent philanthropy," an intuitive and profoundly personal pattern that emerges from our "socializations" much more than our aspirations or professional goals. The key concept is "inherent," a pattern that is both personal and intuitive. Growing up in urban Black communities and socialized by parents and grandparents whose lives were rooted in the rural South, we learned about a collective consciousness characterized by community understanding, determination, and cooperation. This is what makes our lives, actions, and intellectual being "inherent." They are latent much more than manifest and guided by a profound sense of history.

Thus, when we reflect on our developmental years, we realize our academic paths were structured not only by our aspirations but also by our socializations—we were raised in communities where both family and society shaped our sense of self. Indeed, our surrounding networks of relatives, churches, and schools created a strong sense that future success should benefit the community as well as ourselves. In retrospect, we realize that our development as teachers and scholars was guided by a profound sense of historical destiny.

In a 1999 essay, we quoted two prominent scholars whose views on race and the color line in America and higher education "book-ended" the 20th century:

> Writing at the dawn of the twentieth century, W.E.B. DuBois (1903) meditated on its meaning for African Americans. . . . He wrote: "The problem of the twentieth century is the problem of the color-line—the relation of the darker to the lighter races of men in Asia and Africa, in America and the islands of the sea." Some nine decades later, Clark Kerr surveyed the challenges facing higher education at the close of the century and wrote: "If I had to pick a single theme most likely to be dominant in the 1990s, it would be the 'the racial crisis' in its several forms."
>
> Race has been an abiding and troubling issue throughout all of American history, and, as we face the dawn of another millennium, it is apparent that the color line continues as a daunting challenge. (Blake & Moore, 1999)

The persistence of that legacy—consciously and unconsciously—became our guide. We knew that as African Americans, our competence would frequently be challenged by those who sought to discredit our teaching and scholarship. At a much more profound level, we had to cope with unarticulated, unexpressed, and sometimes unconscious feelings of worth. These sentiments sometimes led us to become protective and modest while, at the same time, we worked harder to achieve and even exceed expectations. As we were told by family and friends, "You've got to be twice as good." The positive outcomes for us were extraordinary. They were the foundation for our inherent philanthropic work.

UNIVERSITY RESEARCH, TEACHING, AND THE PUBLIC GOOD

> He could have added fortune to fame, but caring for neither, he found happiness and honor in being helpful to the world.
>
> —Epitaph on the grave of George Washington Carver

In 1998, we joined the faculty of "Midwestern University" (a research university with about 25,000 students) as professors in educational leadership and policy studies, and graduate studies (Moore) and sociology, and graduate studies (Blake). We were expected to engage in the traditional faculty work of research, teaching, and service at the large land grant university in the central part of a rural state with a small proportion of African Americans. In addition, we were charged with developing a nascent program in African American studies. However, as we observed the academic performance of Black students, we also saw the path we knew we had to follow, even though administrative leaders had given us other instructions and obligations.

Midwestern University was the alma mater of George Washington Carver, who was awarded a BA and then MS soon after slavery ended. Appointed to the faculty, Carver began his extraordinary career as a teacher/scholar on the campus.[1] In his name, the university recruited a growing number of Black students from all over the nation, through generous scholarships. While there was a strong tradition of academic and intellectual excellence on the campus, it was not seen in the academic achievement of Black students. Their 6-year graduation rates were well below the national rates of Black students in comparable institutions. Data from the Office of Institutional Research showed that from 1983 (when the statistics were first collected) until 1994, the 6-year graduation rate ranged from 24% to 34% (Moore & Blake, 2004). Even though these were competent and qualified students, and even though they had generous scholarships covering all their needs, no more than one third of any cohort had graduated for more than a decade.

We saw this as an extraordinary waste of student talent, an abrogation of the spirit of George Washington Carver, and a drain on the African American future. In Washington Carver's words, "There is no short cut to achievement. Life requires thorough preparation—veneer isn't worth anything." We felt that, in addition to our regular faculty responsibilities, we had a moral obligation to address the low graduation rates of Black students, a performance level we perceived as the "legacy of race and the color line."

Our moral obligation was often deeply felt but seldom expressed. We saw ourselves as fulfilling the hopes and dreams of countless women, men, and children who had worked the fields where we now walked, hoping for the day when their descendants could have the opportunity to study and learn all they were denied. Our work was guided by the sacrifices of forebears like Washington Carver and many others.

When we pointed out the academic achievement disparity to senior administrators, we were advised to focus on scholarship and teaching—other campus offices were responsible for student persistence and, in time, they would deal with the issue. Yet there had been no improvement for more than 10 years. We could not ignore this human wastage in our faculty work, and we set out to raise levels of academic achievement for Black students while fulfilling our normal responsibilities.

In our unique ways—learned from years of success in other institutions—
we began to send specific messages to students (Blake, 1985; National Institute of Education, 1984). We expected them to allocate much more time to
their studies and strengthen their academic skills, thereby increasing their
confidence that they could succeed in all courses of study at the university. We
were clear, deliberate, and comprehensive in our approach.

Students had come to expect an "easy time" in some of the courses
offered in African American studies. As well, the undergraduate student
culture at the university encouraged "studying for tests" rather than deep
learning, and students were accustomed to waiting until the last minute
to cram for examinations—practices that contributed to low levels of academic success among Black students. In addition, some Black students
tended to defer required courses in math and the sciences until their last
semester—leaving their entire academic careers hanging on the outcome of
an examination or grade in one course. We met students who—hoping to
graduate—were pleading with instructors to let them get by in a required
course. In some cases, the students claimed the instructors were preventing them from graduating. We saw these practices as anathema to the self-
confidence, competence, and success of students.

We clearly articulated our high goals, and we expected students to rise
to them. We increased the rigor and expectations in every course we taught.
As George Washington Carver said, "Education is the key to unlock the
golden door of freedom." We joined together in teaching a course on African American women, even though it was an overload for Professor Moore.
Our purpose was to show students that, as scholars, we exhibited academic
rigor as well as harmony and joy in our professional and personal lives. The
course ended with students working for high grades and better understanding of the purpose and meaning of their studies. They became messengers
to the larger Black student body about expectations and academic performance as well as long-term goals and consequences.

ACADEMIC COLLABORATION:
FACULTY, STUDENTS, AND THE PUBLIC GOOD

Realizing the challenge of a dramatic increase in the academic expectations
of African American students, we devoted significant time to establishing a
program of group advising/counseling sessions where students could work
together to develop individual and collective strategies to meet high academic expectations. These sessions met biweekly and were led by advanced
undergraduate students we recruited and trained. In separate weekly individual and group meetings, we counseled and "coached" the student leaders

of the discussion groups, focusing on their study habits. Professor Blake had the primary leadership responsibility and attended all the sessions. Other faculty, professional staff, and some graduate students were recruited to participate in counseling/advising meetings.

It should be noted that most of the faculty, staff, and administrators who joined us in this endeavor were White. Student participants—while predominantly Black—were also Asian Americans, Latinos, and Whites. While all were welcomed and fully included, the discussions focused on the academic challenges faced by Black students. Occasionally, the discussions included relevant personal and social issues. With the guidance of faculty, counseling staff, and graduate students, the undergraduate participants worked on strategies for meeting academic goals in all their courses, far beyond those we taught (Fiske, 2004).

We developed these unique discussion groups and special courses outside our normal workloads and other academic responsibilities. Our belief in and commitment to the concept of "inherent philanthropy" overwhelmed personal and private goals as we became enmeshed in our desire to see students fulfill their academic goals and dreams. These are goals and dreams often destroyed by social patterns of student life. We, however, were passionate about promoting and upholding the legacy of excellence epitomized by our forebears and captured by George Washington Carver, who said, "No individual has any right to come into the world and go out of it without leaving behind him distinct and legitimate reasons for having passed through it."

Initially, students were reluctant to attend academically focused discussion groups, but as they realized that many of their professors were present and gave good advice, attendance increased. Occasionally, a senior-level (i.e., vice president, dean) administrator would attend and usually expressed amazement and admiration for the seriousness of all participants. Indeed, some administrators found the meetings to be sources of inspiration and information. In one instance, the chair of a science department sought feedback about student experiences in their departmental courses. After an intense and supportive exchange of views, one faculty member made a persuasive case to students that their counsel to the department chair increased the importance of students being diligent in their work and consistent in their courses. He stressed that by increasing their involvement in the learning process, they were also increasing their responsibility to meet higher expectations. It was a sobering moment for the students. The message was heard and understood. Faculty and administrative colleagues were generous in sharing their time and experiences with students.

Over several years, the comprehensive approach began to have an impact. We had combined higher expectations in our courses with biweekly group sessions on academic strategies for success, which resulted in greater discipline and course preparation by students. In the classroom, in our role modeling, and in supplementary group discussions, we consistently emphasized high expectations and greater time in study and preparation for courses. A sizable proportion of the African American students, as well as many others, became actively involved in this comprehensive approach. We saw a substantial increase in the graduation rates of African American students, exceeding rates in comparable institutions around the country.

SCHOLARLY RESEARCH, STUDENT INVOLVEMENT, AND INHERENT PHILANTHROPY

In an effort to heighten academic understanding and promote deeper learning in the counseling/advising sessions, a small number of undergraduate students were recruited for a special research project. This was a voluntary project without academic credit for students or professional credit for faculty. It was another deliberate effort to promote academic excellence among students while also enhancing the inherent philanthropy of faculty.

We guided the students through a series of interviews with faculty about their careers—focusing specifically on the process by which faculty made the transition from a student taking courses for credit to a scholar committed to the intellectual tasks of constant learning through research and teaching.

In small-group meetings, students reviewed literature on faculty lives and work, studied Institutional Review Board rules and procedures, developed an interview protocol, and applied for IRB approval. In the process of learning how faculty became scholars, undergraduate students unconsciously began the process of becoming scholars themselves. With our guidance, the students conducted interviews with more than a dozen faculty members in a range of disciplines. Student researchers, along with others, analyzed the interview transcripts and developed reports to present at the group counseling/advising discussions.

In their reports, students talked about the lessons learned from the interviews and the relevance to their academic efforts. Furthermore, with faculty permission, students could discuss specific experiences of the participating professors while explaining the details and drawing strong connections with the studying/learning patterns of contemporary students.

All the students—but particularly the women—were enthralled by examples of how female faculty met the challenges of academic excellence during their undergraduate years. Moore inspired students with several descriptions. They strongly identified with her descriptions of entering college from the heart of a family/community and the difficulties encountered in the first year of college:

I was the second one in my [extended] family to go to college. I found that it is not just you going to college; it's you and your whole family going to college. It's a community effort—including the church. Many times they don't know how to help you succeed but they are encouraging you to succeed.

I graduated high in my class in high school but I don't think I was prepared for what I was going to experience in terms of the expectations of faculty and the kind of work I was going to have to do. I studied just the way I would have studied in high school and only halfway through the [first] quarter I saw the handwriting on the wall and I can tell you the day I saw it. I took a test in a science course and they would put your name and grade in the hall, in front of the classroom. I remember starting at the top—expecting my name to be at the top—and going down that list. I was not at the very bottom but by the time I got halfway I was devastated that I obviously had not done well. (Professor, education)

However, it was not only students relating to the early college experiences of a professor; they were educated and informed by her account of moving beyond the initial hurdles to success in college and, eventually, to becoming a scholar.

In the second quarter of my first year I began working for a chemistry professor. I became his secretary, student assistant, research assistant, and lab assistant. He would not write letters but he would tell me what he wanted to write to a person. I would write the letter, give it to him, and he would change it, give it back to me and I would write it over again. I used to get very upset with rewriting all those letters but my writing became very good and my ability to listen to people and pick up exactly what they were communicating became very good.

I learned chemistry really hands on because I set up his labs, I studied with him, and he would talk with me about his lectures. I became a very focused person and I knew exactly what I wanted. I studied all the time and I developed new ways of studying. I would prepare for class, I would go to class and take notes, I'd come back and rewrite the notes, and then I would read the notes into a tape recorder and lie in my bed and listen to the tape. For you to understand what the professor was saying—especially in the sciences—you had to have an understanding before you walked into the room. This is particularly true of the scientific terms, because I think that is what threw me and throws lots of students. The terms in science are not ones you hear every day, but the professor uses them like you hear them every day.

My chemistry professor continued to mentor and work with me in my undergraduate years, through graduate school and my early professional career, although sporadically and many miles apart. He was the first person to congratulate me on my international HIV/AIDS research, shortly before his death. (Professor, education)

In presenting their research, students saw similarities to their own situations, but they also learned how they could raise their levels of academic success. A faculty member in one of the natural sciences spoke of the importance of active involvement in the learning process—a lesson first learned at a historically Black college or university (HBCU), where he encountered inspiring faculty who had high aspirations:

The Black professors want to make sure you represent them and the school well. He [a science professor] made you work very, very, very hard but if you accomplished what he wanted you to accomplish or what he thought you could accomplish then you performed quite well. But there are a number of people like that. There wasn't just one individual; there were numerous individuals and I think being exposed to that was the catalyst to a degree. (Professor, natural sciences)

Through their research, students learned that many faculty developed creative study/learning strategies while they were undergraduates. They shared these insights with participants in the discussion groups. These included such practices as rewriting their notes immediately after a lecture, and reviewing the notes before the next lecture. One faculty member told them about developing the practice of studying for 10 hours each weekday, with academic honors as an outcome.

Students were sobered by lessons faculty learned from their families and communities:

See, when we were growing up we were always told this: "You've got to be twice as good." Now, that meant you had to be twice as good if you wanted to make it in the White man's world. I know that's what my father meant. . . . That's how I saw it so I couldn't afford to waste away my time at [an HBCU]. I had to come out of there with an established record so I could compete in the world. (Professor, administrator)

One of the important aspects of the public good in these discussion/counseling groups was the full participation of White faculty. Often they described life experiences that were similar in social origins but also very different. As students analyzed these life experiences and discussed them, they gained valuable insights—the positive consequences of diversity and the public good. Examples from two participants illustrate what students were learning.

A social scientist spoke of being the first member of his family to go to college and how he made the transition to student and then scholar.

> No one in my immediate family had ever graduated from college and I was not an outstanding high school student. In high school I found enjoyment in reading not just for the sake of reading but I grew into or I fostered a sense of reading to know things that although there may not be a direct payment or benefit that somehow I think I evolved—I just wanted to know things. I thought the fastest way of learning was through reading and processing information so I was actually a much better college student from the first day on campus than I was a high school student. I just made up my mind that I had to set time apart every day and devote it to my class work.
>
> The first thing I did every evening is I recopied my class notes from that day. What really amazed me is that I would take a page of notes in class but when I recopied them they would be two and a half pages because I added a great deal of important information I did not put down the first time. Then I would start to work on the reading assignments and try to integrate them into the notes. That is how I learned you just cannot read the information and highlight it. I developed a system that the second and third time through something I would have another sheet of paper and outline the information I was reading, or draw a diagram or make a table. I think this worked for me because I am visual.
>
> I think the biggest mistake we have made in the past 30 years is saying that learning has to be fun. The outcome is exciting and fun, but the process is sometimes very rough and boring. But you have to learn the concepts; you have to learn the basic information to get to the next level. (Professor, social sciences)

Another professor in the humanities was moved by the example of students conducting voluntary research to learn how faculty made the transition from students to scholars. Not only was he the first in his family to enroll in college, but by the time he did, he was already married with a growing family. He was a commuting student, and his family gave him a different rationale for going to college.

> All of my family was in the construction industry, doing very well economically. I was the first one to go to college. They said this is your chance to get a real education and learn what the world is like

and develop yourself as a person. They thought of education as an opportunity to learn about the world—to really study and understand the world.

Because I had a family I had to get a job—and I worked full time in the library. I was able to raise my grade point average by taking fewer courses. If you have to choose I say it is better to take even a course less than your full load sometimes so you can get on to something and really do it. I saw some students who were really focused on things and they were going to do well. They really worked hard and did a lot better.

I did not get many chances to study with other people—it was very individualistic—and I suggest the opposite to my students today. I encourage them to study in groups; I think it is a much better way to work. Working with other people you get all kinds of good feedback and you learn more teaching than doing anything else. If you are telling other people about stuff, if you are the one who is explaining, that is when you learn. It forces you to really learn it because you have to say it out loud—so it's good. (Professor, humanities)

Not every example or lesson the students learned from their interviews of faculty dealt exclusively with academic issues. Some were profoundly personal and exemplified the transformational impact of their own commitment to the public good. Blake's interview revealed the ways academic expectations and personal identity were both linked and transcended. He told students that, in graduate school, his White professors pushed him to extremely high levels of academic achievement—levels that were intellectually attainable but personally discomforting. The discomfort was assuaged by his deep knowledge and understanding of Black achievers he had studied before entering undergraduate school:

There were White professors who were challenging me intellectually and there were Black spirits who were holding up my soul. One of these "Black spirits" was George Washington Carver—I identified with George Washington Carver. I had a profound sense of inferiority that I did not understand. . . .

I identified with George Washington Carver in the same way because as an adolescent I learned about how he had been stolen by slave traders and his master traded him for a horse—a very fine steed— but the message was this high achiever, this outstanding scientist, as a child was only good enough for a horse. That was another kind of identification. I used to recall the story of Booker T. Washington who as a child had shirts made out of gunnysacks that would scratch and irritate his skin.

Those spirits always persuaded me that no matter how deep your despair and privation, you could ultimately achieve and conquer. (Professor, sociology)

We were scholars and teachers, but as faculty members, who were multicultural and multiracial, we were preceptors. We were people who sought the public good to motivate and lead students to lives of service reflective of our origins and our expectations. The philanthropic goal of service for the public good was inherent in our success.

INHERENT PHILANTHROPY IN FACULTY WORK AND STUDENT ACADEMIC ACHIEVEMENT

At Midwestern University, research and teaching were our primary activities. Yet our commitment to the public good inspired us to also focus on the inherent philanthropy in promoting higher levels of academic achievement for African American students.

After 3 years of diligent work, the graduation rates of Black students showed the impact of our efforts. The graduating classes of 1998–2000 (entering classes of 1992–1994) showed little change in previous outcomes—still, only about a third of the entering students were graduating within 6 years. However, in 2001, that rose to 43.5% in the graduating class of 2001, an unprecedented increase that strengthened our belief that we had developed effective strategies for reaching students. Indeed, every rise in the graduation rates inspired us to work even more intensely and involve more faculty, administrators, and students in the process. The continuing rise in graduation rates—at times surpassing 50%—shows that the commitment of all participants led to positive outcomes for students (Moore & Blake, 2004).

CONCLUSION

During our entire time as faculty at Midwestern University, inherent philanthropy was a major component of our work. We knew we had to maintain our teaching and research apart from our intense efforts at advising, counseling, and supporting students. We had created an alternate academic culture for African American and other students who sought to meet the expectations of families, communities, and their history in ways they seldom articulated.

Our faculty work was guided by experiences and understandings that emerged from the collective consciousness of Black Americans. Shaped in slavery, honed by oppression, committed to our faith and belief in the intrinsic values of humankind, it guided us to new heights in higher education.

Inherent philanthropy is a constant reward. As Washington Carver so profoundly reflected, "When you can do the common things of life in an uncommon way, you will command the attention of the world."

NOTE

1. George Washington Carver was born into slavery in Missouri about 1864 (the exact year is unknown). As a child, he developed a keen interest in plants. He eventually made his way to Iowa and in 1891 was the first African American to enroll at Iowa State University. He completed his bachelor's degree in 1894 and his master's degree in 1896. He was the first African American appointed to the Iowa State University faculty. He later joined the faculty of the Tuskegee Institute in Alabama. He gained an international reputation for his research, teaching, and outreach (Iowa State University, 2011).

REFERENCES

Blake, J. H. (1985). Approaching minority students as assets. *Academe, 71*(6), 19–21.

Blake, J. H., & Moore, E. L. (1999). The color line: The enduring challenge in higher education. *Metropolitan Universities: An International Forum, 9*(4), 77–80.

Fiske, E. B. (2004, Spring). Student success. *Lumina Foundation Focus*, pp. 5–23.

Iowa State University. (2011). George Washington Carver Collection, RS 21/7/2, Special Collections Department. Available at http://www.add.lib.iastate.edu/spcl/arch/rgrp/21-7-2.html

Moore, E. L., & Blake, J. H. (2004). Retention and graduation of Black students: A comprehensive strategy. In I. M. Duranczyk, J. L. Higbee, & D. B. Lundell (Eds.), *Best practices for access and retention in higher education* (pp. 63–71). Minneapolis, MN: Center for Research on Developmental Education and Urban Literacy, General College, University of Minnesota.

National Institute of Education (U.S.). (1984). *Involvement in learning: Realizing the potential of American higher education. Final report of the study group on the conditions of excellence in American higher education*. Washington, DC: National Institute of Education.

Payton, R. (1988). *Philanthropy: Voluntary action for the public good*. New York, NY: American Council on Education/Macmillan.

CHAPTER 8

Professors Acting for the Public Good

Beyond the "New Normal" to the Academy We Choose

Gary Rhoades

In the current political economy of U.S. higher education, there is little incentive for faculty to engage in voluntary action for the public good. Academe's corporatization and commercialization operate in the opposite direction. Amid the search for disruptive innovation; reduced per capita state support; and demands for greater efficiency, productivity, and revenue generation—"the new normal"—there is reduced structural room, and even a disincentive, for public interest–oriented behavior.

Nevertheless, some forms of philanthropic activity, as Robert Payton (1988; Payton & Moody, 2008) defines it, "voluntary action for the public good" (p. 3) are remarkably vibrant among professors, whether in the actions of individual faculty or of faculty groups. The forms and meaning of academic work have been delimited by academe's restructuring over several decades. Yet many academics are engaged in voluntary activities that advance the public good and challenge the current systemic restructuring, countering the attendant policy pressures.

Notwithstanding repeated calls in policy circles to accept the new normal, current structural adjustments represent an acceleration of decades-long patterns. In this chapter I speak to three patterns that work against professors pursuing public good activities beyond the expectations of their formal roles and their narrow material interests. For each pattern I offer counterexamples of professors individually and collectively engaging in philanthropic activity that challenges the new normal. I speak to a concept of higher education that professors can, and do, choose (Rhoades, 2006). Our current path is not inevitable. The economic entrepreneurialism playing out in the pursuit of short-term, self-interested gains in revenue and prestige for individuals and institutions is not the only possible course. We can choose socially entrepreneurial philanthropic paths oriented to social gains and benefits for the public good. It is a matter of public policy as well as private action.

The 4-decade rise of academic capitalism (Slaughter & Leslie, 1997; Slaughter & Rhoades, 2004) has redefined conditions of academic work and conceptions of how academe serves the public good. The emerging knowledge/learning regime centers on corporate and market logics of maximizing managerial control and minimizing production labor costs in restructuring academe. It also reframes the public good as being served by infusing private motives, activities, and benefits into academe, rather than by separating public and private domains. Under such a formulation, professors—and their universities—are said to serve the public good by optimizing their private gain.

Accordingly, incentive structures are put into place, as are resource allocation systems that gauge and reward productivity in outputs measured by short-term revenue gains. Thus, in research there is a dramatically increased focus on commercializing knowledge through technology transfer and translating research (generally publicly funded) into marketable products. Institutional patent policies (and broader intellectual property and copyright policies) are structured to reward individual inventors and universities. They do not provide for reinvesting a portion of publicly subsidized proceeds for public benefit (Rhoades, 2001). The reputed public gain is derived from bringing this knowledge to market, for the public to pay for again.

A second example of a structural shift toward market behaviors in academic research can be detected in state, system, and organizational resource allocation metrics. The ascendant, now dominant, emphasis is on funded research that generates revenue. Under performance-based allocation protocols of states and systems or under responsibility-centered allocation systems of institutions, unfunded research counts for little in assessing units and allocating resources based on research productivity. So, too, in public policy discourse what was once defined as "basic" or "fundamental" is now characterized as "curiosity-driven" research, as if it is a self-indulgent curiosity. What matters is research that commands resources and has material payoff.

With these two examples of academic capitalist policies, I turn now to the three structural patterns referenced earlier. The first systemic shift that constrains professorial philanthropy is a heightened demand for accountability and increased productivity—from trustees, public commissions, funders, and others who shape policy. There are ever narrower, short-term measures of productivity that focus on generating outputs and revenues. Such metrics get translated into evaluation and resource allocation systems; they affect how and to what purpose faculty spend their time. They reduce faculty's discretionary time, so central to the "loose coupling" (Weick, 1976) that has long defined higher education organizations and academic work.

That discretion is important because actions oriented to the public interest take away from activities oriented to private gain for the institution.

A second systemic shift is the changing structure of employment. Over two thirds of the academic workforce now works in contingent positions, outside the due process security of the tenure track (Rhoades, 2013). The terms and conditions of employment for contingent faculty (full- and part-time) decrease their time and opportunity for engaging in activities above the call of "duty" and make it dangerous for professors, individually and collectively, to critique current working conditions as being counter to students' and society's interests.

Finally, a third systemic shift is the management revolution. Dating back to the 1980s, college leadership has trended toward more active management (Keller, 1983). More strategic direction by managers has meant less discretionary space for professors, particularly given an academic capitalism that privatizes professional space in the academy. Consequently, there is reduced opportunity and openness for expressing competing, dissenting ideas. In this context, working for the public good questions the institution's strategic direction and at times even challenges one's employer in risky ways.

Although the above patterns all hinder professorial philanthropy, the following sections include examples of professors nevertheless working for the public good. The examples draw on my experience over 2 1/2 years as general secretary of the American Association of University Professors (AAUP) and weave together data from academic studies of professors, including professors' own collective agency.

"PRODUCTIVITY" AND DISCRETIONARY GIVING: TAKING TIME TO CARE FOR THE BROADER GOOD

Academic capitalism prioritizes and privileges activities with short-term revenue potential. Professors and departments that fail to seek or generate revenue are framed as being "subsidized" by more "productive" academics and units. Philanthropic activities reduce the time spent producing revenue and increase the likelihood of faculty being seen as not carrying their weight.

These values are now embedded in resource allocation mechanisms as well as in the normative fabric of academic work and discourse. Many private and public universities have introduced some form of "responsibility center management," also known as incentive-based budgeting (Priest, Becker, Hossler, & St. John, 2002). The idea is to rationalize budgeting and incentivize productivity, which is generally reduced to producing revenue (Hearn, Lewis, Kallsen, Holdsworth, & Jones, 2006). Public institutions are increasingly subject to performance funding metrics established by states and systems.

Accountability pressures and budgeting mechanisms can affect professors' time allocation (Leslie, Oaxaca, & Rhoades, 2002), suggesting that professors have been reducing time on "service" (e.g., departmental, college, and university committee work) that is largely unrewarded. The study found that faculty were not committing as much time to this relatively discretionary area of activity as they once had.

Scholarship on academic capitalism suggests that it is not simply a matter of external corporate entities impinging on the academy (Slaughter & Rhoades, 2004). Rather, academic capitalism's market logic is embedded in decisionmaking and the everyday discourse of academics. Consider external grant money. It is common to hear professors speak of how much money they "bring in" to the institution. So, too, it is not unusual to hear academic administrators say that faculty need to generate more grant revenues. In some units, such as medical schools, faculty are often required to generate part of their academic salary through grants.

In this context, time is commodified and "academic capitalism requires both the reification of time and an internalization of the importance of managing time in a demonstrably efficient manner" (Walker, 2008, p. 484). There is a "cult of efficiency" with a moral dimension, translated into the good (i.e., productive) use of time. In "global time" (Walker, 2008) time is accelerated: There is a sense that we have no time, because work (and thus productivity) has no time bounds. With the expansion of communication technologies, the slippery boundaries between work and leisure have become increasingly fluid. Such "social ordering" of time (Perlow, 1998) can lead to reduced faculty time for philanthropy.

Yet there are important examples of faculty's engaging in activities that fall outside the parameters of "productive" (i.e., revenue-generating) work. One study (Kiyama, Lee, & Rhoades, 2012) speaks to the involvement of faculty members and student affairs professionals in an early outreach program for lower-income parents in a high-minority district. The program aims to enhance college access for underserved populations in a way that will yield benefits years down the road for both the individuals and the institution. For the faculty it is "service" in the broadest sense, going beyond working on departmental, college, or university committees or with professional associations. As participating faculty perceive their involvement, it is both voluntary and for the public good (see also Paul Shaker, Chapter 14, this volume).

What increases the potential for faculty to be involved in such service is the relative, but declining, loose coupling of faculty's not clocking in and not being held accountable for every minute of work time. Professors' commitment to the public good animates service that goes beyond the organization's call for (and reward of) formal duty to a larger sense of professional and social responsibility (see Kezar & Gehrke, Chapter 15, and Tierney &

Perkins, Chapter 13, in this volume). Therein lies the wellspring of professors devoting time to philanthropic activities. Their individual and collective agency is all the more impressive given the policy pressures and social structures that delimit the time for professors to engage in such action.

Faculty Agency in Individually Pursuing Philanthropic Action

Significant proportions of the professoriate devote time to philanthropic service. One significant national data source regarding this activity is the University of California–Los Angeles's Higher Education Research Institute (HERI) survey of undergraduate teaching faculty (the Faculty Survey of Student Engagement [FSSE] discussed elsewhere in this volume is also useful in this regard). The HERI survey reveals that 43.7% of full-time faculty members at baccalaureate institutions engage in 1–4 hours per week of community or public service (Hurtado, Eagan, Pryor, Whang, & Tran, 2012). Another 7.1% engage in 5–8 hours, and 2.6% engage in 9 hours or more of such service. Such service at the level of 1–4 hours per week is even more prominent in public 4-year colleges (51.3%), Catholic colleges (49.8%), and other religious colleges (51.4%).

This dedication of time goes beyond time devoted to the committee work that is at the core of professors' "service" responsibilities. Thus, 58% of faculty surveyed indicated that they spend 1–4 hours per week on committee work and meetings; another 23.7% said they spend 5–8 hours per week in such activities (10.7% spend more than 8 hours a week).

Most professors act on public service goals. In response to the question "During the past 2 years, have you engaged in public service/professional consulting without pay?" 57.1% indicated that they had. That is a much higher percentage than those who responded they had engaged in paid consulting outside their institution (36.4%). It also provides a contrast to the shift in institutions from a model of service-for-free to a fee-for-service model that involves charging students for various items.

Closer to one's academic home, the vast majority of academics are committed to an academic citizenship that goes above and beyond what professional and organizational incentive structures would encourage. Over three quarters of faculty (77.7%) responded that "mentoring the next generation of scholars" was very important or essential to them; 20.7% indicated they engaged in mentoring new faculty "to a great extent." That could be interpreted as academics wanting to reproduce themselves. But it suggests that professors' orientations extend well beyond the confines of immediate "productivity" to include shaping a future they will not be part of.

Beyond themselves, the involvement of professors in advising student clubs is also an indicator of philanthropic action: 43.6% of faculty in 4-year institutions have "advised student groups involved in service/volunteer work." Nearly one-fifth (18%) have taught a service learning class, extending their teaching from the campus into the community, with significant time and energy commitments. The numbers are higher in religiously affiliated institutions.

Having briefly noted the relationship between institutional type and faculty philanthropy (a greater structural or personal proclivity to giving as one moves down the academic hierarchy), there are other dimensions along which professors' philanthropy is socially patterned. A consistent pattern is that faculty of color are more likely to engage in service. Drawing on 1993 data from the now defunct National Survey of Postsecondary Faculty conducted by the National Center for Education Statistics, Bellas and Toutkoushian (1999) found that Black and Latino faculty devoted more time to service than did Anglo- or Asian Americans. Moreover, Black and Latino faculty devoted more time to professional service outside the institution and to unpaid activities at the institution. Emily L. Moore and J. Herman Blake (see Chapter 7, this volume) illustrate this propensity, reporting their own work, as does Thomas Nelson Laird's analysis of FSSE data (see Chapter 5, this volume).

One social structure at play here is that given the fewer numbers of faculty of color, there may be greater pressures from on- and off-campus constituencies for these faculty members to engage in voluntary activities related to representing and serving the needs of communities and students of color. Yet as Benjamin Baez (2000) has revealed, involvement in such service activities, particularly in "race-related critical agency" (aimed at changing inequitable social structures), is at the core of many faculty of color's identity. It is personally rewarding and important as a point of emotional connection given that many faculty of color work in predominantly White institutions.

The power of social structures in patterning professors' philanthropy is evident in the variations by academic rank, which is to say, by job security. The pressure to produce is greater in the pre-tenure years of faculty. Not surprisingly, then, the percentages of faculty engaged in community or public service was higher for tenured (46.9% of associate and 44.9% of full professors) than for untenured faculty (38.7% of assistant professors) (Hurtado et al., 2012, p. 50). Similarly, higher percentages of tenured professors engaged in public service/professional consulting without pay than did assistant professors, perhaps because of greater opportunities.

Just as clearly, then, as social structure affects patterns of individual behavior, so can individuals act in ways that run counter to those structures. They can also work collectively against the press of those structures, a form of agency to which we now turn.

The Collective Agency of Professors in
Service to the Public Good

As general secretary of the AAUP, I was consistently impressed by the commitment of groups of faculty to devoting their energy to fulfill a long-standing professional role as guardians of the public interest. That commitment played out at many levels of activity. In some cases, it was professors' involvement in a campus "chapter," a voluntary association organized principally for the greater good of the community of scholars at a particular institution, but also beyond. In others, it was professors' commitment of time and energy to a "state conference" (the state-level organization that has officers, committees, and activities). And in still other cases, it was professors' involvement and service to the national association. That holds aside faculty members at the local, system, and national level who take leadership positions in collective bargaining units and activities (though many would categorize these activities as "self-interested," much of the work is for nonmembers and for goals and benefits that do not directly benefit the professor in question).

Whatever the level and the activity, these professors are defending abstract principles that are at the core of the association. Arguably, most fundamental among these is the principle of academic freedom—an intangible value. Oftentimes, the faculty involved in defending that principle are not directly implicated in the alleged violation. Yet large numbers of faculty devote significant amounts of time to defending the principle that itself is at core a recognition of the professoriate's duty to advance the public good by the pursuit of truth wherever it leads.

Professors engage in this collective, philanthropic work in a variety of capacities. One form of involvement is with the drafting of amicus briefs on various issues, including academic freedom. Generally, AAUP Litigation Committee members (an advisory committee of the national organization) are law professors who give an extraordinary amount of their time in deliberating on what issues to take up and then in drafting and commenting on briefs. Another form of involvement is in drafting policy statements and doing other work under the purview of the association's various standing committees, the most prominent of which is Committee A (on Academic Freedom and Tenure). Professors serve on investigative committees that are tasked with exploring the facts of a particular inquiry that has been fielded by the staff and been defined as a complaint implicating the AAUP's academic freedom provisions, embedded in the "Recommended Institutional Regulations on Academic Freedom and Tenure." These faculty are working on behalf of not only all faculty current and future but also a society that depends on free inquiry—a public good.

The numbers of faculty involved in the AAUP in these capacities is limited but significant. And the AAUP is just one example of an association that is not built into a professor's career path, in contrast to a disciplinary association. The argument can be made that involvement in the latter is not philanthropic because faculty benefit personally, on their vita, in service credit, and in reputation. But the purpose of the AAUP, as with many such nonprofits formed by professors, is to protect some version of the public trust. Indeed, the origins of the AAUP lie in the idea of professors safeguarding that public trust in higher education. The AAUP's 1915 "Declaration of Principles" explicitly states that "it seems desirable at this time to restate clearly the chief reasons, lying in the nature of the university teaching profession, why it is to the public interest that the professional office should be one both of dignity and of independence." Similar motives can be seen underlying a range of voluntary organizations of professors.

CONTINGENT EMPLOYMENT AND GIVING ABOVE AND BEYOND ONE'S PLACE

For many years scholars have focused on the systematic increase in the numbers and proportion of faculty working in part-time positions (Gappa, 1984; Gappa & Leslie, 1993; Rhoades, 1998). In the 1970s, these faculty members accounted for about one quarter of professors. Over time, their share of the instructional workforce has doubled: Currently, faculty in part-time positions represent 49.3% of professors nationally (Rhoades, 2013).

More recently, scholars have begun to recognize the rise and significance of full-time, non-tenure-track faculty, who account for nearly one-fifth of faculty (Baldwin & Chronister, 2001; Finkelstein, Seal, & Schuster, 1998). Although most attention in this category of academic employee has been accorded to faculty who are "teaching without tenure" (Baldwin & Chronister, 2001), many non-tenure-track faculty are researchers on "soft" (research contract) money. That does not include postdocs, who are also a growth segment of the academic workforce.

The structure of contingent employment compromises faculty's opportunities to engage in philanthropic activity in terms of time, place, and space. The most obvious structure is that of time, especially in the case of part-time faculty. Yet even full-time contingent faculty are generally constrained by time: They are on short-term (usually annual or 3-year) contracts, and there is a premium on using time "productively" (e.g., in higher teaching loads) in ways that the institution values so as to secure continued employment.

Moreover, the formal structure of job descriptions can also delimit the academic and external citizenship of contingent faculty in terms of place.

Particularly for professors in part-time teaching positions, job duties and pay are circumscribed by the classroom. Most such faculty are paid neither for class preparation nor for advising students outside class. Their place of employment is literally the classroom and nothing beyond. More than that, contingent employment generally does not provide for these academics' involvement in shared governance activities (departmentally and organizationally) (Kezar & Sam, 2013; Levin, Shaker, & Wagoner, 2011). Partly, this is a function of employers not recognizing or remunerating contingent faculty for this work. But it is also a function of professional hierarchy, of tenure-stream faculty not recognizing or providing a place for contingent colleagues' involvement in decisionmaking. Both considerations reduce the opportunity for philanthropy.

A third structural constraint on contingent faculty's philanthropy is the relative and often total lack of due process and academic freedom protections accorded them. Limited employment security provides a disincentive for acting to advance the public good. Nevertheless, there is ample evidence of adjunct faculty acting in the public good. The time individuals voluntarily commit to students outside the classroom is but the most obvious of many contributions to students' well-being. On a collective level, the conscientious commitment of contingent faculty to advocate the cause of quality higher education for all who can benefit is a consistent reason offered for continuing to teach under challenging, unrequited conditions.

Giving "Beyond the Office," or Actually, Beyond the Classroom

With "'Beyond the Office'" in the heading above, I offer a play on words to emphasize the working reality of many contingent faculty. "I gave at the office" is a standard expression used to decline a request to give to a charity. It invokes the reality that for some companies and organizations, including universities, charitable contributions can be deducted from employees' paychecks. Yet large numbers of contingent faculty, particularly those in part-time positions, lack private office space (as well as other "benefits" such as insurance, retirement contributions, or technology support). The HERI survey of faculty in 4-year institutions (Hurtado et al., 2012) found that less than one-fifth (18.4%) of respondents had use of a private office (see also the Delphi Project: http://thechangingfaculty.org). Even fewer contingent faculty are remunerated for meeting with students in that space. The numbers are higher in community colleges, where 70% of the faculty are in part-time positions. Nevertheless, considerable proportions of contingent faculty work beyond the constraints of contingency, giving well beyond the boundaries of the narrowly defined spaces and roles for which they are paid.

A survey of "back to school" employment practices in hiring contingent faculty (Street, Maisto, Merves, & Rhoades, 2012) points to faculty's philanthropic commitment to their students and to quality education. These professors' voices are captured in open-ended responses about the effects of their working conditions on students. Last-minute class assignments undercut faculty's ability to prepare for classes. Yet many faculty do prepare for weeks and months before classes start, without remuneration: "Every semester, including this one, when I teach a new course I spend weeks of unpaid time doing course planning" (p. 8), said one respondent. Similarly, at best these faculty receive last-minute access to various instructional resources, so they end up paying for such materials out of pocket: "I try not to let the lack of resources/material support affect my students. It does definitely have an impact on my bank account, though. I often incur the cost of printing and copying syllabi, handouts, and other materials needed" (p. 14), noted another.

Other national survey data also point to the philanthropic commitment of contingent faculty. A 2009 survey of community college faculty (CCSSE, 2009) found that 40% of faculty working in part-time positions do not advise students outside class. However, flipping that around, and considering that most part-time faculty are not paid for advising, most part-time faculty do devote time to students outside class in what could and should be seen as acts of philanthropy. Relatedly, a paper on how "contingency undermines the teaching mission" (Sowards, 2014) maps the constraints of contingency in meeting benchmarks underlying the National Survey of Student Engagement that contribute to quality learning environments. Whether in "active and collaborative learning," "student-faculty interaction," "supportive campus environment," or "enriching educational experiences," Robin Sowards, an adjunct activist and labor leader, speaks to how contingent employment compromises faculty's ability to meet these standards. Yet many contingent faculty go well beyond the classroom and paid duties to do precisely that (see Nelson Laird, Chapter 5, this volume, which addresses data from the parallel FSSE).

Collectively Changing the Place of Contingency for Quality Higher Education

An impressive collective demonstration of philanthropic activity among contingent faculty is the energy, time, and resources put into building nonprofit organizations focused on enhancing quality higher education. One such organization, the New Faculty Majority (NFM), exemplifies an advocacy group focused on the nation's greater good. There is a dimension of self-interest in the creation of such an organization, but also a dimension of public interest in its work.

On the main page of the NFM website, in bold, is "Quality Higher Education." That emphasis plays out in an NFM mantra (not unique to it) that faculty working conditions are students' learning conditions. Thus, in one of NMF's signature events, "Campus Equity Week," the NFM (2013) press release indicates that the "central principle . . . is that high-quality education depends practically and ethically on professional and just working conditions for all faculty." (A number of events held across the nation as part of Equity Week focused on student debt. NFM is keeping the greater good of the nation in focus even as it seeks greater equity for contingent faculty.)

Beyond such examples, there is a dimension of public good advocacy that defines NFM leaders. As with many nonprofit leaders, their work is directed toward a public good that extends beyond the immediate interests of those involved as they consider future generations of both teachers and students—all of which are the basis for an improved society and quality of life. NFM's work is akin to the "social movement unionism" of some service sector labor groups (Johnston, 1994). In the words of one leader, "A national strategy must recognize that the 'new majority' faculty are now part of the working class and that their concerns include both economic and job security as well as the desire to defend and improve education for their largely working-class students" (Berry, 2005, p. 48).

SPEAKING UP AND SPEAKING OUT: CLAIMING SPACE FOR THE PUBLIC INTEREST

The logic of the private sector marketplace redefines colleges as best serving the public interest by optimizing their short-term, revenue generation gains. It has involved nonprofit higher education institutions engaging more in market behaviors, extending more privately branded space, and attending more to brand protection. It also has translated into universities aggressively asserting intellectual property rights (relative to faculty and corporations) and managing academics and units in relation to their revenue-generating possibilities. Academic managers not only leverage revenue-seeking behaviors but also exercise greater influence in realms that are more traditionally the purview of academics. They do so in ways more aligned with a corporate rather than an academic logic, reducing the public space for debate and for speaking on behalf of the public interest, diminishing the university's civic-minded activities.

Amid heightened demands for productivity oriented to centrally defined strategic objectives, it is has become more difficult to speak out on many topics, but especially for academic activities and units not supporting institutional priorities. As I traveled to campuses of all types in my role as AAUP general secretary, I repeatedly encountered a sense of fear. It was not rare for faculty members to express concern about speaking out for fear of retaliation (and in the case of non-tenure-track faculty of being "nonrenewed"). The language of academic managers that calls for faculty to be "team players" and to "get on board" with the direction being charted contributes to that. It is difficult in that context to raise questions without running the risk of being labeled and dismissed as a "troublemaker," an "obstructionist," or simply someone unwilling to face "the new realities." And administrations have vigorously fought against groups of contingent faculty at private universities seeking the right to organize unions, claiming that such efforts bring unnecessary friction to a collegial environment.

In a very few cases, the central push for improved "branding" and "messaging" that come with academic capitalism has translated into efforts to restrict interaction with the press. In a more broadly chilling development, however, a 2006 court case outside higher education, *Garcetti v. Ceballos*, has played out on some campuses with administrations claiming that faculty do not have the freedom to speak out critically about administrators and institutional policies. Such developments led the AAUP to craft a 2009 statement, "Protecting an Independent Faculty Voice: Academic Freedom after *Garcetti v. Ceballos*" (available on the AAUP website, www.aaup.org). A corporate mentality in regard to internal dissent delimits public space in academe. Nevertheless, significant numbers of professors continue speaking up and speaking out, acting in the public good, individually and collectively.

Speaking Up and Speaking Out, Claiming Public Space Individually

The commitment of professors to preserving the academy as a public space and to maintaining—if not expanding—that space for the public good can take different forms. Consider the responses of professors to a question about the personal goals that are "very important" or "essential" to them (Hurtado et al., 2012). Nearly one-fifth (18.8%) identified the goal of "becoming a community leader." Over one quarter (28%) had a goal of "participating in a community action program." Those numbers are higher in public 4-year colleges (33.7%) and in Catholic (34%) and other religious (33.1%) private 4-year colleges. Against all pressures of job security, the numbers are also higher for more junior faculty and faculty who do not have the security of tenure: 42.1% of instructors, 33.2% of lecturers, and 30.9% of assistant professors identified the goal of "participating in a community action program," as compared with 21.7% of full and 26.6% of associate professors.

Professors also have public good goals in relation to their undergraduates. As might be expected, the responses that the vast majority of faculty identified as "very important" or "essential" relate to critical thinking (99.5%), mastering knowledge in the discipline (94.1%), and preparing students for graduate and advanced education (75.2%) or employment (78.3%). Yet slightly over half (52.1%) believe that the goal to "encourage students to become agents of social change" is important, while 44.5% believe in the goal to "instill in students a commitment to community service." Clearly, a conception of a duty to the public good is at least an aspect of what it means to be a professor.

As noted earlier, significant proportions of faculty act on those motivations, advising student clubs involved in service work, teaching service learning courses, and undertaking a broad array of activities without remuneration or "credit." More than that, 42.5% of faculty have within the past 2 years "collaborated with the local community in research/teaching," and 37.4% have used their research "to address local community needs." Further, 15.2% have written op-ed pieces or editorials, speaking out in the public space. Most of these activities are philanthropic: elective, discretionary, and unrewarded by employing institutions.

Speaking Up and Speaking Out, Collectively Claiming Public Space for the Public Good

During my time as general secretary, the AAUP published its report about the threat of the *Garcetti* case to academic freedom and the public interest (AAUP, 2009). The aim of the statement was to strengthen and expand academic freedom, to protect public space for debate *on campus*. Historically, academic freedom as a concept has centered on freedom in classroom teaching, research, and extramural speech. The new policy statement focuses on the significance of speech about institutional policy and practice, emphasizing the value of an independent faculty voice, including, but not restricted to, the realm of formal shared governance. That is important in a more corporatized environment. The policy addresses why professors' independent voices are central to ensuring that the public interest is served in the "new normal." Subsequently, the association launched a successful campaign to incorporate language in faculty handbooks and collective bargaining agreements protecting professors' academic freedom in speech about institutional matters.

During the time of the Great Recession, with cuts in state budgets, dramatic increases in tuition, and cuts in academic programs, there emerged nationally various groups to save the public university. They were concerned not only with preserving funding, but also with the threats posed by the privatization of universities' public space. The discourse of these groups was about sustaining a public interest orientation, in the commitment to affordability and access and to the broader purposes of education. With the growth in new populations of students, a duty to the public good requires articulation of why the national interest is better served by policies ensuring access to broad educational opportunity than by those tracking lower-income, immigrant, and nontraditional students into less resourced institutions, fields, and careers.

One such national group is the Campaign for the Future of Higher Education (CFHE). Launched in May 2011, the campaign is a nationwide grassroots coalition of leaders from faculty and staff unions and organizations. Its aim is to ensure affordable, quality higher education for all who can benefit and to foreground voices and issues that are overlooked in public policy. Although campaign members have significant responsibilities to their own organizations, a philanthropic commitment to advancing the public good animates the campaign.

There are also international organizations, such as Scholars at Risk, which take up similar goals of speaking out for the public good. This association defends academic freedom by providing support and safe harbor to scholars who are facing abuses around the world. Originating at the University of Chicago in 1999, it has expanded to launch the Network for Education and Academic Rights (NEAR) and to partner with the Institute of International Education in creating a Scholar Rescue Fund, advancing academic freedom in the public interest in a globalized and interdependent world.

CONCLUSION: PERSISTENT AND PREVALENT FORMS OF PROFESSORIAL PHILANTHROPY

In May 2009, when the country was reeling from the Great Recession, I spoke at the New Jersey AAUP state conference. Such conferences are places where members come together to discuss issues that can affect but also go beyond the local "chapters" or bargaining units to which faculty belong. Conferences are centered on advancing the AAUP's core principles and furthering the faculty role of protecting the public interest through safeguarding those principles, and this one was illustrative of a broader range of commitment.

The setting was an old union hall at the Labor Education Center of Rutgers University; the flags of blue- and white-collar unions hung from the aged, pine walls. The president of the New Jersey AAUP opened the meeting by singing a haunting rendition of an 1854 song written by Stephen Foster, called "Hard Times Come Again No More." The song's message, expressed in the opening stanza, is that society's more fortunate should address the plight of the poor: "Let us pause in life's pleasures and count its many tears, while we all sup sorrow with the poor."

Mere months after the U.S. economy's collapse, that message resonated. Although it was sung amid unprecedented state budget cuts to higher education and, in some states, furloughs of faculty, the state's AAUP leader was focusing attendees' attention on the less fortunate outside the academy and on the academy's larger purpose in serving the broader public interest. She was asking them to put the assaults on professors and their institutions in the larger context of the populations and purposes we serve. That is philanthropic leadership, in the face of academic capitalism. It is an anecdote of a fleeting moment, but also an emblem of the profession's promise and sometimes fulfilled duty.

From one campus to another, policymakers and managers are speaking about a "new normal," of needing to focus on generating revenues and economic development. Yet individual professors continue to focus on service and students. So, too, groups of faculty are pursuing and advancing the public purposes of American higher education. Similarly, the least secure, contingent members of academe are individually giving of themselves in and beyond the classroom and are undertaking collective efforts nationally to enhance the quality of working and learning conditions in the academy for the benefit of students and educational quality.

Finally, nationwide, professors are individually and collectively reasserting the significance of an independent faculty voice in shaping their institution's future in ways that call the academy to its public interest ideals. At the center of that is a commitment to better serving the growth demographics of prospective students that historically have been underserved, with an affordable, quality higher education. Philanthropy in the professoriate is alive and well. Whether as individuals or groups of academics, many professors are acting for the public good, recognizing the real "new reality." Unless we turn to those purposes and to more fully fulfilling the promise of American higher education to be the equalizer, not the divider, as the minority becomes the majority, higher education will drive us to become, more than we already are, a nation of haves and have-nots, with a weakened middle class.

REFERENCES

AAUP. (1915). 1915 declaration of principles on academic freedom and academic tenure. Washington, DC: American Association of University Professors. Available at http://www.aaup.org/file/1915-Declaration-of-Principles-onAcademic-Freedom-and-Academic-Tenure.pdf

AAUP. (2009). Protecting an independent faculty voice: Academic freedom after *Garcetti v. Ceballos*. Washington, DC: American Association of University Professors.

Baez, B. (2000). Race-related service and faculty of color: Conceptualizing critical agency in academe. *Higher Education, 39*(3), 363–391.

Baldwin, R. G., & Chronister, J. L. (2001). *Teaching without tenure: Policies and practices for a new era*. Baltimore, MD: The Johns Hopkins University Press.

Bellas, M. L., & Toutkoushian, R. K. (1999). Faculty time allocations and research productivity: Gender, race, and family effects. *The Review of Higher Education, 22*(4), 367–390.

Berry, J. (2005). *Reclaiming the ivory tower: Organizing adjuncts to change higher education*. New York, NY: Monthly Review Press.

CCSSE. (2009). *Making connections: Dimensions of student engagement*. Austin, TX: Community College Survey of Student Engagement.

Finkelstein, M. J., Seal, R. K., & Schuster, J. H. (1998). *The new academic generation: A profession in transformation*. Baltimore, MD: The Johns Hopkins University Press.

Foster, S. (1854). *Hard times come again no more (Foster's Melodies No. 28)*. New York, NY: Firth, Pond.

Gappa, J. M. (1984). *Part-time faculty: Higher education at a crossroads*. ASHE-ERIC Higher Education Research Report No. 3. Washington, DC: Association for the Study of Higher Education.

Gappa, J. M., & Leslie, D. W. (1993). *The invisible faculty: Improving the status of part-timers in higher education*. San Francisco, CA: Jossey-Bass.

Hearn, J. C., Lewis, D. R., Kallsen, L., Holdsworth, J. M., & Jones, L. M. (2006). "Incentives for managed growth": A case study of incentives-based planning and budgeting in a large public research university. *The Journal of Higher Education, 77*(2), 286–316.

Hurtado, S., Eagan, K., Pryor, J. H., Whang, H., & Tran, S. (2012). *Undergraduate teaching faculty: The 2010–2011 HERI faculty survey*. Los Angeles, CA: UCLA, Higher Education Research Institute.

Johnston, P. (1994). *Success while others fail: Social movement unionism and the public workplace*. Ithaca, NY: ILR Press of Cornell University Press.

Keller, G. (1983). *Academic strategy: The management revolution in American higher education*. Baltimore, MD: The Johns Hopkins University Press.

Kezar, A., & Sam, C. (2013). Institutionalizing equitable policies and practices for contingent faculty. *The Journal of Higher Education, 84*(1), 56–87.

Kiyama, J. M., Lee, J. J., & Rhoades, G. (2012). A critical agency network model for building an integrated outreach program. *The Journal of Higher Education, 83*(2), 276–303.

Leslie, L. L., Oaxaca, R. L., & Rhoades, G. (2002). Revenue flux and university behavior. In D. M. Priest, W. L. Becker, D. Hossler, & E. P. St. John (Eds.), *Incentive-based budgeting systems in public universities* (pp. 111–135). Northampton, MA: Edward Elgar.

Levin, J. S., Shaker, G. G., & Wagoner, R. (2011). Post neoliberalism: The professional identity of faculty off the tenure-track. In B. Pusser, K. Kempner, S. Marginson, & I. Ordorika (Eds.), *Universities and the public sphere: Knowledge creation and state building in the era of globalization* (pp. 197–219). New York, NY: Routledge.

New Faculty Majority (NFM). (2013). Campus equity week events to raise awareness of how contingent faculty inequities affect quality of higher education [Press release]. Available at http://www.campusequityweek.org/2013/resources/media-releases/media-release-campus-equity-week-events-to-raise-awareness-of-how-contingent-faculty-inequities-affect-quality-of-higher-education

Payton, R. (1988). *Philanthropy: Voluntary action for the public good*. New York, NY: American Council on Education/Macmillan.

Payton, R., & Moody, M. P. (2008). *Understanding philanthropy: Its meaning and mission*. Bloomington, IN: Indiana University Press.

Perlow, L. A. (1998). Boundary control: The social ordering of work and family time in a high-tech corporation. *Administrative Science Quarterly, 43*(3), 328–357.

Priest, D. M., Becker, W. E., Hossler, D., & St. John, E. P. (Eds.). (2002). *Incentive-based budgeting systems in public universities*. Northampton, MA: Edward Elgar.

Rhoades, G. (1998). *Managed professionals: Unionized faculty and restructuring academic labor*. Albany, NY: State University of New York Press.

Rhoades, G. (2001). Whose property is it? Negotiating with the university. *Academe, 87*(5), 38–43.

Rhoades, G. (2006). The higher education we choose: A question of balance. *The Review of Higher Education, 29*(3), 381–404.

Rhoades, G. (2013). Disruptive innovations for adjunct faculty: Common sense for the common good. *Thought & Action, 29*, 71–86.

Slaughter, S., & Leslie, L. L. (1997). *Academic capitalism: Politics, policies, and the entrepreneurial university*. Baltimore, MD: The Johns Hopkins University Press.

Slaughter, S., & Rhoades, G. (2004). *Academic capitalism and the new economy: Markets, state, and higher education*. Baltimore, MD: The Johns Hopkins University Press.

Sowards, R. (2014). *Faculty contingency: Problems and solutions*. Presented at Ontario Confederation of University Faculty Associations of British Columbia, Burnaby, BC, February 27.

Street, S., Maisto, M., Merves, E., & Rhoades, G. (2012, August). *Who is Professor "Staff": And how can this person teach so many classes?* Center for the Future of Higher Education. Available at http://futureofhighered.org

Walker, J. (2008). Time as the fourth dimension in the globalization of higher education. *The Journal of Higher Education, 80*(5), 483–509.

Weick, K. E. (1976). Educational organizations as loosely coupled systems. *Administrative Science Quarterly, 21*(1), 1–19.

Part III

PHILANTHROPY AS AN ASPECT OF ACADEMIC PROFESSIONALISM

CHAPTER 9

Faculty Behaving Well

Dwight F. Burlingame

Exploring how faculty contribute to the public good through the philanthropic aspects of their work is challenging because of the many and diverse ways in which a variety of motives—some acknowledged, some unrecognized—affect how the vocation of education is practiced. Robert Payton's (1988) broad definition of philanthropy as "voluntary action for the public good" (p. 3) is a guiding concept for the contributors to this volume, and it forms the foundation of my own personal understanding of how faculty act philanthropically—giving time, money, and talent for the benefit of the common good formally and informally, intentionally and unintentionally, recognized and unrecognized.

Such a broad definition that encompasses so many aspects of faculty work has practical and even political value in helping explain a profession that is often viewed by the general public—as well as policymakers—from a reductionist perspective. To many, philanthropy means only giving money, and when faculty give to their own institutions they are dismissed as self-serving. Although this volume attests to the fact that faculty work is much more philanthropic than simply donating money, even this unambiguous activity and the contributions that faculty make to raising money from others, require justification lest they be twisted from the public good into a private benefit.

PHILANTHROPY AND HIGHER EDUCATION AS WE KNOW IT

Philanthropy—private, voluntary giving of time, talent, and money—has long played an important role in the development and diversity of higher education, particularly in the United States (Drezner, 2011). Most often this history is focused on the role of private donors in shaping the creation of new institutions of higher learning: from the founding of Harvard and other early private colleges; to the creation of women's colleges, Black colleges, and teachers' colleges; to—more recently—the creation of special-focus colleges with religious, social, or economic purposes.

Philanthropy in higher education has been acknowledged, cultivated, and increasingly valued as billion-dollar capital campaigns proliferate—and meet their goals. Interestingly and fittingly, Harvard University announced in fall 2013 the beginning of the largest capital campaign in the history of higher education worldwide—$6.5 billion (Powell, 2013). One wonders when the first trillion-dollar campaign—fueled by ambition and inflation—will get underway at some college or university in the pursuit of philanthropy. The latest Harvard campaign tends toward the traditional claims for how the money will be used:

> [It is intended that] 45% of the fundraising proceeds will go to research, faculty needs, and teaching and learning; 25% will go to financial aid and the student experience; 20% to buildings and capital projects; and 10% in flexible funding to foster new initiatives and faculty collaboration. (Powell, 2013, para. 13)

Clearly, faculty will be one of the principal beneficiaries of the anticipated giving, showing the cyclical nature of giving and receiving.

Giving to the university has an intrinsic value, and those gifts further a contribution to society that is foundational to almost every college and university. At some level, the structure and rationale for the societal role of higher education and potential of philanthropic giving to advance that role inevitably influence the sense faculty have of themselves and their work, as an outcome of organizational culture, if nothing else.

Financial support for bricks-and-mortar projects, support for research initiatives (including those with targeted focus such as cancer research or environmental issues), for scholarships and financial aid, and for specific programs (such as women's studies or Jewish studies, or even philanthropic studies) are examples of external philanthropic forces shaping the intellectual life of campuses. Rarely do large gifts come to a university unrestricted (McClintock, 2000). Instead, donors nearly always have a specific intent.

Often, private donors were and continue to be alumni with hopes and dreams for their alma maters. Many alumni also serve as leaders of corporations, foundations, and other organizations with resources they are able to direct. Peter Dobkin Hall (1992), a historian of philanthropy, noted that "no single force is more responsible for the emergence of the modern university in America than giving by individuals and foundations" (p. 403), emphasizing once again the integral—if often unspoken—importance of philanthropy to higher education. Traditions of self-help, mutual aid, reciprocity, and giving to others have existed for all time in the human condition and among all ethnic and racial communities, and philanthropic traditions within American higher education are no different (Drezner, 2011). And within the academy, faculty members are typically among the most important personal connection that individuals have with the institution.

FACULTY AS FUNDRAISERS

Many would argue, and believe, that what faculty members do in their daily tasks is in fact part of their "economic" expectations—what they are being paid to do. Those holding such a perspective are no doubt in the majority, and they cannot see how any dimension of faculty work is philanthropic or voluntary, no matter either how significant the actual contribution of time, money, or expertise might be from the faculty member's perspective or how intentionally philanthropic the "extra" effort might be.

This argument can become circular very quickly. I have come to believe that we all have mixed motives for doing what we do. For an external observer to determine at what point an activity becomes philanthropic for another person is a futile activity. Intent is a critical factor, and only the philanthropic actor can know when an act is intended to be philanthropic—regardless of how others might view and assess the action. Observers may not know or appreciate when an act or an extension of an act may be voluntary—beyond what is required, compensated, or even expected.

Faculty participation in United Way campaigns or participation in a "day of service" would generally be considered philanthropic, even by the cynics among us, while staying late on campus to meet with a student or responding to email inquiries without regard to whether it is a weekend or weekday or serving on a nonprofit board as a subject matter expert probably would not be. Yet these latter examples may be just as philanthropic as the former explicit action of giving money or formal volunteerism.

But what about faculty giving money to their own institution—or helping professional fundraisers in seeking donations from alumni, students, their parents, corporations, foundations, and others that could potentially benefit them in their faculty work?

Beyond their own giving, faculty increasingly join with professional fundraisers in donor calls. They participate in "thanking" opportunities for donors, they listen carefully to donor expectations and interests, they engage with potential donors in developing research that informs practice and policy, and they provide feedback to development officers on cultivating new donors and renewing and "upgrading" existing philanthropic givers.

The pattern for engaging faculty members in development activities is much like the development of the dean's role 30-plus years ago (Hall, 1993).

Certainly in most public and private comprehensive colleges and universities in the United States today, we see significant fundraising activities taking place that are designed to raise needed resources to support the activities of the various subunits of the institution. Centralized control of fundraising has given way to decentralized systems that recognize the important principle that more funds will be raised when there is increased engagement with more donors by the persons who are carrying out the activities for which potential donors have an interest—the faculty.

It is typical for job announcements for a dean's position to stipulate that the preferred candidate has fundraising experience. Since dean candidates typically come from the professorial ranks, fundraising experience will have come from one's role as a faculty member or department chair. The expectation for the deans' experience with potential donors is not unlike the expectations for the president of a college in the early history of American higher education (Curti & Nash, 1965). Seeking donor support is a growing expectation for presidents. Indeed, fundraising is now so well defined as a presidential trait that candidates must often have a *proven* track record in fundraising to be considered seriously. It is not enough just to be willing.

Fundraising is thus driven deeper into the institutions and into the ranks of academic and professional employees. Faculty members are often called on to be extensions of the school's fundraising activities, with the development staff providing orientation and training (and even a critique when things do not go as anticipated on a call with a donor). Faculty are offered as an example, if not proof, of the value of the investment based on results in teaching and learning, research, or community engagement. When faculty can "show" results through their work—especially when the results are presented along with successful and articulate students—potential donors have a credible basis on which to invest in the future.

Perhaps one of the oldest "truths" of fundraising is that people give to people. This is particularly true if donors want to give to the people who are directly carrying out the mission of the organization or cause in which they have an interest. Faculty are one of the most important "people" groups to higher education donors and potential donors. Such engagement of faculty members with donors and fundraising may even inspire faculty members to become donors themselves (Shaker, 2013a).

Voluntary behavior can be encouraged and fostered among faculty while maintaining its voluntary or discretionary nature. It is no coincidence that Harvard's announcement of its new campaign was accompanied by a program featuring a "panel of faculty members representing biology, business, medicine, philosophy, and law [who] discussed the importance of both basic and applied research" (Powell, 2013, para. 30). Development staff are calling on faculty to assist with fundraising campaign planning,

shaping, and implementation and to serve as educational and policy advocates in the public sphere.

Faculty members play an important part in identifying potential individuals who have the interest and the capacity to engage with the institution—including their own colleagues. This is especially true in the case of
alumni who faculty believe, with appropriate engagement, might become
donors. Whether the gift is a current one or is deferred or planned, the
advice and counsel of the faculty member will be important to the development professional. Faculty knowledge of the potential donor will be important to determine the priority for engagement and solicitation activities and
for the deployment of employee time—which is, largely, a philanthropic
gesture by at least the faculty, for whom such engagements occur outside
defined duties.

Gifts from external donors are catalysts for innovation even beyond the
instrumentality they make possible—whether donated money is used for
release time or equipment or assistance or travel. Faculty can be inspired by
the generosity of others to an extent far beyond a direct return on a financial
investment as they work to find cures for disease, in programs for underserved populations, and even to make their own substantial philanthropic
gifts after witnessing the effects of others' contributions. Moreover, many
significant gifts come through donors' estate plans and are realized long
after those who assisted in raising the funds are gone. In this case, it is the
discipline, the university, and society that benefit, far into the future.

The new Harvard campaign strikes a common chord for all college and
university fundraising. Harvard president Drew Faust announced the campaign with a call to action most presidents would share:

> The Harvard Campaign calls on us to articulate and affirm the fundamen-
> tal values and purposes of higher education in a world transformed by
> globalization and technology, a world filled with promise for improving hu-
> man lives, a world in which talent recognizes no boundaries, and in which
> creativity and curiosity will fuel the future. (Powell, 2013, para. 5)

Through the university—*through the work of faculty*—donors contribute
to the public good, and so do their agents, the faculty who teach, conduct
research, and apply their knowledge and experience to the communities of
which they belong.

So it is little wonder that faculty are asked to be the intermediary with
potential donors, to join directly in raising resources, and to do so while not
shirking their paid duties. Through the voluntary donation of their time, they
are themselves behaving philanthropically as they reach out to the several
constituencies of possible donors: foundations, corporations, and individuals.

Foundations: The most common engagement of faculty is with foundations as an applicant or principal investigator on a research proposal or other grant request. Whether the foundation is a corporate, private, family, or community foundation, the personal engagement of the faculty with the foundation staff will be the basis for a more successful philanthropic relationship, assuming, of course, that the proposed project meets the need of the foundation to accomplish its goals—especially meeting the societal need addressed in the foundation's mission.

Corporations: Corporate giving is increasingly tied to businesses' strategic goals, making the expertise of faculty ever more important in building what may become philanthropic relationships. As the faculty panel reacting to news of the new Harvard campaign said, in "the differing roles of businesses and universities in knowledge generation, . . . universities are uniquely suited to create knowledge, while businesses are best able to develop and apply that knowledge" (Powell, 2013, para. 33). There is a relationship of mutual benefit between corporations and universities in which faculty often provide entrée.

Individuals: The Voluntary Support of Education Survey (Council for Aid to Education, 2012) found that about $28 billion was given from all sources to education, and of that amount approximately 44% came from individuals (26% from alumni and 18% from nonalumni). Foundations gave approximately 30% and corporations approximately 17%; organizations gave 9% and religious organizations 1%. Aside from alumni, students, their parents, and other individuals with whom faculty have meaningful relations (even when not known to the faculty, whose influence may have gone unnoticed at the time), individual university colleagues are now a growing part of the potential audience for fundraising efforts by faculty as on-campus fundraising campaigns become increasingly popular, and current, former, and retired faculty and staff are seen to make gifts from the tens of thousands to the millions of dollars (Shaker, 2013a, 2013b).

RECOGNIZING FACULTY ENGAGEMENT

Primary outcomes of philanthropic engagement are twofold: collective and individual. On the one hand, institutional communities are built and nurtured through philanthropy, while, on the other, individual faculty themselves may benefit personally. Much of the attention to philanthropy in higher education is focused on the institution, the collective community, as made clear in the references to Harvard's new campaign. Despite the lofty rhetoric to the contrary, several of higher education's own competing values actually encourage faculty to withdraw from the collegial life around their institution (Gappa, Austin, & Trice, 2007). Faculty at many institutions are encouraged to reduce time devoted to teaching to a minimum while focusing on research and writing for their "discipline"; they are advised to avoid committee appointments, participation in community engagement, and even assisting students if not directly related to their research agendas because all will not further their careers.

However, according to David Brown and KerryAnn O'Meara (2011) research shows faculty scholarship "done in isolation from interdisciplinary colleagues and collaboration with peers suffers, so there is very little win-win in this trend toward isolation" (p. 15). Major changes are not likely to take place overnight, but openly acknowledging the role of faculty philanthropy can connect more faculty more deeply to their place—their academic home—with highly positive results for the academic community. Involvement by faculty in fundraising activities is just one example of an opportunity for engagement.

FRAMING THE PHILANTHROPIC WITHIN ACADEMIC WORK

Payton's broad definition of philanthropy and the adoption of this formulation by many suggest that the human wish for purpose and meaning in life can be realized through one's work, including academic work. The organizational culture, therefore, within which professionals and in this case, faculty, operate is key to actualizing how they behave philanthropically. Perhaps Edgar Schein (1992) captured best the notion of organizational culture when he summarized it as the rituals, values, actions, or behaviors within a climate that make a whole. Noting further, unsurprisingly, that organizational culture is "hard to define, . . . analyze . . . , measure, and . . . manage" (p. 12), Schein anticipates the challenges of thinking about academic work in the context of philanthropy.

The nature of the academic community has changed over time, and the need for today's professoriate to find meaning in their work beyond monetary gain is perhaps more critical than ever if for no other reason than the psychological need for intrinsic "compensation" for the increasing portion of the academic workforce (both part-time and contingent faculty) that is compensated at ever-lower comparative rates (Kezar & Sam, 2010). This suggests that the satisfaction generated through philanthropy can play an important part in building faculty commitment to the institution's mission and values, particularly in support of the academic ethos that attends to the public good through education, research, and service. This could be the case especially to the extent that access to education remains a public good and not a private benefit.

Although I met Robert Payton after I was a full-time academic professional, he was my teacher. His concept of philanthropy, combined with his practice of the profession of teaching, provided a powerful model and example. Deep reflection on just what the concept of voluntary action for the public good meant within my institution caused me to see just how applicable the concept is to faculty work at all levels, but especially to higher education, where faculty typically have considerably more freedom and discretion in the use of their time and the exercise of their rights than other teachers. Some in the K–12 setting and, certainly, many in the community college sector might well make a similar claim for the presence of a philanthropic aspect to their teaching and service. And, of course, teaching and other academic work takes form in the context of a specific setting and culture.

In the history of higher education and philanthropy, we have seldom seen works addressing the philanthropic role of the faculty. This internal perspective on what is taught by faculty, how they convey their ideas of a civil society, how they interact with each other as well as with their students and other constituents of the institution, and how they honor a professional commitment to the public good merits much further discussion and debate. The role of faculty in fundraising as discussed is but the more highly visible way in which faculty act philanthropically. Is there a similar case to be made for the professional practice of faculty as philanthropic through their inherently altruistic role in providing education as a vehicle toward a better life for all?

With great admiration for Payton's wisdom and in view of his role as my teacher, I modify his definition of philanthropy by adding one simple word to the definition—*intended*. Philanthropy is voluntary action *intended* for the public good. This change has been motivated by my observation over many years that people in all walks of life have adopted altruism, or a concern for others, as the motive for philanthropy, including teachers at all levels. I have come to appreciate, in my colleagues and myself, just how important intention is in self-defining what we do and why we do it. On reflection, we know that altruism is not the single motive for defining philanthropy, and, in fact, it is probably not the desired operational motive for our understanding of this aspect of human behavior. This is particularly true since most of human action is motivated by a concern for oneself as well as for others. Recognizing and reflecting on intent is key to leading a philanthropic academic life. (For a comprehensive review of altruism and its role in defining the human condition, Post, Underwood, Schloss, and Hurlbut's 2002 collection, *Altruism and Altruistic Love*, provides a useful context for the philanthropic nature of all work, especially academic work.)

Prevailing evidence clearly indicates that both altruism and egoism are at work in the human condition as a cause for any philanthropic action that occurs. This argument is especially convincing within the faculty work environment when one considers William Dean's reflection that "altruism elevates the moral agent and diminishes the moral object (the one to whom the altruistic act is aimed). Therefore, even on its own terms, the use of altruism can be morally counterproductive" (personal correspondence, October 1992). To this formulation, we might add "intention."

Scholars in many fields of study, typically in philosophy, religion, education, psychology, sociology, and, most recently, philanthropic studies, have studied helping behavior. In an earlier essay, I reviewed much of the work that contributed to my operational idea that "altruism and egoism come together in the moral person to form a cooperative venture to achieve nearly all ends in society. Our actions are neither pure egoism nor pure altruism but some form of both, coalesced if you will" (Burlingame, 1993, p. 2).

By operationalizing my definition of philanthropy using our understanding of "helping behavior" we can avoid one of the contested issues of Payton's definition as "voluntary action for the public good." "Philanthropy as voluntary giving and receiving (of money and/or effort) intended for public purposes" (Burlingame, 1993, p. 6) may provide a more value-neutral definition, as Mike Martin (1991) has argued, which leaves room for moral assessment to be done in individual cases—and allows room for considering "intent." Philanthropy is viewed differently from various cultural and economic positions. What has been claimed to be philanthropic may not, in fact, have been so. Therefore, by including the moral judgment in the definition of philanthropy, "we still allow for the moral discourse to be applied to individual cases and at the same time include the moral 'sentiment and imagination' as it is applied to communities" (Burlingame, 1993, p. 7).

Two other clarifying elements inherent in the broad definition of philanthropy may be needed to accept faculty work as philanthropic. First, *voluntary* is most closely construed to mean that the act is not being compensated or politically (socially, religiously) coerced. It is intended as giving without profit or payment. Behavior done willingly is not always voluntary. For example, I may pay my taxes willingly in my role as a good citizen, but this is not voluntary. Faculty will turn in their grades willingly but this is not voluntary.

Second, to accept faculty work as philanthropic, it is important to consider the difference between what many claim is a philanthropic act and, conversely, a life's work with philanthropic aims. From the classic writings of Aristotle forward, through the biblical authors, Maimonides, Islamic scholars, and other great philosophers, it becomes clear that being generous and acting with gratitude (being philanthropic) is a matter of character—living a life of meaning for good ends—as well as intent. Even when the "good" person is compensated, is it not possible to go beyond defined or expected duties to give more and thus act philanthropically while being paid?

Is this not the life of a faculty member: not only giving voice to one's self development (egoism) but also providing example and encouragement to others to do well (altruism) through the teacher's deliberate actions, perhaps including donating to the teacher's own institution or actively soliciting others to donate? No PhD program of which I am aware has newly certified graduates—many of whom become faculty—take an oath to contribute to the public good, but there is an implied commitment to use one's newly acquired and certified education in exactly this way. Perhaps there should be the academician's equivalent of the Hippocratic oath.

In this context I am reminded of two great examples of faculty members (indeed, philanthropists) who edited works for the series Philanthropy and Nonprofit Organizations that I coedit for the Indiana University Press—William Jackson (2008) and Amy Kass (2002, 2008). Their books are philanthropic gifts to any who read them; through the intellectual work of these faculty editors, collections of ideas about giving and volunteering are made available and accessible. And, as Kass (2002) notes in her introduction to her first collection, *The Perfect Gift*, "we can choose or refuse to be philanthropic. We can give and serve well or poorly. But we cannot choose whether or not to have such choices" (p. 3). She further notes that "we are all, in the root sense of the term, philanthropists . . . thus 'philanthropic' describes the disposition to promote the happiness and well-being of one's fellows" (p. 3). Or as my teacher Robert Payton would often say, there is a "philanthropic imagination" at work in us.

Giving and receiving implies a relationship of at least two parties. Philanthropy is a social relation that is very fluid: One may be a donor and then become a receiver (Schervish & Havens, 1997), a role reversal common in academic settings where faculty benefit from the gifts of external donors yet themselves donate to their own workplace. The fact that there are economic rewards for certain acts of philanthropy does not mean that the act is not also philanthropic. The intellectual work of faculty for "public purposes" could be the most contested claim by critics of defining (at least aspects of) faculty work as philanthropic. It is, however, the public good of the intellectual work and of the benefits of education itself that is essential for a good society (Sulek, 2010; Tierney & Perkins, Chapter 13, this volume), which arguably requires educated citizens. I believe that most faculty worry about the lives of their students and others, just as they worry about the state (values, culture, and purpose) of the institutions in which they work. Like most donors (philanthropists), faculty want to make a difference. Their philanthropic action is a way in which they can fulfill that aspiration—both by direct contribution of resources and by engaging intentionally in improving the lives of students and (through them) the public good. The same can be said for philanthropically intended research and civic engagement.

Ironically, at the same time it is this broad, Payton-defined sense of philanthropy that allows for the realization that philanthropy can also be wasteful and ineffective, it can be a saving grace to some and ridiculous to others, it can blur the boarders of the other sectors, and it can be "the social history of the moral imagination" (Geertz, 2000, p. 8). Thus acting in one's self-interest will not automatically produce misanthropic consequences. Likewise, acting altruistically does not always produce philanthropic results. "Philanthropy is best described and understood when its definition takes into consideration concepts that include both the interest of self and the interest of others. Or, as Tocqueville so elegantly defined it, 'Self-interest rightly understood'" (Burlingame, 1993, p. 8).

REFERENCES

Brown, D., & O'Meara, K. (2011). Engaged faculty: An interview with KerryAnn O'Meara. *Higher Education Exchange*, 14–23.

Burlingame, D. F. (1993). *Altruism and philanthropy: Definitional issues*. Essays on Philanthropy, No. 10. Indianapolis, IN: Indiana University Center on Philanthropy.

Council for Aid to Education. (2012). *Voluntary support for education survey 2011*. New York, NY: Council for Aid to Education.

Curti, M. E., & Nash, R. (1965). *Philanthropy in the shaping of American higher education*. New Brunswick, NJ: Rutgers University Press.

Drezner, N. D. (2011). *Philanthropy and fundraising in American higher education* (ASHE Higher Education Report, Vol. 37, No. 2). San Francisco, CA: Jossey-Bass.

Gappa, J. M., Austin, A. E., & Trice, A. G. (2007). *Rethinking faculty work: Higher education's strategic imperative*. San Francisco, CA: Jossey-Bass.

Geertz, C. (2000). *Local knowledge: Further essays in interpretive anthropology* (3rd ed.). New York, NY: Basic Books.

Hall, M. R. (1993). *The dean's role in fund raising*. Baltimore, MD: The Johns Hopkins University Press.

Hall, P. D. (1992). Teaching and research on philanthropy, voluntarism, and nonprofit organizations: A case study of academic innovations. *The Teachers College Record, 93*(3), 403–435.

Jackson, W. J. (Ed.). (2008). *The wisdom of generosity: A reader in American philanthropy*. Waco, TX: Baylor University Press.

Kass, A. A. (Ed.).s (2002). *The perfect gift: The philanthropic imagination in poetry and prose*. Bloomington, IN: Indiana University Press.

Kass, A. A. (Ed.). (2008). *Giving well, doing good: Readings for thoughtful philanthropists*. Bloomington, IN: Indiana University Press.

Kezar, A., & Sam, C. (2010). *Understanding the new majority of non-tenure-track faculty in higher education: Demographics, experiences, and plans of action* (ASHE Higher Education Report, Vol. 36, No. 4). San Francisco, CA: Jossey-Bass.

Martin, M. W. (1991). *Philanthropy, virtue, and responsibility*. Unpublished paper.

McClintock, B. R. (2000). Trends in educational fundraising. In P. M. Buchanan (Ed.), *Handbook of institutional advancement* (3rd ed., pp. 367–373). New York, NY: Council for Advancement and Support of Education.

Payton, R. L. (1988). *Philanthropy: Voluntary action for the public good*. New York, NY: American Council on Education/Macmillan.

Post, S. G., Underwood, L. G., Schloss, J. P., & Hurlbut, W. B. (Eds.). (2002). *Altruism and altruistic love: Science, philosophy, and religion in dialogue*. New York, NY: Oxford University Press.

Powell, A. (2013, September 21). Harvard kicks off fundraising effort. *Harvard Gazette*. Available at http://news.harvard.edu/gazette/story/2013/09/harvard-kicks-off-fundraising-effort/

Schein, E. H. (1992). *Organizational culture and leadership* (2nd ed.). San Francisco, CA: Jossey-Bass.

Schervish, P. G., & Havens, J. J. (1997). Social participation and charitable giving: A multivariate analysis. *Voluntas: International Journal of Voluntary and Nonprofit Organizations, 8*(3), 235–260.

Shaker, G. G. (2013a). The generosity of an urban professoriate: Understanding faculty as donors and academic citizens. *Metropolitan Universities, 23*(3), 5–25.

Shaker, G. G. (2013b). Faculty and staff as prospects and donors: Giving on campus. In N. D. Drezner (Ed.), *Expanding the donor base in higher education* (pp. 123–137). New York, NY: Routledge.

Sulek, M. (2010). On the modern meaning of philanthropy. *Nonprofit and Voluntary Sector Quarterly, 39*(2), 193–212.

CHAPTER 10

Faculty Work as Philanthropy

Doing Good and Doing It Well

Richard C. Turner

This chapter, like so many recent commentaries on higher education (Bousquet, 2008; Gappa, Austin, & Trice, 2007; Nelson, 2010; Olson & Presley, 2009) accepts the fact that higher education will change deeply in the coming decades and that the pressures on faculty and students, especially because of the recent economic downturn, will change the way people pursue education in the future. As faculty respond to these changes, they need to spell out the values and assumptions that shape their work in ways that they have rarely had to do before. If, as Cary Nelson (2010), Marc Bousquet (2008), and Frank Donoghue (2008) all argue, American higher education is headed toward greater and greater corporatization, then some very basic faculty values, especially those aspects of faculty work shaped by their public and nonprofit contexts, will be challenged, and probably lost, without active and careful attention on the part of current university faculty. Much of what will be lost in the corporatization of universities will be the generosity and devotion that characterizes much faculty work. The philanthropic values that permeate faculty approaches to their roles and responsibilities are as important to faculty work as their expertise or their contributions to institutional aspirations. According to Donoghue (2008), corporate values and corporatized universities are generally inimical to traditional faculty roles (p. 22), and especially to the philanthropic aspects of faculty work. Unless Donoghue is right that it is too late to resist this trend (p. xi), faculty need to make a special effort to ensure that the philanthropic elements of their work remain central in whatever new definition of faculty work emerges. That special effort begins at least by entering into extended conversations about faculty work as philanthropic and how faculty might capture those achievements.

One very important aspect of faculty work—its philanthropic dimension—has too often been left unstated and unrecognized. Briefly, the

elements of faculty work that might be called "philanthropic" include contributions to the common good of an academic institution as well as to
society at large; the choices faculty make to help students and colleagues
improve their work and their prospects for short- and long-term success;
and the contributions of time, expertise, and creative energy to making a
class, a campus, a discipline or a profession better, beyond what is ordinar-
ily expected. The complexity of faculty roles and responsibilities make it
difficult to draw the line between what faculty are required to do and what
they contribute over and above their duties, but the clarification of what
such a line means is crucial in defining the significance of faculty work.
Doing good work and proving that it is done well is possible in academic
communities just as it has been possible for nonprofits to meet the challenge of accountability. Nonprofit managers have the responsibility, arising
from their sense of mission, to measure and document their contributions.
As faculty focus explicitly on the philanthropic aspects of their work, they
may find valuable the process of documenting and evaluating their contributions, just as nonprofits have.

Furthermore, faculty need to clarify the special characteristics of their
work in a nonprofit setting. (Public universities are not technically nonprofits,
but faculty in public universities usually operate within the same values and
traditions as their colleagues in private, nonprofit institutions.) In order to
represent the value and significance of their work, faculty need to articulate
the special roles and responsibilities that they have by virtue of working in a
nonprofit organization or its equivalent. Faculty have management responsibilities and accountability to their constituents, but these elements differ
significantly from what exists in corporate environments and require special
attention to the rules that shape nonprofit organizations.

Articulating the philanthropic values and dimensions of faculty work
will also enable faculty to develop assessment practices that capture how
well they are contributing to the common good. Measuring impact and success is presumably a goal of those calling for more businesslike practices
in universities. Leaving aside the question of how well businesses measure
their impact, faculty certainly should welcome opportunities to spell out
their achievements and demonstrate the extent of their contributions.

WHEN FACULTY WORK IS PHILANTHROPIC

Faculty contribute to a series of common goods. Their work contributes
to the creation of citizen leaders for the improvement and the guarantee
of the future of democratic societies. Most universities make this claim for
their work, and liberal education initiatives are especially likely to point to

the creation of better citizens as a goal and an important outcome. Faculty members also help to prepare their students to become responsible citizens within their own academic communities. Faculty contribute to the advancement of the discipline or profession within which they work through both their scholarly contributions and their professional service to the discipline or profession. Advising students, reviewing colleagues' scholarly work, and participating in the structures of professional organizations are all part of this work. The principle of stewardship of the disciplines as enunciated in Chris Golde and George Walker's *Envisioning the Future of Doctoral Education* (2006) emphasizes the responsibilities academics have to ensure the success of succeeding generations of scholars, a perspective that resembles philanthropic values. Adrianna Kezar, Tony Chambers, and John Burkhardt (2005) make a compelling case not only for the contributions higher education makes to the public good but also for the need to pursue an extended conversation on how higher education can re-establish its charter from the public it serves.

Faculty gifts come in a wide range of activities and represent a complex set of personal and professional values. Faculty contribute to the academic life of the institutions in which they work through service on governance committees, task forces, administrative positions, and other duties necessary to the health and success of the institution. Some of this work is expected, but the flexibility of faculty responsibilities makes it possible for some faculty to contribute more than others. Each of these roles has the potential for making a contribution beyond what is expected. Faculty can develop the measures for identifying the degree and quality of each claim, although the kind and degree of a measure may differ with each aspect of faculty work—that is, research, teaching, or service. Faculty need to be willing to substantiate the claims for success they make just as professionals in other nonprofit settings do. Aspiring to do good is a worthy goal and evidence of a fine disposition and something any well-intentioned person can lay claim to. Proving that some good has resulted from well-intentioned actions is the responsibility and mark of a professional. Most disciplines and professions have some standards of minimum or exemplary practice that inform peer review, but those standards rarely spell out any maximums expected of professionals, thus creating an ambiguity about what duties professionals owe beyond an expected minimum. Faculty who demonstrate contributions above what is expected have a legitimate claim to making a gift.

Faculty work contributes to a larger mission and a common good that often reflect the highest aspirations of democratic societies. Furthermore, faculty often do what they do out of a sense of their work as a calling, sometimes a giving back, sometimes a chance to make a difference in a complex world. Faculty work tends to share more with philanthropy, as "voluntary action for the public good" (Payton & Moody, 2008, p. 12), and voluntary association than with standard employer–employee relations, in which the employee trades labor for money. The "voluntary" part of the definition carries special importance in thinking about faculty work, as it underscores the independence and individual commitment that characterizes faculty work. William Sullivan's *Work and Integrity* (2005) captures the central place of independence in its discussion of professional work as a vocation:

> But this sense of calling is a core feature of professionalism. To carry this off successfully requires considerable individual discernment and capacity for initiative and judgment; although the basic structures of professional work are institutionally constructed, the specific forms of an individual's practice and career are very much a personal accomplishment, involving a lifetime of creative invention as labor. (p. 15)

The integral sense of independence in faculty work enables the idea that faculty can donate the time, energy, and expertise available to them after they have fulfilled their prescribed duties. In contributing to their institutions' commitments to the public good through successful completion of their duties, faculty are just doing their job. But extraordinary efforts beyond what is expected constitute a gift.

This pervasive sense of vocation and its related insistence on internally defined missions mean that faculty guard fiercely the integrity of and the control over their work, whether in the classroom, in the lab, or in the community. Faculty get a paycheck every month and they come to the office every day (well, almost every day), but they tend to perceive their allegiance as owed to their peers in the profession and the recipients of their good works—most immediately their students, more broadly their other constituent communities. They are more properly seen as nonprofit managers or, in some cases, social entrepreneurs, than as employees joined together in a labor organization (although some faculty have chosen to unionize) or as individual employees depending on bosses for direction and continued approval.

Perhaps most obvious as a philanthropic characteristic of faculty work is the extraordinary amount of discretionary time, energy, and expertise that faculty invest in their teaching, research, and service (Braxton & Bayer, 1999; Shils, 1978). Indeed, most faculty have already invested years in acquiring their expertise before they begin a job as a faculty member. This contribution often far exceeds the compensation most professors receive, thus moving their work beyond trading labor for money to the level of a gift. That is, once faculty members (and this could be said for many other professions as well) put in more time, energy, or expertise into an activity than what might be necessary to do the job expected of them, they have made a gift of that time, energy, or expertise. There seems to be a "line" that differentiates what faculty do as their jobs according to societal and institutional expectations and what they do over and above that constitutes gifts. Just as people donating money draw on the wealth ("wealth" being those resources they have beyond what they need to support themselves) at their disposal, faculty make choices to give of their resources beyond what is necessary and so make a gift of this "extra" effort. In *The Gift*, Lewis Hyde (1983) makes the case that people operate in an exchange economy, where labor, talent, or achievement is exchanged for money, or in a gift economy, where people give of their labor, talent, or achievements without any promise of return but with a hope that the gift will enhance the life or lives it touches. In this sense Stanley Fish's *Save the World on Your Own Time* (2008) may have missed the point about faculty work and faculty commitments. Fish argues vehemently that faculty responsibilities are limited to teaching what they are expert in and that faculty should not aspire to goals beyond that expertise. In fact, much of the work faculty do and that Fish decries as outside the bounds of proper faculty interest is "on their own time," contributed over and above expectations.

Perhaps the second most striking aspect of faculty work as philanthropy lies in the commitment most faculty make and its resemblance to what is often referred to in specifically religious contexts as a vocation or a calling. In some religious institutions the devotion to work that amounts to a calling may be part of the explicit expectations grounded in the nonsecular commitments of the institution, the faculty, and the students. When the same devoted behaviors are central to faculty work in an institution without an explicit religious mission, these actions may be best seen as philanthropic. The authority that warrants so much of what faculty do seems to rest in some higher cause or greater good that faculty have identified as the reason for making such an absolute commitment to something more than the elements of a job description.

Sometimes the greater good is the advancement of a discipline or profession, sometimes the altruistic goals of an institution, and sometimes the improvement in the lives and prospects of clients or students. Faculty often are no more specific than using the phrase "my work" when referring to what they do, but that work usually implies something important and valuable not only in the view of the individual but also for society in general. In a recent essay, J. Hillis Miller (2009) expresses this absolute dedication to the work: "Any professor must carry on the search for truth wherever it takes him, unconditionally" (p. 78). Searching for truth may operate at the highest level of generality, but advancing knowledge is still a specific public good. The independence of faculty work means that few faculty limit their sense of mission to some directive received from an institution or administrator. Indeed, Edward Shils (1978) has made an impressive case for the almost absolute independence of faculty work in defining the academic ethos as based on an individual quest for truth and knowledge. Many faculty remain stubbornly unaware of an institution's mission and goals even as they make deep commitments to their own sense of contributing to a higher good. Often, faculty have adopted that sense of mission from the training they received within their disciplines or professions. Like many workers driven by a commitment to a cause, faculty fail to draw distinctions between their work lives and their personal lives, a blurring of roles that seems to recognize a higher authority, if not a specifically religious one, as the warrant for the focus and dedication. This sense of dedication to a higher purpose may be admirable in its intention and often helpful in its impact, but it leads to organizational anomalies in an academic community. Academic communities have learned to depend on these anomalies, but a changed, redefined, "corporatized" environment may not welcome implicit arrangements as well.

The need for independence is crucial for faculty to maintain control over their work, and that control is essential to faculty making the contributions to which they aspire. Nelson (2010) emphasizes the importance of faculty independence in understanding the basis for academic freedom. Faculty do indeed require an extraordinary amount of independence and control over their time in order to ensure the integrity of their work (Baldridge, Curtis, Ecker, & Riley, 1978). As Nelson (2010) points out, that independence comes from their participation in a discipline or a profession, something that sets a presumably higher standard for their work because all professions have a duty to advance the public good. Shils (1978) is clear about the primacy of faculty expertise in developing the shape of an academic community and faculty roles within it.

As Sullivan (2005) suggests, this independence is balanced by the responsibility to operate within the values and expectations of the discipline or profession and as articulated by the theory and practice of peers. That responsibility extends to working for institutional goals, student success, and constituent communities' interests. But these obligations lie with the faculty member and are not always initiated or pursued by these constituencies or measured by them, although constituents should measure the impact of work done for their benefit. These related assumptions parallel the way people who feel called to work approach their missions. This independence, which enables faculty members to make decisions about contributing their time to the needs of individual students, provides a benefit to the institution or the public good in ways often not anticipated in their job descriptions. (Indeed, in the past, few faculty would accept a job description, something most employees get as a matter of course.) Guidelines for faculty work usually reside in advancement criteria that are peer review rubrics rather than job descriptions. Faculty work has occurred traditionally in a climate of understanding and trust, and it fits less well within the terms of explicit contracts.

Another distinct philanthropic element of faculty work is the presence of what looks like serial reciprocity in the terms faculty use to talk about why they do what they do. Serial reciprocity is the habit or commitment to pay back a gift or favor, not by returning it to the giver of the gift, but by passing along an equivalent or greater gift to someone else to honor or recognize the original giver and gift (Moody, 1993). Serial reciprocity is often part of the explanation philanthropists provide for their giving. Faculty often talk about the special debt they owe to a teacher who inspired them or otherwise prompted them to pursue their work. Faculty talk about paying back the gift they feel they received in their undergraduate or graduate educations by making equivalent opportunities available to their students. Perhaps not all these memories of exceptional undergraduate teachers are accurate, but the point still stands. Even when students enroll in expensive institutions expecting superior instruction, their response to better-than-the norm for that institution feels like a gift.

Faculty owe their students and their discipline the best work they can do, but they also "bestow" their leadership and special genius on the same groups to which they are responsible in other ways, and often to projects and initiatives that they deem to need their unique talents and expertise. For instance, faculty members fulfill their obligations to serve an institution by participating in committee work within shared governance structures. Fairly often, members of a committee will make a special commitment to a project that comes within the committee's sphere of responsibility. Similarly, faculty often invest time and energy in student initiatives on the premise that the extra work will be especially valuable to the students. These faculty practices suggest the line between expectations and gifts. Or rather, the same act may appear merely as what tuition is meant to purchase or it may appear as something extra that a faculty member has given. Similarly, one student may regard a faculty member's work as part of a labor/money exchange while another student in the same class (who presumably derived some extraordinary benefit) perceives the instruction as a gift. This ambiguity arises in part from the pervasive absence of job descriptions in faculty appointments. A delineated list of faculty roles and responsibilities would clarify the line between expectations and gifts even if it would pauperize the rich engagement so many faculty have with their academic communities.

Liberal education is based on the notion that what a teacher or researcher does has its impact in the long term and often in ways unanticipated by either student or teacher. This gap between an instructor's action and its ultimate consequences parallels the criterion the Internal Revenue Service uses to determine a gift—the donor must relinquish control over the commodity. When faculty invest special effort in students, in their institutions, or in their disciplines, they usually expect that the outcome of that investment will be evident later and at a significant remove from the act of giving itself. Liberal education almost always defines its expectations in terms of long-range and complex outcomes. Liberal education often has short-term, job-related consequences as well, but its long-term impact is most frequently emphasized and thought to have the greatest value.

FACULTY AS NONPROFIT MANAGERS

So, faculty may be philanthropists. But they also need to do what philanthropists do—answer to the responsibility to make the case for the relevance of their doing good. Faculty can focus their work as philanthropists not so much by rehearsing how they will distribute millions once they win the lottery but by thinking of their roles as nonprofit mangers, or perhaps social entrepreneurs in some cases, whose efforts serve dual purposes, and their work as contributions to the aspirations and goals of their students, their campuses, and their disciplines or professions and communities. Although faculty quite rightly protest against their work being measured as if it were part of a corporation, they still need to recognize the managerial responsibilities inherent in working in a nonprofit environment, and especially a contemporary one. Faculty enhance their control and the coherence of their activities when they place their work in the context of what nonprofits do. Working within an academic community allows faculty to approach their work as philanthropy if they first define their academic context as a nonprofit venture. Like nonprofit managers, faculty can then create a context where professorial achievements are recognizable and definable as philanthropic and are distinct from the work and the measures of achievement within the other two sectors—business and government.

Faculty, as well as many others engaged in the work of universities, need to pay more attention to the nature of the nonprofit environment in which they work. Perhaps universities find themselves boxed in by the call for corporate-like values and practices because they have not made the case for their contributions as proper to a nonprofit organization. Faculty need to develop the rationales and justifications for what they do. The constituents of academic communities—students, trustees, community partners, and others with an interest in the consequences and impacts of faculty work— have asked for an account of faculty work. The ability of faculty to create the atmosphere of trust and independence they need to complete their responsibilities depends on providing a convincing response to this request. By definition, constituents have a right to explanations of the importance and relevance of faculty work, but those accounts ought to grow out of an understanding of faculty work appropriate to the nonprofit nature of the context within which the work occurs. Perhaps there was a time when faculty and their constituents shared an understanding of the implications of the nonprofit work universities do and so there was a broad warrant from society for faculty to pursue the missions entrusted to universities. But no such general understanding currently exists; even many faculty and administrators would be hard pressed to explain the public good served by universities and the implications of their work for supporting the claims universities make for what they do.

One very important difference between for-profits and nonprofits is that the people who pay for nonprofit services often differ from those who receive them. Most for-profits trade goods or services for money and the transaction is fairly straightforward. Nonprofits often provide goods or services donated by someone other than the agent or nonprofit manager. Universities charge fees to students, but those fees often do not cover the cost of the instruction students receive. Thus, although many students have the impression that they (or their parents) are paying for their education, that payment also is subsidized by government and private donor support. Faculty are in the front line of this ambiguity as they interpret their responsibility of carrying out university missions to educate the students who see themselves as trading money for credits and, ultimately, certification of training. Faculty who accept Fish's (2008) version of faculty work teach their discipline or profession well and thoroughly within the expectations of their professional or disciplinary code, and leave it at that. Others, whose work advances the goals of the institution as well as meeting disciplinary and professional expectations, go beyond the mere certifying of student achievement and products to ensure student learning within the institution's claims for success. Furthermore, faculty who bring their expertise to bear on solving problems or enhancing life within local and regional communities make doing good a part of their professional life.

All the pressures on higher education emphasize the urgency for faculty to regain control over the conduct of faculty work and its meaning for American higher education, and that means looking closely at how being in the nonprofit context shapes faculty work and explains many of the values and practices at the center of faculty roles. Elizabeth Boris's article on nonprofits in *Philanthropy in America: An Historical Encyclopedia* (2004) offers a series of characteristics of nonprofit organizations, and many of those characteristics capture the extent to which faculty work is distinctly a part of nonprofit institutions and very different from corporate practices.

A NEW COMPACT FOR FACULTY WORK

Had things stayed the same, perhaps all faculty members could have maintained the genteel tradition of not bragging about the good one does, of letting the work speak for itself. Such informal recognition processes, very common in nonprofit organizations, are often not tolerated in corporatized environments and so are under particular threat when institutions take business as an organizational model. But the pressures on higher education (e.g., cuts in public funding, board activism, decline of the profession's prestige, increase in non-tenure-track faculty in classrooms) and the need for a new compact regarding faculty work require that faculty spell out the philanthropic dimensions of their work and incorporate that recognition into whatever new understanding emerges. Spelling out these dimensions makes possible a valuable response to the pressure on faculty to document their impact and achievements, something that nonprofit managers have now had to do for decades. That new enunciation of faculty values and aspirations must be explicit about what drives faculty work in ways that academic cultures have failed to do in the past.

The demand for accountability and the increasingly frequent attacks on universities' rights to pursue traditional missions come from many sides. The professionalization of faculty work ignores the specific missions of local institutions in favor of contributions to a discipline or profession. Fish (2008) argues against universities making claims beyond providing specific instruction in specific fields of expertise without any reference to the impact of those efforts on students or any other traditional constituents of faculty work. And faculty claims for the impact of their work have been seriously undermined, if not exactly attacked, by the hiring patterns of the past 3 decades, patterns that have left tenured and tenure-track faculty outnumbered and alienated from the majority of contingent faculty, who do most of the teaching on many campuses. Finally, traditional roles and responsibilities have been abrogated by the call for universities to adopt business models in their operations and in their conception of themselves. This corporatization of American higher education, especially as it has been enacted in for-profit universities, reshapes priorities in conversations about university resources and measures of success and might render traditional university missions irrelevant.

Recognizing the philanthropic nature of faculty work enables all members of academic communities to see the centrality of faculty work and create the structures necessary to facilitate this work. In a time of rapid and radical change, academic communities need to recognize and sustain the philanthropic aspects of faculty activities. Faculty need to invest the time and energy to foreground the philanthropic aspects of their work and embrace their responsibilities as nonprofit managers. Kezar et al. (2005) lay out the scheme for how faculty can promote the conversation about how higher education contributes to the public good (pp. 317–325) and that process will serve faculty well in engaging academic communities in the philanthropic elements of faculty work. University officials need to recognize the contributions of faculty and enable them to continue the philanthropic elements of faculty work even as they lead their institutions through periods of change. The giving and volunteering that characterize academic communities provide the cohesion needed for the pursuit of the policies and practices that warrant the claims for contributions to the public good.

As universities move forward into much changed economic and cultural environments, faculty need to carry with them a coherent sense of the work they do, especially the core values that regard their work as an act of giving and as a calling. Faculty, by virtue of their participation in disciplinary and professional communities, are answerable to broader constituencies than their institutions even though those responsibilities are pursued in concert with the duties faculty have to their institutions. Those entrusted with a university's success need to recognize and incorporate the philanthropic aspects of faculty work in an institution's goals and values. If faculty are going to be asked to accomplish their work in high-pressure environments and to offer reasonable assessments of that success (Gappa et al., 2007), they need to trust that what they do is understood by students, administrators, and other constituents as including a contribution to a greater good. Faculty can attend to the greater good and still participate in the management structures of an academic community if academic managers and others who have a stake in evaluating faculty activities (trustees, accrediting bodies, state governing bodies) recognize the special philanthropic dimension of faculty work.

REFERENCES

Baldridge, J., Curtis, D., Ecker, G., & Riley, G. (1978). *Policy making and effective leadership*. San Francisco, CA: Jossey-Bass.

Boris, E. T. (2004). Nonprofit sector. In D. Burlingame (Ed.), *Philanthropy in America: An historical encyclopedia* (Vol. 2, pp. 355–360). Denver, CO: ABC-CLIO.

Bousquet, M. (2008). *How the university works: Higher education and the low wage nation*. New York, NY: New York University Press.

Braxton, J. M., & Bayer, A. E. (1999). *Faculty misconduct in collegiate teaching*. Baltimore, MD: The Johns Hopkins University Press.

Donoghue, F. (2008). *The last professors, the corporate university, and the fate of the humanities*. New York, NY: Fordham University Press.

Fish, S. (2008). *Save the world on your own time.* New York, NY: Oxford University Press.

Gappa, J. M., Austin, A. E., & Trice, A. G. (2007). *Rethinking faculty work: Higher education's strategic imperative.* San Francisco, CA: Jossey-Bass.

Golde, C. M., & Walker, G. E. (Eds.). (2006). *Envisioning the future of doctoral education: Preparing stewards of the discipline.* San Francisco, CA: Jossey-Bass.

Hyde, L. (1983). *The gift: Imagination and the erotic life of property.* New York, NY: Vintage.

Kezar, A. J., Chambers, T. C., & Burkhardt, J. C. (Eds.). (2005). *Higher education for the public good: Emerging voices from a national movement.* San Francisco, CA: Jossey-Bass.

Miller, J. H. (2009). The university, with conditions. In G. A. Olson & J. W. Presley (Eds.), *The future of higher education: Perspectives from America's academic leaders* (pp. 73–82). Boulder, CO: Paradigm.

Moody, M. P. (1993). *Pass it on: Serial reciprocity as a principle of philanthropy.* Essays in Philanthropy, No. 13. Indianapolis, IN: Indiana University Center on Philanthropy.

Nelson, C. (2010). *No university is an island: Saving academic freedom.* New York, NY: New York University Press.

Olson, G. A., & Presley, J. W. (Eds.). (2009). *The future of higher education: Perspectives from America's academic leaders.* Boulder, CO: Paradigm.

Payton, R. L., & Moody, M. P. (2008). *Understanding philanthropy: Its meaning and mission.* Bloomington, IN: Indiana University Press.

Shils, E. (1978). The academic ethos. *The American Scholar, 47*(2), 165–190.

Sullivan, W. M. (2005). *Work and integrity: The crisis and promise of professionalism in America* (2nd ed.). San Francisco, CA: Jossey-Bass.

CHAPTER 11

Toward a More Perfect Union

Thought Meets Action in the Philanthropy of
State Humanities Councils

Elizabeth Lynn

Like other kinds of professionals, faculty members give and serve in their communities in order to advance the common good. They may do so as citizens, contributing something with no connection to their academic knowledge, as when an economist coaches her daughter's soccer team. But faculty also contribute to community organizations *through* their academic expertise—as, for example, when a sociologist serves on the board of the Urban League and conducts a survey of local minority-owned businesses. Both contributions qualify as forms of philanthropy, broadly defined as "voluntary action for the public good" (Payton, 1988, p. 3).

In this chapter, I consider one way in which humanities faculty have been inspired and encouraged to engage philanthropically in communities across America: through the programs and the boards of state humanities councils. The state humanities council movement offers an especially useful insight into faculty philanthropy because of the widespread perception that the humanities have little to do with the nitty-gritty of life, the policy issues and actions that make an actual difference in communities. That perception, in itself, can become a self-fulfilling prophesy: Perceived as irrelevant to civic life, humanists may choose to stay on campus where their hard-earned knowledge and skills are more readily respected and engaged.

Yet, as this case study of the state council movement will show, since the early 1970s many humanities scholars have been putting their knowledge and expertise to work for the public good. Through state humanities council programs, faculty members have led hundreds of thousands of community conversations and book discussions, moderated innumerable public panels, given talks as "Road Scholars" in large and small towns across America, assisted with multiple museum exhibits, organized library archives, and much more. Taken together, America's public humanities programs constitute what former National Endowment for the Humanities chairman Jim Leach (2011) has rightly called the "finest outreach education in the humanities in the world today."

The programs of the councils thus constitute a significant form of humanities faculty philanthropy. But equally significant—indeed, in their transformative potential, perhaps more significant—are the volunteer boards of the state humanities councils. Through these boards, scholars have joined together with other citizens to determine what the humanities can do for American public life—and then acted to realize their evolving vision with imagination and endeavor. In the process, the councils have often transformed the scholars themselves, igniting their interest in civic life and expanding their philanthropic identity.

If we want to understand philanthropy as a dimension of faculty work, we ought to take a closer look at the power of the state humanities council movement, both for engaging humanities faculty more effectively in their communities and for releasing the inherent civic energy of the humanities in American public life.

ORIGINS OF THE STATE HUMANITIES COUNCILS

The year 1965 was a *signature* one in American legislative history. Between April and November, President Lyndon Baines Johnson signed the Voting Rights Act, Elementary and Secondary Education Act, Higher Education Act, Water and Air Quality Acts, and Social Security Amendments that created Medicaid and Medicare. Tucked in among these landmark Great Society programs was the National Foundation on the Arts and Humanities Act, which established the National Endowment for the Arts (NEA) and the National Endowment for the Humanities (NEH).

Six years later, with much less signatory flourish, the novice NEH started an experiment of its own. Under pressure from Congress, though inwardly unsure about the merits of the enterprise, the NEH launched a test group of six "state-based programs" to explore how best to engage humanities scholars with the American public.

That little experiment yielded unexpectedly exciting results. By 1973, 42 states had established voluntary "committees" of humanities scholars and public members, who were working together energetically to regrant NEH dollars for public humanities programs in their state, through which humanities scholars could share their expertise on public policy issues with the out-of-school adult public. By 1976, the public policy focus had softened somewhat but the movement itself had grown. Now every state in the nation had one of these committees—or councils as they came to be called.

By 1981, the NEH was able to report that in the preceding year alone, 15,000 scholars had participated in public humanities programs and 30 million Americans had benefited from these efforts (Gibson, 1982).

Today, there are 56 state humanities councils—one for every state and territory—governed by "mixed" volunteer boards of faculty scholars and citizens. These councils receive more than one third of all NEH program funds (over $40 million in FY2011) and they raise almost as many dollars in state and private funds. Each year they conduct thousands of programs nationwide, often with humanities faculty members serving for little or no compensation. Indeed, for humanities faculty, the state council movement has become a primary platform for contributing their time, talent, treasure, and thought on behalf of the common good.

Yet this platform was not part of the NEH's plan from the start. How did it develop? How did this uncertain experiment become a defining dimension of the work of the NEH—and a spark for faculty philanthropy that connects the humanities to the common good?

NOT EVEN A GLINT

The animating purpose of the NEH was to secure recognition and a share of federal funding for America's "academic humanists"—scholars of history, literature, language, and other disciplines, who had professionalized in the late 19th and early 20th century and who increasingly saw themselves as members of a guild rather than as members of an educational institution or community. In the trenchant words of Ellen Lagemann and Harry Lewis (2012):

> As their affiliations shifted from educational institutions to academic guilds, faculty members identified themselves more with national professional communities than with the local residential communities in which their institutions were located. With this cosmopolitanism came a related shift in professional identity: professors' disciplinary affiliations trumped their status as teachers. (p. 17)

Even if humanities scholars wanted to engage philanthropically in their communities, the standards of the profession increasingly oriented them toward their own guilds.

But while humanists increasingly defined themselves through their research, they were being overshadowed by colleagues in the sciences. Federal funding for the sciences had grown rapidly in the years after World War II, first through research support, particularly from the military, and then through the establishment of the National Science Foundation in 1950. In the words of Barnaby Keeney, who would chair the first national commission on the humanities, and later, the NEH itself, "The results created an imbalance in the universities and colleges–despite the evident benefits for education in general. Federal funds were relatively abundant for the sciences, but they were entirely lacking for the humanities and the arts" (Keeney & Culligan, 2002).

In 1963, the American Council of Learned Societies, the Council of Graduate Schools in the United States, and the United Chapters of Phi Beta Kappa Society organized a National Commission on the Humanities, hoping to address this imbalance in funding and to promote the value of research and teaching by academic humanists. The commission brought together university professors and presidents, business and professional leaders, and school administrators to study the state of the humanities and make recommendations to Congress.

A year later, the commission published its report, recommending, as expected, that the president and Congress establish a National Humanities Foundation. As Robert Connor (1993) has observed, the report offered three key arguments in favor of allocating federal funds to support the arts and humanities. First, these funds would begin to correct the imbalance with science by supporting research in the humanities. Second, they would help America secure its international cultural status on the world stage by supporting the arts and thus help win the Cold War against the Soviet Union. And third, they would strengthen democracy itself by creating better citizens.

In putting forward this last argument, the writers of the report made several claims that were later redacted in the following declaration in the 1965 legislation—a declaration that has served as a veritable proof text for the NEH and the state councils ever since:

> Democracy demands wisdom and vision in its citizens. It must therefore foster and support a form of education, and access to the arts and the humanities, designed to make people of all backgrounds and wherever located masters of their technology and not its unthinking servants. (National Foundation on the Arts and Humanities Act of 1965, Sec. 2)

This brief but by now iconic statement introduced two key arguments for the value of the public humanities, both of which opened the door for faculty to understand the nature of contributions they might make to society as informed volunteers.

One argument might be called the *principle of access*—the doctrine that all citizens, regardless of background and "wherever located," deserve access to the humanities. The principle of access underlies a broader tradition of education for democracy, manifest in the land grant movement of the 19th century and the public educational broadcasting movement of the 20th.

A second key argument embedded in the proof text is what we might call the *democracy needs argument*. This argument asserts a direct link between the humanities and good citizenship in the form of a syllogism: *Democracy needs citizens who have X. The humanities cultivate X. Therefore, democracy needs the humanities*. This syllogism would appear time and again in the following decades to justify the value of the humanities for American democracy, with X redefined in light of the particular concerns of each era. Thus, to jump ahead to the 1980s: *Democracy needs citizens who appreciate difference. The humanities cultivate appreciation of difference. Therefore democracy needs the humanities*. Or, in the early years of this century, after the attacks of 9/11: *Democracy needs citizens who appreciate American history and values. The humanities cultivate appreciation of American history and values. Therefore, democracy needs the humanities*.

The Humanities Commission Report was widely circulated and well received, and its recommendations were soon realized. In 1965, the National Endowment for the Humanities was established, equipped with a mission to cultivate democracy and vision in all citizens, but animated by a particular interest in supporting and forwarding the work of academic humanists.

The new endowment accordingly structured its activities into three divisions: research, education, and public programs, with the last designed to support existing national and regional cultural institutions, such as libraries and museums. State-level public humanities councils were not even a glint in the NEH founders' eyes, much less part of their original plan. One might say that the NEH began as an ironic reversal of Kennedy's famous statement, despite the language of access and democracy. The NEH was asking what the country could do for humanities professors—not what they could do for their country.

RISE OF THE STATE-BASED PROGRAMS

The idea of the state-based programs only emerged 5 years later, and under instructive circumstances. The year was 1970. The NEH was up for reauthorization, and it was being pressed by congressional supporters to do something that would help the American people understand the need for continued funding. "The humanities" then, as now, were a hard sell at home. The NEA had state agencies to support the arts, and these agencies were making their own case effectively. Unlike artists, however, humanists were increasingly tucked away on college and universities campuses. The situation presented difficulties for congressional representatives who had to defend humanities expenditures to their own constituents. If no one knew what the humanities were, how could they be explained?

Under duress from Congress, the NEH agreed to experiment with "state-based programs" in the humanities in six states, starting in 1971. Thus begun a self-conscious experiment—both organizationally and programmatically—with the humanities in American public life. As John Barcroft, the director of public programs for the NEH, wrote in a 1972 memo, "No one in the country quite knows what a public program in the humanities is, nor do they know what kinds of resources they need to draw upon in order to mount one" (cited in Mitchell, 2006, p. 196). He might well have added that humanities faculty did not yet know that they had the capacity to make a real, practical difference in the lives of their communities by stepping out of the classroom and the library and engaging with fellow citizens as volunteers contributing their knowledge, expertise, and experience.

THE VOLUNTEER COMMITTEES

Starting out, the Division of Public Programs at the NEH decided to experiment with three different organizational models, each tested out in two states:

1. In Maine and Oklahoma, it authorized *state arts agencies* to do humanities programming.
2. In Georgia and Missouri, it created humanities programs within *university extension services* or divisions of continuing education.
3. In Wyoming and Oregon, it created a new freestanding organization, in the form of a *volunteer committee*. The committee could include representation from existing agencies with an interest in particular forms of the humanities (historical societies, libraries, colleges, or archives, for example) and could also include citizens from different domains (public members, as they came to be known), but they were all expected to share an interest in bringing the humanities to the public.

Within a year, the results of this part of the public humanities experiment were in—and they were definitive. In a Goldilocks moment, the NEH found that the arts agencies did not focus enough attention on the humanities, and the continuing education agencies did not engage a wider public. But the volunteer committees were just right. In the words of one chronicler, "The NEH had discovered that volunteer state committees were the most effective bodies for delivering humanities programs to the public audiences which the Endowment wished to reach" (The State Program of the National Endowment for the Humanities, 1994, p. 6). And humanities faculty were among the volunteers.

In fact, these new committees of humanities scholars and citizens were unexpectedly energetic and passionate. As one state committee member put it: Washington, DC, realized that it now had "a tiger by the tail." In the words of another observer, "The program is releasing energies in the humanities in local contexts more effectively than would happen in a program centralized in Washington, D.C." (The State Program of the National Endowment for the Humanities, 1994, p. 7, fn 12).

What exactly was the nature of this "energy?" This, it seems to me, is worth exploring as we seek to understand how and why faculty serve the common good. Why did these committees of scholars and citizens take off in the way they did? What can we learn from the engagement of humanities scholars with the public that can help us better understand the philanthropic dimensions of faculty work?

There are three features of these volunteer committees that are especially noteworthy and helpful to our consideration of the philanthropic nature of faculty work.

First, the committees brought together people who were not usually in conversation with one another, crossing boundaries that seemed, by the 1970s, to divide disciplines, institutions, and—most notably—academic professionals and the lay public. To offer one example, the Indiana volunteer committee formed in late 1971 began with the dean of Indiana's only "evening college," another educational administrator, an historian, a librarian, and a philanthropist. These five Hoosiers were invited to Washington, DC, where, for the most part, they met one another for the first time. As the historian in the group, Robert (Bob) Burns (1993) of Notre Dame, later recalled, "There was a professor from Evanston coming, a professor from Bloomington coming, and then . . . a librarian from Terre Haute and a public citizen. Well, I mean, this was like nothing I had ever heard of before. . . . This was off the wall" (p. 8). Burns's comment underscores how isolated faculty had become in their own subdivided worlds of work—and how exciting it was to discover, or begin to recover, a sense of connection to fellow citizens through shared interest in a larger community.

Second, the volunteers shared a devotion to their mission, which was to connect the humanities to the public, and a unifying sense of being explorers on a new frontier. As the philanthropist or "public citizen" in the group, Virginia Ball, explained in a 1993 interview, the mission created a powerful cohesive force across the group's many differences. "It was a strong committee," she observed, "[and] I think it was strong because it was so diverse. And [yet] we all worked together, everyone was pulling together. It was a very cohesive group . . . very cohesive toward our projects or our real philosophy of getting the academics, the humanities into the public" (p. 16). Indeed, mused Ball, a veteran of many other civic groups and organizations, "it was an interesting experience—probably the most interesting, really, I've ever done" (p. 9).

And third, as the mission itself ensured, the people who joined these committees (or at least the people who stayed) were "both/and" people. They were deeply interested *both* in ideas *and* in their larger communities. In the words of NEH staffer Todd Phillips (n.d.), these were people who had a "dual capacity for abstract thought and pragmatic activity"—and not just a capacity, but a passion, for both. Of course this characterization applied equally to faculty as it did to citizens—both of whom were volunteering in new ways.

The result was board discourse that was at once intellectual and practical, a compelling combination not easily found in most academic or civic settings. As Kenneth Gros Louis (1993), an Indiana University English professor who served on the Indiana board, recalled:

> That was probably one of the most memorable things about having served on the committee. . . . It brought together academics and non-academics to try to agree on what to support, fund, promote, in the humanities. And those are some of the best discussions, much better than any discussions I ever had with the English department where we were all academic[s]. And, I suspect, much better than the mayor of Wabash . . . would have had with the city council, all of them non academics. (p. 16)

Gros Louis's comment invites us to consider how much better many conversations could be—both on campuses and in communities—were faculty and civic leaders encouraged to work together more regularly for the common good.

THE GREAT PUBLIC POLICY EXPERIMENT

The volunteer committees were organizational experiments. But they were also, at heart, social experiments. Through these programs, the NEH sought to "reintroduce" humanities scholars to the American public—creating a meaningful relationship where one no longer existed. As NEH chairman Ronald Berman somberly remarked in his 1973 address at the first national meeting of the state committees, "The state-based program . . . bears the

burden of reintroducing the humanities into American life at the most immediate level—at the level of the individual adult citizen" (p. 4). Looking
back on that time in 1993, Indiana committee member Virginia Ball re-
membered the sense of "burden" well. "We were charged to bring the ivory
tower of academia down to the public. . . . And, as I say, neither of them
really cared whether the other one existed!" (p. 5).

In order to help the academy and the public learn to care for one another,
the Division of Public Programs initially added a third element to the programmatic mix: public policy. The state-based programs were charged with
focusing on public policy issues of interest to the out-of-school public, organized around state themes, and drawing on the expertise of humanities scholars. By targeting out-of-school adults, the programs would not intrude on the
other research and education agendas of the NEH. By focusing on public
policy, they would hopefully solicit broad participation and add some "moral
urgency" to the mix (NEH, 1973, p. 77). By including humanities scholars,
they would demonstrate the relevance of the humanities to the lives of ordinary Americans and provide a public venue for the scholars' service. And
by adopting state themes, their activities would have greater focus and unity.

The new state-based programs put public policy into their organizations' titles (as in the Maine Council for the Humanities and Public Policy
or the Vermont Committee on the Humanities and Public Issues) and went
to work trying to figure out how to operationalize the program mission. Not
surprisingly, different states interpreted and implemented the mission in
different ways. Indiana, for instance, defined public policy as matters on
which the public could vote, and put humanists into dialogue with members
of the public on these issues, allowing them to put their expertise to use for
public purposes. California, on the other hand, focused more intensely on
theoretical interplay, developing discussions among humanists and policy
specialists, and chose not to worry too much about public engagement.

The overall effect of the public policy framework, however, was to redefine the humanities as a kind of policy expertise, embodied in the person of
the humanities scholar. Throughout the 1970s, as a result of these programs,
faculty members were invited into a variety of settings, from hospitals to
town halls, to share their expertise. They sat on panels alongside government officials and policy analysts, offering historical perspective on waste-
water management or a philosophical critique of the concepts of justice
underlying urban development policies. They led discussions of literature
with municipal planners, as in the case of the "Circuit Riders" program in
the state of Maine. They moved into medical schools as philosophers in residence, joining staff meetings as members of the health care team.

The experimentation was energetic—but the results were mixed, both
from the perspective of the public and from the perspective of the faculty

members. Marvin Hartig (1993), who served as the first chair for the Indiana committee, described the challenge of the reluctant humanist:

> One of the things that we found out in the first year in the programming was that humanists around the state, they seemed to be quite reluctant to get involved. They had never done anything like this. They perhaps thought our [theme], the role of the family in government, was too social science oriented. And they couldn't envision how philosophy, history, literature, etc. applied to that objective. . . . I think it was mainly they didn't know how to apply their ideas to these problems of public concern. (pp. 21–22)

It became easier over time, Hartig said. The committee held regional meetings of 30 or 40 humanists. "And [the director, Marty Sullivan] would talk to them, giving examples of how you can involve the knowledge in the fields of history, philosophy, literature, take that knowledge and apply it to everyday problems. And show them that this is what we wanted them to do. Then that would instill a lot more interest" (Hartig, 1993, p. 22). Indiana's outreach effort was effective: By 1976, the committee calculated that it had involved a total of 1,748 humanists in its programs in the first 5 years of its existence. Reflecting on this accomplishment, the committee leadership observed that "statistics can in no way reflect quality, but note should be made of the high level of humanistic input from these professional people" (Indiana Committee for the Humanities, 1977, p. 4).

The committee wanted humanists involved from the start, in design and implementation. "We wanted [the humanists] to work on it from day one. Not have somebody else dream up the idea and say, "Oh, now this is where we're going to have a humanist come in and that person will do this, and this, and this. We wanted them to be involved from the beginning. And once that happened, . . . the programming was much more effective" (Hartig, 1993, p. 22).

In 1976, as part of its Congressional reauthorization, the NEH lifted the public policy mandate and the state theme requirement as well, allowing state councils to interpret their mission of "bringing the humanities to the public" in a much broader range of ways. The Great Public Policy Experiment had not quite worked as hoped. But the volunteer committees were a singular success. Committees were now active in all 50 states—an energized new network of scholars and citizens drawn from a wide range of occupations and perspectives. "Nearly one thousand individuals now serve on the state committees," wrote the NEH National Council. "They include business and labor leaders, farmers, university presidents, members of minorities, judges, housewives, retired people, scholars, public librarians and many others" (National Council on the Humanities, 1977, p. 1).

THE MISSION

Volunteer committees had passion, they had funding, and they had a unique mission—to bring the humanities to the American public. At the same time, precisely because it was unique, the mission was open to interpretation.

The result, from 1971 forward, was a passionate, well-funded, sincere, and continually evolving attempt to work out, on the ground, just what the humanities can and should be to the American public. We have already seen how one early interpretation of that mission—the Great Public Policy Experiment—played out. What follows is a quick sketch of the various ways the mission has been interpreted across the years, categorized (no doubt too neatly) by decade. In brief, these interpretations of mission reflect shifting ideas not only about *what the humanities essentially are* but also about *what a democratic citizenry needs from its humanities scholars*.

1950s–1960s: Cultivating the Individual

- Humanities as *wisdom*, embodied in classic texts and questions of Western culture
- Classic format: study group
- Goal: autonomous individuals

Exemplary statement: The humanities . . . as an underlying attitude toward life . . . centers on concern for the human individual: For his emotional development, for his moral, religious and aesthetic ideas, and for his goals—including in particular his growth as a rational human being and as a responsible member of society.

—Report of the Commission on the Humanities
(American Council of Learned Societies et al., 1964, p. 1)

1970s: The Great Public Policy Experiment

- Humanities as *expertise*, embodied in scholars' testimony on public policy issues
- Classic format: panel presentation
- Goal: informed voters

Exemplary statement: The humanities . . . provide an historical and philosophical context for the choices which we must make as a society. . . . And it is for this reason that we make grants to support the work of the state-based committees.

—National Endowment for the Humanities (Berman, 1973, p. 4)

1980s: Multiculturalism

- Humanities as *difference*, embodied in interrogation of self and encounter with others
- Classic format: the symposium, led by scholars in the humanities
- Goal: prepared pluralist

Exemplary statement: Humanistic learning is implicated in the essential question of what it means to be human. It explores how people over time and in different cultures have answered that question in different ways and through different forms of expression so that finally we may confront the same essential questions in our daily life, in our own time and place.
> —A Report to the Congress of the United States on the State of the Humanities (American Council of Learned Societies, 1985, p. xv)

1990s: Public Culture

- Humanities as *insight*, embodied in public scholarship and civic discourse
- Classic format: national conversation
- Goal: thoughtful Americans

Exemplary statement: The improvement of American cultural conversation is the most important task of the humanities community in the last decade of this century.
> —National Task Force on Scholarship and the Public Humanities (Quay & Veninga, 1989, p. 18)

2000s: Civic Engagement

- Humanities as *connection*, embodied in practices of reflection and dialogue
- Classic format: community conversation
- Goal: engaged citizens

Exemplary statement: The Maryland Humanities Council brings communities together, promoting conversations about important issues. We encourage Marylanders with different backgrounds and viewpoints to see, hear and learn more about others and themselves. We believe that only informed, engaged citizens can build healthy, democratic societies (Maryland Humanities Council Mission Statement, 2014).

CONCLUSION

What does this brief foray into the rich history of the state humanities council movement suggest about the philanthropy of faculty work, in the fields of the humanities specifically but more broadly as well, as a platform from which to consider the voluntary engagement of faculty for all disciplines in enhancing the public good of their communities? I leave that question open for discussion, but I want to conclude by emphasizing three relevant lessons we might take from this story.

First, the National Endowment for the Humanities was established to strengthen and support the scholarly work of America's humanists. Yet through this very act, Congress was also drawn to notice the lack of interaction between academic humanists and the American public. The state humanities councils were created to bridge this gap, by "bringing the humanities to the American public" and showing how scholars could serve the public good.

Second, through its evolving interpretation of that mission, the council movement has demonstrated remarkable philanthropic imagination. Decade after decade, councils have identified and sought to address key challenges at the heart of American public life as these rose into view— challenges directly related to the preparation of citizens for life in a democracy—challenges of cultivating autonomous individuals, informed voters, prepared pluralists, thoughtful conversationalists, and engaged community members, work often undertaken by faculty.

Third and most important of all, through their volunteer committees or boards and through the activities and programs that engage faculty in communities across their respective states, councils created new philanthropic networks of active citizens who were diverse in background and beliefs, yet commonly interested in both thought and action, in ideas and in their own communities. The surprising energy of these boards points to some deeper possibilities for the philanthropic role of faculty members in our communities and country.

> How can universities encourage greater nonprofit/public board involvement by faculty as a way of releasing the civic energy inherent in the encounter between thought and action?
>
> How can faculty participation in community organizations be encouraged, supported, and expanded at a time when pressure on faculty to do more within their own disciplines and departments is also on the rise?

For humanities faculty members, the state humanities council movement has provided a much-needed platform for contributing time, talent,
treasure, and thought to the public good. In making their contributions,
these scholars invite us to reflect on the societal value of their philanthropy—and the need for institutions of higher education to recognize that value as a part of their own contribution to the public good.

NOTE

An earlier version of this chapter appeared as "An Ongoing Experiment: State
Councils, the Humanities, and the American Public," Dayton, OH: Kettering
Foundation, 2013.

REFERENCES

American Council of Learned Societies, Council of Graduate Schools in the
    United States, and United Chapters of Phi Beta Kappa. (1964). *Report of the
    Commission on the Humanities*. New York, NY: American Council of Learned
    Societies.
American Council of Learned Societies. (1985). *A Report to the Congress of the
    United States on the state of the humanities and the reauthorization of the
    National Endowment for the Humanities*. New York, NY: Author
Ball, V. (1993). *Interview by E. Racette*. Bloomington, IN: Indiana University Oral
    History Research Center.
Berman, R. (1973). The endowment's public programs. In *Proceedings: National
    meeting of state-based committees* (pp. 1–7). Washington, DC: National
    Endowment for the Humanities.
Burns, R. (1993). *Interview by E. Racette*. Bloomington, IN: Indiana University
    Oral History Research Center.
Connor, W. R. (1993, May 12). Testimony of the FY-1994 appropriation for the
    National Endowment for the Humanities. U.S. House of Representatives,
    Subcommittee on Interior and Related Agencies. In the National Humanities
    Alliance Digital Library. Available at http://www.nhalliance.org/advocacy/
    testimony/testimony-on-the-fy-1994-appropriation-for-the-nat.shtml
Gibson, D. (1982). Foreword. In C. Buckingham, M. Sherman, & S. Weiland (Eds.),
    What portion in the world: New essays on public uses of the humanities. Papers
    presented at the National Conference of State Humanities Councils, 1981
    (pp. 3). Minneapolis, MN: National Federation of State Humanities Councils
    (ERIC ED233617).

Gros Louis, K. (1993). *Interview by E. Racette*. Bloomington, IN: Indiana University Oral History Research Center.

Hartig, M. (1993). *Interview by E. Racette*. Bloomington, IN: Indiana University Oral History Research Center.

Indiana Committee for the Humanities. (1977). "A Measure of Indiana Humanities: 1971–1976." Indiana Humanities. Indianapolis, IN: Indiana Humanities Report.

Keeney, B., & Culligan, J. (2002). The National Endowment for the Humanities. *Encyclopedia of Education*. Encylopedia.com. Available at http://www.encyclopedia.com/topic/United_States._National_Endowment_for_the_Humanities.aspx

Lagemann, E., & Lewis, H. (2012). *What is college for? The public purpose of higher education*. New York, NY: Teachers College Press.

Leach, J. (2011, November 5). *Re-imagining the American dream: The humanities and citizenship*. Speech at the National Humanities Conference, St. Petersburg, FL. Available at http://www.neh.gov/about/chairman/speeches/re-imagining-the-american-dream-the-humanities-and-citizenship

Maryland Humanities Council. (2014). About us. Available at www.mdhc.org/about-us

Mitchell, K. (2006). Conclusion: The academic as public historian. Available at http://www.neh.gov/files/divisions/fedstate/scholar_as_public_historian.pdf

National Council on the Humanities. (1977, February). Comments on the Endowment's reauthorizing legislation and the programs of state committees for the humanities. Portland, ME: Files of the Maine Humanities Council.

National Endowment for the Humanities. (1973). *Proceedings: National meeting of state-based committees*. Washington, DC: State Based Program, Division of Public Programs, National Endowment for the Humanities.

National Foundation on the Arts and the Humanities Act of 1965 (P.L. 89-209). Available at http://www.neh.gov/about/history/national-foundation-arts-and-humanities-act-1965-pl-89-209

Quay, J., & Veninga, J. (1989). *Making connections: The humanities, culture, and community*. American Council of Learned Societies Occasional Paper No. 11. Available at http://archives.acls.org/op/op11quay.htm

Payton, R. (1988). *Philanthropy: Voluntary action for the public good*. New York, NY: American Council on Education/Macmillan.

Phillips, T. (n.d.). *Untitled history of state humanities councils. Section D: Summary overview of the sample states, and conclusion*. Unpublished manuscript. Washington, DC: Files of the Federation of State Humanities Councils.

The state program of the National Endowment for the Humanities: A brief history. (1994). Unpublished manuscript. Washington, DC: Files of the Federation of State Humanities Councils.

CHAPTER 12

How Do Faculty in For-Profit Institutions Serve the Public Good?

Denise Mott DeZolt

Whereas the mission of an academic institution provides its overall goal and direction, faculty in both the nonprofit and for-profit sectors bring that mission to life in all its aspects, including curriculum development, teaching, scholarship, creativity, and community engagement. From the perspective of the for-profit sector, this chapter examines current factors and trends in the academy that impinge on faculty's capacity to exercise discretion in how they spend their time, including how much time and effort they devote to enhancing the public good even when much of that time and effort comes from their actions as practicing professionals that, in turn, qualify them to be faculty. The increase in part-time and non-tenure-track faculty, the changing regulatory landscape (especially in for-profit higher education), and the influence of online education are significantly affecting faculty productivity and engagement across their professorial life cycles. Similarly, faculty recruitment, selection, orientation, evaluation, and development influence the extent and nature of faculty engagement in philanthropic endeavors, especially within the for-profit sector.

This volume has embraced a definition of philanthropy as "voluntary action for the public good" (Payton, 1988, p. 3). If for-profit colleges and universities were asked to consider this definition of philanthropy, the typical response would likely be that for-profits do not pay for voluntary actions. Yet the nature of faculty work within for-profits may not be fairly and accurately understood—by the media, by public officials, by accreditors, and even by the for-profit institutions themselves. Little analysis and fact-based evidence exists to permit an adequate assessment of just how much "voluntary" action for the public good there might be. More important, scant attention has been allocated to the fact that many—indeed, most—for-profits are the beneficiaries of voluntary actions by their academic employees, whose very contributions to the public good in their professional practice or even in the exercise of their civic duty not only make them better teachers and scholars but also actually help the for-profits contribute to the public good of local, regional, national, and international communities. This issue warrants thoughtful research, and in so defining what the essentially important question is regarding how all institutions—including for-profits—contribute to the public good, we may need a broader scope than "voluntary action for the public good." At nonprofits and government institutions, a presumption is that faculty direct part of their discretionary time to the public good in lieu of personal advancement or recognition, and, because they are not paid as much as they might earn elsewhere, they are sacrificing and thus volunteering some proportion of their time (see Genevieve Shaker, Chapter 6, this volume); yet cannot the same argument be made for faculty who contribute to the mission of for-profits even when their voluntary actions for the public good occur though their professional or civic—as opposed to academic—lives and when the institution explicitly relies on these contributions to the public good to ensure a high quality of learning and student success? For many faculty employed by institutions that rely on part-time or adjunct faculty, the nature of faculty work—the experiences, knowledge, and social actions that underlie it—are more nuanced and complex than may be assumed.

This chapter proposes an academic culture that not only could enhance faculty commitment, capacity, and competence in the scholarship of engagement but also could recognize the multifaceted ways that faculty in all higher education institutions are engaged in work that serves the greater—public—good. Across all educational sectors, philanthropy may be inclusive of faculty engagement in institutional initiatives such as service learning, professional and community service, and research that focuses on social change or community engagement for the benefit of others. The looming question is, to what extent is philanthropic work possible within for-profit institutions? While much of this chapter proposes a model for such work, it also highlights the ways for-profit institutions and their faculty contribute to the public good.

CONSIDERING THE FOR-PROFIT SECTOR: SHIFTING FACULTY DEMOGRAPHICS

In the past 20 years faculty demographics have moved from primarily full-time tenure-track faculty to a large body of contingent, nontenured, full- and part-time faculty, influenced heavily, but not solely, by the growth in both the number and size of for-profit institutions and in distance education (Charlier & Williams, 2011; Curtis & Thornton, 2014). Despite criticisms and reservations, this trend is likely to continue unless there is a sea change. Additionally, innovations in the varieties of instructional approaches and modalities (e.g., MOOCs, competency-based education, self-paced and adaptive learning models), the need for new faculty models as a result of shrinking resources, and shifts in college enrollments have contributed to this transformed academic landscape. According to the 2012 Digest of Education Statistics, in fall 2011, there were 1.5 million faculty members in degree-granting institutions, evenly divided among full- and part-time (Snyder & Dillow, 2013). While the number of faculty increased between 1991 and 2011 from 33% to 40% of university personnel, during this time frame, both the number of institutions granting tenure and the percentage of faculty with tenure declined. Specifically, tenure-granting institutions went from 63% in 1993–1994 with 56% of full-time tenured faculty to 45% in 2011–2012, with a concomitant drop in tenured faculty to 49%. These declines are attributable in part to the increasing number of institutions in the for-profit sector, only a limited number of which grant tenure.

However, according to Kena et al. (2014), "Despite the faster growth in the number of faculty at private for-profit institutions over this period, approximately 9% of all faculty were employed by private for-profit institutions in fall 2011, while 63% were employed by public institutions and 28% by private nonprofit institutions" (p. 187). Thus, the trend toward an ever increasing reliance on a nontenured, non-full-time faculty workforce crosses sectors and raises concerns about the level of faculty participation, commitment, quality of instruction, and impact on student outcomes, particularly as faculty members piece together a semblance of a living wage by working for multiple institutions, often without benefits or a sense of job security. Issues concerning the changing nature of faculty work are endemic across all sectors, not only the for-profit one.

Concurrent with these trends are increased public scrutiny and regulatory expectations that for-profit higher education deliver meaningful academic and employment results with local and global impacts. Criticisms about the composition of the academic workforce at for-profits have been leveled, but little attention has been given to one of the characteristics of faculty most often employed in the for-profit sector. One could argue that instructional delivery in for-profit institutions is in itself a philanthropic contribution, given that many faculty are practitioner-faculty expected to bring academic credentials informed by professional practice to the learning environment and to support students in meeting their program outcomes— without additional income or reward for this value-added contribution to learning. Because they are themselves engaged in both professional and civic communities, practitioner-faculty have the potential for embedding learning in the civic and professional values on which the public good relies.

Yet with an intensifying focus on employability as a major student outcome, faculty at public, nonprofit, and for-profit institutions alike may, in fact, be challenged to fit greater external community engagement into an already intensely demanding situation. Adding to the complexity of faculty engagement is the trend among many accrediting bodies to make explicit their expectations of institutions' accountability for contributions to the public good, placing faculty in the middle of competing demands and expectations. Thus, shifts in faculty demographics have implications for how institutions maintain their commitments to the public good and engage their faculty members in philanthropic endeavors, particularly in service to the community, including research. Although these demographics and trends affect both non-pofit and for-profit institutions, our consideration continues its focus on faculty in the for-profit sector, where perceptions about the culture and values of for-profits color assumptions about their faculties' "voluntary action for the public good."

Despite the increasing number of faculty in the for-profit sector, there is no consistent body of scholarship on their academic and professional backgrounds, competencies, responsibilities, or participation in governance and curricular engagement (Allen, 2013). Further, there is a paucity of research on their philanthropic engagement from either a service or a social change research perspective. Even the factors that would contribute to such engagement are little discussed. The for-profit sector itself might do well to address these gaps, bringing analysis and evidence to bear on an actual understanding of presumed practice.

Fostering Faculty Engagement in Philanthropy in the For-Profit Sector

To contextualize the following sections, by *faculty engagement* I mean the cultural norms and processes by which faculty are able to participate fully in their roles across the institution regardless of their status; to recognize the importance of their role in facilitating student learning; to profess a sense of connection and affiliation with the institution; and to report satisfaction with their roles, their relationships with staff and administration, and their contributions to student success, including the voluntary investment of time, expertise, and energy on behalf of students. Such engagement is inclusive of their participation in service beyond the academy and with socially oriented research. What then is the role of the institutional mission in faculty engagement in philanthropic behaviors?

Just as strategic planning, organizational structure, and new program offerings need to be driven by and aligned with the institutional mission, so, too, does faculty engagement in philanthropic endeavors such as their service to professions and communities, as well as engagement in social change research (Franz, 2009, 2011). Faculty members who understand, believe in, and adopt the mission of the institution will reify it in their interactions with colleagues, administrative leadership, support staff, and students and will extend that mission to their service and research activities.

Such alignment also ensures the faculty's capacity to sustain the curriculum, serve students, and promote engagement by reflecting their knowledge of and involvement with the evolving needs of the community. Therefore, to promote faculty participation, clarity is needed regarding how and what aspects of philanthropy are embodied in the mission; what "philanthropy" as construed by the mission actually means and thus what faculty actions or behaviors serve as the objective correlatives of these values; how those values would be observed and evaluated; and how key external stakeholders would describe the overt manifestation of these values. An institution with civic engagement as part of its mission would likely seek faculty who not only have the appropriate academic credentials but who also apply their learning in meaningful service to their local communities, who can bring real-world examples of such engagement into the instructional environment, and who can engage in action-oriented research—all with an awareness of this aspect of mission and with an intentionality about how to direct their time, talent, and even treasure to these ends.

One example of a private, for-profit higher education entity that manifests its mission in a high sense of purpose—to contribute to local and global good—is Laureate International Universities, a global network of more than 75 higher education institutions in 30 countries. The 70,000 staff and faculty (approximately 67% faculty) serve approximately 800,000 students worldwide. Each institution is locally situated with its own mission, recognitions, and accreditations, yet all are committed to quality education for their students that meets both employer needs and the demands for addressing real-world issues. Across all institutions, faculty, staff, and students are engaged with local communities through their service work and research as part of the Here For Good initiative (see http://laureatehereforgood.net). For example, for the past 7 years, through the Dr. David A. Wilson research award, Laureate has provided two $50,000 grants each year to faculty members across seven universities who proposed exemplary research projects in teaching and learning innovation that could potentially have global impact (see http://www.laureate.net/HereforGood/Awards/David-A-Wilson-Award-for-Excellence-in-Teaching-and-Learning). In 2014, recipients from the University of Liverpool (UoL) online programs and Universidad Europea de Madrid (UEM) were awarded for their research on modeling interpersonal dynamics of retention (UoL) and for content language integrated learning (UEM). Past recipients include Walden University in the United States, Universidad del Valle de Mexico in Mexico, Universidad Andres Bello in Chile, Universidad Peruana de Ciencias Aplicadas in Peru, and Universidade Potiguar in Brazil.

Most recently, two graduates from Universidad Peruana de Ciencias Aplicadas were recipients of the 2014 Here for Good award as they were recognized for their work to bring more sustainable housing options to the people of Southwestern Peru. They were awarded $10,000 to continue their work.

Laureate exemplifies what Steve Gunderson (2012) describes as public–private–philanthropic partnerships within global organizations. For example, over a decade ago, Laureate partnered with UoL, a member of the United Kingdom's Russell Group and ranked in the top 1% of universities worldwide, to offer its fully online graduate programs for working professionals. Further, Laureate and UoL collaborated to establish the university's first campus in China—Xi'an Jiaotong-Liverpool University, a not-for-profit, research-based university that offers undergraduate degree programs and graduate programs to more than 5,000 students at its campus in the city of Suzhou. Most recently, Laureate partnered with Monash University, one of Australia's top institutions and ranked in the top 1% of the world's universities by Times Higher Education World University Rankings, to operate Monash South Africa, a leading higher education provider in Johannesburg. In addition to its university partnerships, Laureate has partnered with the government of the Kingdom of Saudi Arabia to establish new technical vocational institutions. Since its 2010 opening of Riyadh Polytechnic Institute, Laureate has been selected to establish six additional institutions.

Building Capacity

Many of the faculty in the for-profit sector are recruited and selected for their practitioner orientation, even in those institutions that serve graduate students and that often privilege theory over practice. Infusing one's practice into the curriculum serves to bring it alive in meaningful, real-world contexts and, when effectively implemented, supports student learning outcomes. Conceivably, such a cadre of faculty may easily be able to demonstrate their contributions to the community good by virtue of their work, volunteerism, and participation in professional and civic organizations. These data, however, even if collected, are rarely available or reported in any standard way, thereby making meaningful assessments and comparisons difficult at best.[1]

A further challenge arises when faculty are then expected to supervise and engage in research activities. Individuals who otherwise maintain full-time positions elsewhere, often in major roles such as a school superintendent or business leader, and who also teach, do not always have the time, inclination, opportunity, and sometimes even the skill set to conduct and publish research, especially research designed for an academic audience. In some instances, institutions need and want faculty to publish in large part to meet professional and accreditation standards and to enhance the reputation of the institution. Again, documenting faculty engagement in public good research in the for-profit sector is complex in part because of the large cadre of part-time and contingent faculty who may work for a range of other institutions, conduct research and publish in various capacities, or do not report the nature or breadth of these activities in any standard fashion to the for-profit institution that relies on them. Yet these practitioners may well have exceptional records of influence in their own professional communities and the civic communities of which they are a part. Such civic-minded work may not be done at the behest of the for-profit institution, but these actions are very much a part of what makes the academic work of these faculty effective and relevant to its educational mission.

Because data documenting such faculty work for the public good either do not exist within for-profit institutions or are not publicized, these institutions need to determine and be explicit about what they value among practitioner faculty, especially with regard to what is termed here as philanthropic engagement—to contributions to the public good regardless of their origin, but linked to the mission of the university or college that employs them. Faculty development and compensation or reward systems need to be comparably aligned. Additionally, with rare exception, for both full- and part-time faculty in many for-profit institutions, opportunities for rank or advancement, a clear career path, or an expanding role within the institution are typically intangible, at best, and are often even less clear, as philanthropic engagement is not factored into success as a faculty member. Further, a commitment to systematic data collection and transparency of results would provide an evidence base for understanding, recognizing, and perhaps even rewarding such engagement, especially when the linkage to institutional mission is clear.

Attracting the right faculty from the outset saves both the institution and potential faculty invaluable time and resource allocation. To attract the appropriate faculty, institutional capacity needs must be carefully defined and aligned with sound business practices—as well as mission. Position announcements would subsequently include factors such as possessing the sufficient academic credential in the discipline necessary to teach at the program level; a record of teaching, research supervision, or mentoring experience; licenses or certifications particular to the position and professional field; specific experience in a range of instructional responsibilities (e.g., course instruction, course development, mentoring, outcome assessment);

and the ability to provide timely and substantive feedback to students at the appropriate developmental level. Scholarship and service activities, particularly those that extend into the community, also should be clarified and defined, since institutional reputation and capacity to meet student needs can be damaged in communities where there is a mismatch of expectations and knowledge or experience; communities similarly suffer. Faculty who understand the institutional expectations of their roles and responsibilities, know the criteria by which they will be evaluated, and have the competencies and tools necessary for success are well situated. To that end, robust faculty orientation, training, ongoing development, and recognition and reward systems that also honor philanthropic engagement (O'Meara, 2008) may provide faculty with foundations for success and demonstrate institutional commitment to a sustained relationship with those faculty along with the institution's commitment to the community—whether local, regional, or global.

Examining several accredited for-profit institutions (e.g., American Public University System, University of Phoenix, Capella University, Walden University) revealed a variety of ways that information about faculty roles and responsibilities are publicly available. However, there was very little reference to types of scholarship or community engagement beyond a preference for active participation in the profession in the area of teaching. Additionally, these same factors were minimally (e.g., an expectation for a record of scholarship), if at all, explicit in position descriptions, except in the case of those searching specifically for faculty with applied research experience. Faculty handbooks in which these matters may be more explicit are typically not publicly available.

Building Competence

To promote engagement of faculty in the for-profit sector in philanthropic service and research, it may be necessary to ensure that faculty have the opportunity to learn and to execute the philanthropic core competencies as determined by their institutions. An array of participatory engagement models exist, typically building on or extending one another, that could inform how to facilitate, develop, and promote faculty engagement (Boyer, 1997; Franz, 2009; Heckert, 2009; O'Meara & Niehaus, 2009; Sandmann, Saltmarsh, & O'Meara, 2008). These models support a highly contextualized approach that situates the multiple facets of engagement in the context of institutional mission, disciplinary demands, and community needs. Such models may be particularly relevant to colleges and universities in the for-profit sector that serve adult learners, are mission driven to serve the greater good, and see the interrelatedness of student outcomes that lead not only to employability but also to civic engagement behaviors and social change-oriented research.

Enabling faculty to be consistently productive citizens in terms of philanthropic engagement requires dedication to development and evaluation around key performance indicators or quality standards. Engaging faculty in their own evaluation process and development planning provides another avenue for continued participation in and commitment to active engagement. Using consistent formative and summative evaluation timelines, measures, and protocols that include self-evaluation, supervisor evaluation and feedback, and indirect and direct measures of philanthropic behaviors (including assessments from community stakeholders) creates an opportunity for both institutional and individual commitment to a common expectation. Timely, evidence-based, and substantive feedback on progress toward and contributions to institutionally recognized philanthropic endeavors provides individual faculty members with benchmarks. From this information, a set of leading practices may emerge to further evolve institutional expectations and commitments. As part of the review process, faculty can then prepare for their next development opportunities by identifying short- and long-term goals, with behavioral outcomes, an action plan, and a timeline for executing on those goals. Because regional accreditors in the United States (and some quality assurance bodies in other nations) have explicit requirements that institutions document their contribution to the public good, both the data and systematic reviews can provide a key response to the growing demands for public accountability—regardless of sector.

Building Commitment

Previous sections have addressed practices that may prepare or support faculty for successful engagement in philanthropy particularly in the for-profit educational sector. Beyond success, though, is the notion of thriving as a faculty member—continuing to develop as a professional with evolving competence and expertise, as a citizen with a growing awareness of how personal actions contribute to the public good not only as a citizen but also explicitly as a practicing academic professional and as a person with a sense of personal well-being—that is, as one who participates meaningfully in the student learning experience, who contributes time and talent in service to the institution's internal and external constituents, who engages in public good-oriented research, and who continues to develop within, in part because of the institution. Also, thriving faculty members are committed to and promote the vision, mission, and outcomes of the institution and the communities—civic, professional, personal, academic—of which they are a part.

A culture that facilitates such a faculty constituency would show a respect for diverse theoretical, teaching, and learning perspectives, in word and in practice, and would provide opportunities for active participation in philanthropic endeavors. Further, institutions demonstrate commitment to faculty engagement by expectation setting, recognition, and reward processes (Kezar & Maxey, 2013) and research support opportunities, both financial and in terms of practical research skill development. Again, on review of public websites of several for-profit institutions, information is disseminated about specific faculty who participate in their communities, their professions, and through applied research, though it is unclear how systematically these endeavors are recognized, rewarded, or financially supported.

Given the increasing number of faculty in the for-profit sector and the apparent lack of research on their engagement in philanthropic endeavors, such as service learning, service to the community, or social change-oriented research, the sector has the opportunity to further demonstrate its commitment by reimagining commonly held notions of faculty in terms of their commitment and skills in instructional delivery, scholarship, research, and creativity, and service within and external to the institution. Of particular relevance to this volume, is how research focused on the multiplicity of ways in which faculty, via their professional and clinical contributions, their applied research, and their engagement in professional and community organizations may lead to a deeper understanding of how this ever-growing group of educators manifests their philanthropic endeavors.

The University of St. Augustine for Health Sciences (USA), a regionally accredited for-profit physical and occupational therapies institution with multiple programmatic accreditations, demonstrated that 90–95% of core faculty across three campuses engaged in some form of community service over the past year. Obtaining these data required specific outreach and fostered a recognition of the opportunity for more systematic data collection related to philanthropic endeavors of the USA faculty (R. Willis, personal communication, June 6, 2014).

Capella University, a regionally accredited for-profit distance education institution, also with various programmatic accreditations, indicated that their scholar-practitioner faculty are making varied and important contributions to their disciplinary and professional communities. Further though, they noted that evidencing those contributions is sometimes problematic with a dispersed faculty. Additionally, centralized data collection efforts are difficult to scale because of the unique programmatic and specialized accreditation needs (K. Pearce, personal communication, June 24, 2014).

Additionally, a study of faculty conducted by Walden University, a regionally accredited, distance education, for-profit institution with numerous programs that are also accredited, revealed a high level of community engagement of its predominantly contributing (part-time) faculty members (E. Riedel, personal communication, April, 23, 2014). Based on their 2014 Annual Faculty Satisfaction Survey (n = 1,964; 73% response rate), 77% of faculty reported volunteering in the past year for an organization, including religious organizations, educational organizations, and civic organizations. Faculty often participated as organizational advisors and board members for professional and charitable organizations, sharing their educational knowledge with the community. They also credited their social change–oriented mission, and primarily graduate degree–granting institution, with contributing to their engagement. In the same survey, 71% of faculty reported that their university affiliation made them aware of the importance of civic and community service, 38% reported that their work with Walden increased their knowledge and ideas about how to make a difference in society, and 35% said they gained new confidence or commitment in becoming involved in civic and community service (E. Riedel, personal communication, April, 23, 2014).

Relatedly, student doctoral research at Walden must have a social change component. Since 1970, over 5,000 completed doctoral research studies have been supervised by faculty with content and research expertise who ensured that research met a social orientation. In the past 15 years, the research being conducted by graduate students and supervised by their graduate faculty not only includes a social change dimension; those same studies are evaluated against a rubric to assess meeting that condition of their research (see Center for Research Quality, n.d.).

Despite this strong evidence from Walden of a "civically minded" approach, the basic evidence from USA, the challenges noted by Capella, and the featuring of select faculty on publicly available websites of an array of institutions, what remains unknown at this time is the extent to which faculty engagement in philanthropic endeavors is defined, documented, validated, and recognized for its meaningful contributions in the for-profit sector as a whole. Further, how do institutions in the for-profit sector build and sustain a culture of transparency and accountability around faculty commitments to the public good?

Models of faculty engagement referenced in the section on building competence lend themselves well to a possible research model, specifically participatory action research (PAR) (Nastasi, 2008; Nastasi & Hitchcock, 2009; Nastasi et al., 2007a, 2007b; Nastasi & Schensul, 2005). This model situates the researcher in the context of the researched as collaborators in both process and product of research embedded in real-world issues and solutions. By using PAR the institution can examine itself relative to its considerations of faculty engagement, documentation of participation rates, evaluation of research and teaching results, and community impact from philanthropic endeavors. Bonnie Nastasi offers the following comments on the role of such an approach based on her deep experience as a researcher and as a faculty member who has worked successfully both as faculty member and as administrator across non-profit and for-profit higher education sectors engaging in community efforts and applied research in local and global contexts.

A participatory approach can ensure that stakeholders (community, students, academy) have a voice in the development of philanthropic efforts by academic institutions. Using a participatory approach, program planners can involve stakeholders as partners in (a) understanding the needs, resources, and culture of the community; (b) identifying specific goals for philanthropic efforts; (c) designing and implementing programs; (d) evaluating the acceptability, social or cultural validity, and impact of programs; and (e) ensuring that program efforts are sustainable within the community. Such a process can ensure that the organization is devoting its efforts to developing sustainable programs that meet the needs of the community, as viewed by community members, and enhance the role of the institution within the community. Through such efforts, the academic institution can further contribute to the development of capacity by involving stakeholders in education and training to develop stakeholder skills related to program efforts (B. Nastasi, personal communication, May 4, 2014).

CONCLUSION

The changing faculty composition across sectors and the factors that are contributing to it offer both opportunities for and challenges to faculty engagement in philanthropy across the for-profit higher education sector. When considered in the context of a dearth of research or meaningful data on such participation, the for-profit sector finds itself well situated to craft models and processes to further our understanding of faculty engagement in philanthropy using faculty engagement models and a participatory action-research approach. As the examples of Laureate International Universities, Walden University, the University of St. Augustine, and Capella University show, for-profit institutions and their faculties can and do engage in philanthropic work. Further, the faculties at these institutions bring their professional practice and philanthropic service to their teaching and research, as consultants and board members. They also support valuable social change-oriented research, both their own and that of graduate students. By creating and owning its philanthropic agenda, the for-profit sector may be better able to support faculty, students, and communities through philanthropic engagement, while creating a new narrative, a richer discourse on its contributions to the public good.

NOTE

1. Exceptions to this are data from Walden University and University of St. Augustine for Health Sciences, discussed later in the chapter.

REFERENCES

Allen, H. L. (2013). Faculty workload and productivity in for-profit institutions: The good, the bad, and the ugly. *The NEA 2013 Almanac of Higher Education.* Available at http://www.nea.org/assets/docs/2013_Almanac_Allen.pdf

Boyer, E. L. (1997). *Scholarship reconsidered: Priorities of the professoriate.* New York, NY: The Carnegie Foundation.

Center for Research Quality. (n.d.). Walden University. Available at http://researchcenter.waldenu.edu/PhD-Dissertation-Program.htm

Charlier, H. D., & Williams, M. R. (2011). The reliance on and demand for adjunct faculty members in America's rural, suburban, and urban community colleges. *Community College Review, 39*(2), 160–180.

Curtis, J. W., & Thornton, S. (2014). Losing focus: The annual report on the economic status of the profession, 2013–14. *Academe.* Available at http://www.aaup.org/file/zreport.pdf

Franz, N. K. (2009). A holistic model of engaged scholarship: Telling the story across higher education's missions. *Journal of Higher Education Outreach and Engagement, 13*(4), 31–50.

Franz, N. K. (2011). Tips for constructing a promotion and tenure dossier that documents engaged scholarship endeavors. *Journal of Higher Education Outreach and Engagement, 15*(3), 15–30.

Gunderson, S. (2012, May 8). Counterpoint: For-profits and philanthropy. *Inside Higher Ed.* Available at https://www.insidehighered.com/views/2012/05/08/profits-are-partner-not-enemy-philanthropy-essay

Heckert, T. M. (2009). Alternative service learning approaches: Two techniques that accommodate faculty schedules. *Teaching of Psychology, 37*(1), 32–35.

Kena, G., Aud, S., Johnson, F., Wang, X., Zhang, J., Rathbun, A., Wilkinson-Flicker, S., & Kristapovich, P. (2014). *The condition of education 2014* (NCES 2014-083). Washington, DC: U.S. Department of Education, National Center for Education Statistics. Available at http://nces.ed.gov/pubs2014/2014083.pdf

Kezar, A., & Maxey, D. (2013). Dispelling the myths: Locating the resources needed to support non-tenure-track faculty. The Delphi Project on the Changing Faculty and Student Success. Available at http://www.uscrossier.org/pullias/wp-content/uploads/2013/10/DelphiProject-Dispelling_the_Myths.pdf

Nastasi, B. K. (2008). Social justice and school psychology. *School Psychology Review, 37*(4), 487–492.

Nastasi, B. K., & Hitchcock, J. (2009). Challenges of evaluating multilevel interventions. *American Journal of Community Psychology, 43*(3–4), 360–376.

Nastasi, B. K., Hitchcock, J. H., Burkholder, G., Varjas, K., Sarkar, S., & Jayasena, A. (2007a). Assessing adolescents' understanding of and reactions to stress in different cultures: Results of a mixed-methods approach. *School Psychology International, 28*(2), 163–178.

Nastasi, B. K., Hitchcock, J., Sarkar, S., Burkholder, G., Varjas, K., & Jayasena, A. (2007b). Mixed methods in intervention research: Theory to adaptation. *Journal of Mixed Methods Research, 1*(2), 164–182.

Nastasi, B. K., & Schensul, S. L. (2005). Contributions of qualitative research to the validity of intervention research. *Journal of School Psychology, 43*(3), 177–195.

O'Meara, K. (2008). Motivation for faculty community engagement: Learning from exemplars. *Journal of Higher Education Outreach and Engagement, 12*(1), 7–30.

O'Meara, K., & Niehaus, E. (2009). Service-learning is . . . How faculty explain their practice. *Michigan Journal of Community Service Learning, 16*(1), 17–32.

Payton, R. (1988). *Philanthropy: Voluntary action for the public good.* New York, NY: American Council on Education/Macmillan.

Sandmann, L., Saltmarsh, J., & O'Meara, K. (2008). An integrated model for advancing the scholarship of engagement: Creating academic homes for the engaged scholar. *Journal of Higher Education Outreach and Engagement, 12*(1), 47–64.

Snyder, T. D., & Dillow, S. A. (2013). *Digest of education statistics 2012* (NCES 2014-015). Washington, DC: National Center for Education Statistics, Institute of Education Sciences, U.S. Department of Education.

Part IV

FACULTY LEADERSHIP AND COMMUNITY ENGAGEMENT

CHAPTER 13

Beyond the Ivory Tower

Academic Work in the 21st Century

William G. Tierney and Jason F. Perkins

Common interpretations of the phrase *ivory tower* are usually pejorative; "he's off in his ivory tower" suggests that the academic is disengaged from the "real world," studying esoteric pursuits unrelated to societal needs. And yet the original meaning of the term comes from the Song of Solomon and suggests purity (Song of Solomon, 7:4). The ivory tower was a holy place where one contemplated life's great questions. Today the ivory tower—the research university—is not only a place that contemplates life's great questions but also a place that uses the contemplation of such questions toward the public good.

The assumption has been that research ultimately leads to greater understandings and that only in the ivory tower can such knowledge be gained (Adams, 2004). In the 20th century, life in the ivory tower also became infused with the idea of academic freedom (Krell, 2008). If one is removed from society, it presumably becomes easier to critique society's shortcomings without fear of bias or ideology. Those who live in society can more easily be persuaded of an idea not because it is true but because of personal relationships or private advantage. Thus, the idea of the ivory tower leads to core assumptions about academic life. The state gives money to the ivory tower because those in the ivory tower know best how to spend the money without political interference. Those who do research in the ivory tower ought not to have to scurry after funds to do research because it will bias their work. Those who are students ought not to have to pay to be in the ivory tower; the academics should make a determination and then students shall enter.

The ivory tower itself is important to society because it is a fountainhead for the creation and preservation of truth (Sowell, 2009). The value of seeking the truth, however, is under attack and rejected by many (Klein, 2005). Society can no longer afford the basic precepts of the ivory tower, bemoan some. Others acknowledge the costs of the ivory tower (Reiland, 1996) but go further and reject the premise that there should be some place in the public sphere where one contemplates life's questions (Deresiewicz, 2011). The idea that all knowledge is ideological and up for grabs also has enabled critics to point to the ivory tower as a bastion of left-wing ideology (Schrecker, 1986).

Distance from problems certainly has the potential of reducing bias or interference from external agents who have a vested interest in the topics academics study. But at a time when society needs more engaged intellectual leadership, it is no longer a viable strategy to remain monastic. Scholars need to walk their talk. The divide that currently exists between those who are practitioners and those who do research has to be overcome not only for maintaining the relevance of faculty but, more importantly, for the general benefit of society (Plater, 2004). One ought not to claim some sanctimonious privilege because one happens to work in a university. Yet one also should not discount that society has invested in academics the great privilege of learning something in ways that others do not—namely, by reading, writing, and conducting research. That sort of knowledge has to be shared with others, rather than only among one's confreres. Sharing knowledge requires that academics get out of the ivory tower and into schools, homeless shelters, community-based organizations, businesses, and, when the message warrants it, the streets (Votruba, 1996).

For the attainment of such a goal, the professorial reward structure needs to shift. Institutions need a diversity of routes to academic excellence, and some of them will pertain to being involved outside the ivory tower in ways that are too infrequent right now. Academic work needs to have an impact in order to provide a return on society's investment and the privilege accorded to those who seek truth and knowledge. For that to happen, the reward structure and those practices that socialize faculty need to shift in a way that supports engagement rather than disdains it.

Accordingly, our argument here is that academic work needs to change if it is to stay relevant in the evolving contexts of the 21st century. The result is that how work gets rewarded and how academics get socialized also need to change (MacFarlane, 2005, 2007). To make that argument, we begin by discussing what we mean by "the public good" and then turn to a discussion of how we think of tenure and academic freedom. We suggest that academic freedom and tenure need to remain a core value and a structure in the academy, but the sort of work academics are rewarded for needs to change, as does the manner in which they are socialized. We conclude with a consideration of the implications of these changes for the new 21st-century university and highlight the importance of engagement with external constituencies and communities.

HIGHER EDUCATION AS A PUBLIC GOOD

The purpose of this discussion is not to investigate the economic theory of the public good yet again but, rather, to expand on the significance of the term and its relevance to higher education (Tierney, 2006). In particular, we would like to explore its implications for academic work. The rationale for making such a case pertains to what society expects of academics and how those expectations play into the changing notion of the public good (Blackburn & Lawrence, 1995). Segregating the true academic from the general public seemed logical a century ago, based on society's expectations of postsecondary institutions (Votruba, 1996). Universities, and their staff and faculty, have played a central role in the notion of education as a public good, but that notion is changing—or rather, how society views a public good continues to evolve (Holland, 1997). Increasingly, individuals are demanding that academic institutions play an expanded role in helping society resolve the myriad issues that confront us. This involvement has begun to bridge the gap between the academy and the "real world" (Plater, 2011). This shift, in turn, results in a need for academics to evolve as well.

The argument over public higher education as a public good has largely turned on two issues: form and definition (Kezar, Chambers, & Burkhardt, 2005). As with their confreres in K–12 education, those in higher education have debated the issue of assignment of public monies to institutions rather than individuals. Why not let consumers choose how to spend their money rather than force public institutions on them? The call for expanded choices for the consumer has less to do with the quality of the content—curricular offerings—and more to do with the manner in which learning gets conveyed. Public institutions, in general, have geographic and temporal limitations in course offerings. Some would argue that the times when courses are offered are seemingly arranged for the convenience of the faculty rather than the convenience of the consumer. The assumption here is that enabling the citizenry to receive a postsecondary degree is still in the public good and hence deserving of public monies; what is questionable is the organizational form that provides the education.

The implications for faculty work have been clear as well. Insofar as the institution—the public, and, by relationship, the private university—has been defined as a public good, the activities of the faculty have enabled the public good (Calhoun, 2006). Thus, how faculty comport themselves is directly related to the nation's conception of a public good. For example, the notion that faculty work is most appropriately completed within the confines of the ivory tower derives in large part from the disengagement expected by society of academics in postsecondary institutions (Deresiewicz, 2011). As we elaborate below, however, our contention is that just as society's definition of the public good has shifted over time, so too should academe now rethink the stance of the disengaged academic as supportive of the public good. The idea of academics expanding their engagement to the broader public now seems to be a compelling case in support of the public good. That is, faculty have had as a cornerstone of their work the belief that the structure of tenure will protect their basic academic freedom and enable them to pursue the quest for "truth" in the classroom and in their research interests (Plater, 1998). The assumption, of course, is that one's search for truth is purely objective such that individuals remove themselves from society. We turn to a discussion of academic freedom and tenure to expand on our ideas and then elaborate on what a new view of engagement might be.

THE IDEA OF ACADEMIC FREEDOM AND TENURE

The idea of academic freedom in American universities is a little over 100 years old. In the late 19th century, the concept of the American research university took hold as an increasing number of graduate students studied abroad, particularly in Germany. These students returned to the United States with a desire to import the idea of *Lehrfreiheit* (Josephson, 2004). The historian Frederick Rudolph (1962) defined *Lehrfreiheit* as "the right of the university professor to freedom of inquiry and to freedom of teaching, the right to study and to report on his findings in an atmosphere of consent" (p. 412). Although these fledgling faculty desired an atmosphere where freedom of inquiry was possible, the structure of the academy did not adapt to permit these changes. Inevitably, the ideas of new faculty conflicted with the structures of the old university. Eventually members of the disciplines decided that a national faculty group needed to be created, ultimately called the American Association of University Professors ([AAUP] 2012). Within 2 years of its creation, the AAUP had to deal with over 30 cases pertaining to violations of academic freedom.

Tenure developed as a means to protect academic freedom (Neumann, 2009; Tierney & Bensimon, 1996). The assumption was that in order for academic freedom to be protected, a structure was needed that ensured neither internal nor external influence in the work of the academic. Hence, the AAUP introduced the structure of tenure. Tenure enabled faculty to test the boundaries of their ideas. Faculty could therefore feel free to speak, write, and criticize without interference and without fear of compromising their job security (Plater, 1998).

By the end of the 20th century over 95% of all traditional postsecondary institutions in the United States had some form of tenure (Ellison & Eatman, 2008). By the start of the 21st century, despite modifications to the tenure system, including longer probationary periods, post-tenure review, and family-friendly tenure clock policies, the structure of tenure looked pretty much as it had for a half century. Thus, academic work has been enshrined as supportive, if not constitutive, of education as a public good. The ability of faculty to do their work successfully relies on the core value of academic freedom, and tenure is the structure to support it. The assumption has been that the organization of colleges and universities serves to isolate faculty from everyday life so that their work will not be polluted by engagement with society. Indeed, it is this "disengagement" that underlies the unbiased nature of academic work. Until recently, the logic of academic work was in keeping with society's definition of education as a public good. The result was that academic freedom became a hallmark of the academy with tenure as its pillar (Adams, 2007). We turn now to how individuals have learned about being an academic and how the academy judges the quality of one's work.

DEFINING SOCIALIZATION AND ACADEMIC WORK

As tenure became enshrined as a structure safeguarding academic freedom, it resulted in gradual and unintended consequences. Although tenure was originally instituted to enable faculty to take intellectual risks, by the end of the 20th century, it appeared to have the opposite effect (Tierney & Bensimon, 1996). The stakes for getting tenure and promotion had risen so high, and the consequences were so important—lifetime employment in a constricted job market—that rather than take risks, faculty had become risk averse even though the structural intent was the opposite. Academics traded the traditional, high-impact, albeit high-risk project that might yield significant results for the quick publication with minimal findings. If publications were the route to tenure, then the steps to attain tenure were relatively clear. Publish or perish became the mantra, regardless of the quality of output.

Socialization

The professionalization of the faculty led to a relatively cohesive framework about how graduate students became socialized to academic life. On leaving their graduate programs, these new graduates entered the panoply of community colleges, colleges, and universities to discover a sharp disjuncture between what they had been taught and what they were expected to do. Most of these institutions had teaching rather than research at their core (Cochran-Smith & Lytle, 1990). As the new faculty trained at research universities entered these organizations, however, they emphasized their interest in research, at the expense of teaching. The result is that at all institutional types except community colleges, professors have found greater professional rewards (i.e., tenure, promotion, an increase in salary) for doing research rather than teaching.

Although many have pointed out the weaknesses of faculty socialization, there are instances where it has been remarkably successful (Johnson, 2001; Tierney, 1997). In addition to orienting new members to the challenges specific to the new work environment, socialization serves to acquaint them with the organization's culture. Insofar as academic life had enshrined academic freedom, and with it, tenure, and the importance of research in faculty work, the socialization of graduate students can be deemed successful.

The values, beliefs, and attitudes held by faculty reflect their socialization experiences and in essence mirror faculty culture. Socialization is bidirectional (Tierney & Rhoads, 1993). That is, just as the organization informs the socialization experience of new recruits, so too does their entrance affect the organization. Graduate students socialized in conducting research enter an organization and bend the organization's culture toward some purposes and away from others. An example would be the focus on research over teaching. Dunn, Rouse, and Seff (1994) have stated that socialization is "the process by which individuals acquire the attitudes, beliefs, values, and skills needed to participate effectively in organized social life" (p. 375). Ann Bragg (1976) also has pointed out that "the socialization process is the learning process through which the individual acquires the knowledge and skills, the values and attitudes, and the habits and modes of thought of the society to which he belongs" (p. 3). In an article on organizational culture, William Tierney (1988) defined socialization by asking, "What do we need to know to survive/excel in the organization?" (p. 8). Our point here is that the academy has been remarkably consistent: Tenure and academic freedom mirror societal expectations of the public good.

Faculty socialization occurs in two sequential stages. The anticipatory stage involves undergraduate and particularly graduate education (Fadia & Fresko, 2010). In the undergraduate phase, the student begins to grasp the role of the professor and the day-to-day tasks. In graduate school, recruits learn more about the norms of the professoriate as they function within the greater organization. By the beginning of the 21st century, those norms tended overwhelmingly toward research and were internally focused (Torres & Zahl, 2011). Indeed, discussions about teaching or service were largely ignored or disdained.

After graduate school, students enter the second stage of socialization—the organizational stage (Fisher, 1986). Organizational socialization is a cultural process that involves the exchange of patterns of thought and action.

This exchange is specific to the norms and culture of the given organization. Socialization is ongoing throughout an individual's career, although it is particularly intense during the initial years when a new recruit joins the organization. The process of being trained in what is relevant to a given organization most often takes place with a new member. The assumption is that a successful socialization experience will ensure that newcomers will have a smooth transition into the organization and will eventually be successful and in sync with the mores of the organization. For academics, success is often synonymous with attaining tenure. In summary, applying academic freedom and the pursuit of research for its own sake without thought of reward from the organization is ideal, even if it is uncommon.

Academic Work

Although we have discussed the emphasis of research over teaching in various socialization structures, the result of the manner in which we have socialized graduate students to the mores and culture of academe is not limited to this aspect. Rather, the kinds of research and the kinds of teaching also have been critical to the way the academy has conducted itself. Research, for example, has largely been hermetically sealed. There is an incestuous pattern in which peer review operates and how the assessment of the quality of an academic's work is limited to judgment by other academics (Lamont, 2010). Publication in peer-reviewed academic journals has always been more important than articles or documents that make their way into the public sphere. Presentations at specialized academic conferences are of more worth to the assistant professor than if he or she were to speak at a practitioner conference on any number of issues.

These perceptions, in part, make sense given the historic stance of colleges and universities as intellectual monasteries focused on discovering truth. If one were to judge the quality of a carpenter's craftsmanship then one would most likely turn to experienced carpenters. Similarly, when a journal article offers a breakthrough in a given field, one needs to ensure from experts that all the literature has been covered, that the methodology is appropriate, and that the conclusions are fair. This is a great responsibility because laypeople may make use of the findings, but they are not adequate judges of the soundness of the finding. When an article gets published in an academic journal or a presentation is made at an academic conference, the assumption is that the author's/presenter's work has gone through a degree of review that is thorough, complete, and nuanced. The assumption is that listeners can trust what has been written and presented.

Although "teaching, research, and service" has been an academic mantra of what the professoriate is expected to do, service always has been the weakest link in the triad of responsibilities (O'Meara, 2012). Although a large body of research has focused on gauging research quality and teaching effectiveness, almost no effort goes into determining whether the service one performs is of any utility to anyone. Further, service more often than not gets defined as service to one's discipline or profession, or perhaps institution. Therefore, this type of service is not necessarily a general service to the community but is specific to the institution. Examples of such service would include manuscript review for a journal, review of promotion or tenure files, or participation in institutional committees. Such activities, however, actually preserve the status quo for institutions with regard to what gets rewarded. Service gets defined as activities that support the research and functioning of the institution, rather than as intellectual contributions to local communities, for example.

While there is a great deal to be said that is positive about the idea of academic freedom and the structure that supports it—tenure—one outcome is that postsecondary organizations have been largely inwardly focused and have not gone "beyond the ivory tower" (Deresiewicz, 2011). While the inward focus and traditional path of research and teaching have served their purposes in the academy, it is also useful to consider what has been overlooked or avoided as the American college and university have matured over the past century. Our point here is to suggest how one might balance a concern for developing trustworthy findings that at the same time are useful to audiences other than academics. Expanding the utility of research findings to a broader community serves the public better than turning to philosophical ruminations about the meaning of truth, since philosophy—while valuable in its own right—often results in the neglect of problems within the "real" world. If the manner in which one is judged rests largely on one's peers, then those who are not peers are irrelevant. That is, even though most academic work is relevant to one's colleagues and may exhibit mastery of certain material, it can be of no utility to the larger public without losing its value within the academy. Making academic work relevant to the public demands shifting the academy's definition of value.

Moreover, advances in technology and social media are bringing about vast transformations in how individuals process and conceptualize data and information (Obijiofor & Green, 2011; Perkins, 1985). Consider how the newspaper industry has had to weather the rise of alternative technologies and providers of news information along with the decline in its readership and advertising revenue as online newspapers, blogs, and video communities have arisen (Obijiofor & Green, 2011).

Thus, in what follows we flesh out how academic work might be constituted in the 21st century. On the one hand, we wish to consider how academic work might be more philanthropic by reaching out to external constituencies such as local organizations. On the other hand, we also suggest that technological advancements that have led to transformations in the larger society will precipitate changes in the academy. Monasteries, religious or academic, will likely always play a critical role in society. But we question the wisdom and viability of the ivory tower principle if all postsecondary institutions are supposed to act in such a manner. What might an engaged faculty member do with regard to academic work when considering moving beyond the ivory tower?

REFRAMING ACADEMIC WORK

Our assumption, then, is that academic work needs to be more involved with individuals and communities beyond the academy (see also Gary Rhoades, Chapter 8; and Paul Shaker, Chapter 14, this volume). This is not to suggest that every academic on every campus must be involved with schools or nonprofit organizations and the like. However, we are arguing that in the universe of postsecondary education, an environment where the vast majority of entire organizations employ individuals who mostly work and communicate with one another is no longer sufficient. Although faculty outreach and engagement has been a matter of discussion for a generation (Demb & Wade, 2012), there is a considerable question about the degree to which any effort has been made to implement these ideas. Further, implementation would be aided if initial conversations about faculty involvement in outreach were more focused on what faculty "should" be doing, rather than having to deal with the fiscal and technological changes that the academy currently encounters.

We are suggesting that a shift in faculty work is not simply an issue of temporal distribution of effort—spending more hours in activity X than in activity Y—but instead needs to be a cultural transformation. It is clear that if an individual spends an hour or 2 a week in a volunteer activity off-campus some might see the time spent as engagement outside the academy. What we are suggesting, however, is something more far-reaching that brings about different ways of thinking about one's work. If the definition of the public good has shifted more toward the assumption that colleges and universities need to be more focused on external communities, then what might this entail for the professorate?

Rethinking the Reward Structure

Participants in any organization need guidelines about the kinds of activities that are rewarded and those that are sanctioned (Saltmarsh et al., 2009). If the 20th century rewarded research and the ability to convince one's peers about the quality of work, then the 21st century needs to expand the reward structure. One possibility, for example, is what some have called translational research, in which one's work is not merely intended for academic audiences but aims to benefit a broader audience (MacFarlane, 2007). Rather than confine the communication of research outcomes to academic conferences and journals, the academic speaks to practitioner and policy-related groups and broadens publications to various media (Cassuto, 2012a). Such changes might necessitate evaluations that constitute more than external academic peer review and instead involve individuals from various communities.

The result is that publications would appear not only in refereed journals but also in mainstream outlets via articles, op-eds, and blogs or other emerging forms of social media. In the past, a faculty appearance in the mainstream media would be frowned on as a waste of one's time (Hermanowicz, 2011). The assumption was that one should instead be focused on advancing one's academic work through peer-to-peer interaction. We are not suggesting that one will leave peer-to-peer work behind but instead that translating one's work into prose that has utility and understandability to a larger audience becomes critical.

Similarly, service would be a more protean concept rather than a term that has one meaning. While service to one's peers and to the academy may remain important, a more versatile idea would be adopted whereby individuals may work beyond the institution's borders (Holland, 1997). Again, the point is not that one drops one form of service for another but that a process of osmosis is initiated between the academy and the general community. Thus, the needs of the community would get taken into account and the manner in which one's work gets communicated will also be transformed. The result of such changes, however, necessitates varied learning experiences for academics when they are in the academy and when they are graduate students. Recognize, however, that the idea of tenure or academic freedom does not need to be eliminated if academics move beyond the ivory tower. Tenure currently is a structure that rewards one kind of activity and not others (MacFarlane, 2007; Saltmarsh et al., 2009). If those in charge of the academy—faculty and administrators and boards—wish to redefine activities that provide rewards, then they need to be clear in redefining the rules. If tenure remains the main bulwark for academic freedom, then the import of the 21st century is not eliminating tenure but revising the criteria for tenure and promotion (Ellison & Eatman, 2008; Neumann, 2009; Plater, 1998).

Rethinking Academic Training and Socialization

It goes without saying that there will need to be a basic change in the training and thought process in academia. Academic writing, for example, is specialized and sometimes convoluted by the needs of the field. It is safe to say that individuals who write for particular audiences might not necessarily know how to turn academic prose into an op-ed. Similarly, the manner in which one critiques an academic article is very different from the casual critique one will find on anonymous social media outlets. Consequently, Leonard Cassuto (2012b) has opined that if the academy wants to develop a more outward-looking orientation then perhaps communication courses need to be developed that enable graduate students to learn to write and speak in a different register from that of academic discourse.

The tradition and myth has been that graduate students need to spend lonely hours in the library or laboratory or field by themselves if they are to be successful academics. Such a portrait, however, is based on old socialization patterns that presume the traditional, internally focused form of academic work. In the 21st century, an alternative model might be that the graduate student is expected to do volunteer work with a group or agency with whom he or she might eventually be involved or could benefit from involvement. We need to build on and extend the examples of community-based learning that have long connected health fields, law, and some of the other professions with the world beyond the ivory tower, but now with a more intentional sense of reciprocity and mutual benefit. Those in education, for example, might work in schools or as part of a tutoring outreach program. Similarly, an MBA might be able to provide significant service to a homeless shelter with regard to business plans or development, while students in the life sciences could volunteer at a hospital. The point is simply that if involvement with the community is going to be an academic goal, then it also needs to be part of socialization's fabric, and of consequence, part of the instrumental activities of a graduate program.

Popular media also transforms how academics might present themselves and to whom. Whereas sending a paper to senior scholars for their review was a worthwhile undertaking a generation ago, if the purpose now is to get one's work into the hands of the general public, then vehicles such as Facebook and blogs become significant tools. Even Twitter provides academics with a vehicle for popularizing their work in a manner that would have been unthinkable only a decade ago (Jansen & Zhang, 2009). But how one uses such tools relies on adequate training just as one needs training in writing for academic audiences. The well-liked TED Talks or Ignite sessions also incentivize academics to learn how to communicate in new ways (Young, 2011). If such experiments are successful, academics will be much more engaged with multiple communities than they have been in the past. Rather than have a handful of one's confreres read and comment on their work, academics will maintain their core identity while transforming what it means to be an engaged intellectual.

REFERENCES

Adams, M. L. (2007). The quest for tenure: Job security and academic freedom. *Catholic University Law Review, 56*, 67–98.

Adams, M. S. (2004). *Welcome to the ivory tower of Babel: Confessions of a conservative college professor*. New York, NY: Harbor House.

American Association of University Professors (AAUP). (2012). 1940 statement of principles of academic freedom and tenure. Available at http://www.aaup.org/AAUP/pubsres/policydocs/contents/1940statement.htm

Blackburn, R. T., & Lawrence, J. H. (1995). *Faculty at work: Motivations, expectations, satisfaction*. Baltimore, MD: The Johns Hopkins University Press.

Bragg, A. K. (1976). *The socialization process in higher education*. Washington, DC: The George Washington University.

Calhoun, C. (2006). The university and the public good. *Thesis Eleven, 84*(1), 7–43.

Cassuto, L. (2012a, January 8). Let's teach graduate students differently. But how? *The Chronicle of Higher Education*, p. A38.

Cassuto, L. (2012b, May 11). Teaching Ph.D.'s how to reach out. *The Chronicle of Higher Education*, p. A38.

Cochran-Smith, M., & Lytle, S. (1990). Research on teaching and teacher research: The issues that divide. *Educational Researcher, 19*(2), 2–11.

Demb, A., & Wade, A. (2012). Reality check: Faculty involvement in outreach and engagement. *Journal of Higher Education 83*(3), 337–366.

Deresiewicz, W. (2011). Faulty towers. *The Nation*, pp. 27–34.

Dunn, D., Rouse, M., & Seff, L. (1994). New faculty socialization in the academic workplace. *Higher education: Handbook of theory and research, 54*(10), 374–416.

Ellison, J., & Eatman, T. K. (2008). *Scholarship in public: Knowledge creation and tenure policy in the engaged university*. Syracuse, NY: Imaging America.

Fadia, N., & Fresko, B. (2010). Socialization of new teachers: Does induction matter? *Teaching and Teacher Education, 26*(8), 1592–1597.

Fisher, C. D. (1986). Organizational socialization: An integrative view. *Research in Personnel and Human Resources Management, 4*, 101–145.

Hermanowicz, J. (2011). *The American academic profession: Transformation in contemporary higher education*. Baltimore, MD: The Johns Hopkins University Press.

Holland, B. A. (1997). Analyzing institutional commitment to service. *Michigan Journal of Community Service Learning, 4*, 39–41.

Jansen, B., & Zhang, M. (2009). Twitter power: Tweets as electronic words of mouth. *Journal of the American Society for Information Science and Technology, 60*(11), 2169–2188.

Johnson, B. (2001). Faculty socialization: Lessons learned from urban Black colleges. *Urban Education, 36*(5), 630–647.

Josephson, P. (2004). Lernfreiheit, Wertfreiheit: Max Weber and the University Teachers' Congress in Jena 1908. *Max Weber Studies, 4*(2), 201–219.

Kezar, A., Chambers, T., & Burkhardt, J. (2005). *Higher education for the public good*. San Francisco, CA: Jossey-Bass.

Klein, D. B. (2005). The Ph.D. circle in academic economics. *Economic Journal Watch, 2*(1), 133–148.

Krell, R. (2008). The ivory tower under siege: A constitutional basis for academic freedom. *George Mason University Civil Rights Law Journal, 21*(2), 259–298.

Lamont, M. (2010). *How professors think: Inside the curious world of academic judgment*. Cambridge, MA: Harvard University Press.

MacFarlane, B. (2005). The disengaged academic: The retreat from citizenship. *Higher Education Quarterly, 59*(4), 296–312.

MacFarlane, B. (2007). Defining and rewarding academic citizenship: The implications for university promotions policy. *Journal of Higher Education Policy and Management, 29*(3), 261–273.

Neumann, A. (2009). *Professing to learn: Creating tenured lives and careers in the American research university*. Baltimore, MD: The Johns Hopkins University Press.

Obijiofor, L., & Green, K. (2001). New technologies and future of newspapers. *Asia Pacific Media Educator, 11*, 88–99.

O'Meara, K. A. (2012). *Because I can: Exploring faculty civic agency and what supports it*. Kettering Foundation Working Paper 2012-1. Dayton, OH: Charles F. Kettering Foundation, Inc.

Perkins, D. N. (1985). The fingertip effect: How information-processing technology shapes thinking. *Educational Researcher, 14*(7), 11–17.

Plater, W. M. (1998). Using tenure: Citizenship within the new academic workforce. *American Behavioral Scientist, 41*, 680–715.

Plater, W. M. (2004). Civic engagement, service-learning, and intentional leadership. In M. Langseth & W. M. Plater (Eds.), *Public work and the academy: An academic administrator's guide to civic engagement and service-learning* (pp. 1–22). Boston, MA: Anker.

Plater, W. M. (2011). Collective leadership for engagement: Reclaiming the public purpose of higher education. In J. Saltmarsh & M. Hartley (Eds.), *"To serve a larger purpose": Engagement for democracy and the transformation of higher education* (pp. 102–129). Philadelphia, PA: Temple University Press.

Reiland, R. R. (1996). Rising costs, falling value of ivory tower. *Insight on the News, 12*(34), 29–34.

Rudolph, F. (1962). *The American college and university: A history*. New York, NY: Vintage Books.

Saltmarsh, J., Giles, D., O'Meara, K. A., Sandmann, L., Ward, E., & Buflione, S. M. (2009). Community engagement and institutional culture in higher education: An investigation of faculty reward policies at engaged campuses. In S. H. Billig,

B. E. Moely, & B. A. Holland (Eds.), *Creating our identities in service-learning and community engagement* (Vol. 10, pp. 3–29). Charlotte, NC: Information Age.

Schrecker, E. W. (1986). *No ivory tower: McCarthyism and the universities*. Oxford, UK: Oxford University Press.

Sowell, T. (2009). *Intellectuals and society*. New York, NY: Basic Books.

Tierney, W. G. (1988). Organizational culture in higher education: Defining the essentials. *Journal of Higher Education, 59*(1), 2–21.

Tierney, W. G. (1997). Organizational socialization in higher education. *Journal of Higher Education, 68*(1), 1–16.

Tierney, W. G. (2006). *Trust and the public good: Examining the cultural conditions of academic work*. New York, NY: Peter Lang.

Tierney, W. G., & Bensimon, E. M. (1996). *Promotion and tenure: Community and socialization in academe*. Albany, NY: State University of New York.

Tierney, W. G., & Rhoads, R. A. (1993). Enhancing tenure, promotion, and beyond: Faculty socialization as a cultural process. *ASHE-ERIC Education Report, 93*(6).

Torres, V., & Zahl, S. B. (2011). On becoming a scholar: Socialization and development in doctoral education [Review]. *Journal of College Student Development, 6*(52), 761–763.

Votruba, J. C. (1996). Strengthening the university's alignment with society: Challenges and strategies. *Journal of Public Service and Outreach, 1*(1), 29–36.

Young, J. R. (2011, March 4). TED conference turns professors into stars. *The Chronicle of Higher Education*, p. A10.

CHAPTER 14

Philanthropy and Education Faculty

Renewing Engagement with Teachers and Schools

Paul S. Shaker

> The things in civilization we most prize are not of ourselves. They exist by grace
> of the doings and sufferings of the continuous human community in which we
> are a link. Ours is the responsibility of conserving, transmitting, rectifying,
> and expanding the heritage of values we have received that those who come
> after us may receive it more solid and secure, more widely accessible and more
> generously shared than we have received it.
>
> —John Dewey, *A Common Faith*

This chapter explores the ways faculty members in education participate in professional philanthropy. Countless acts of generosity flow between professors interested in practice and corresponding professionals in their places of practice. Remarkable collaborative programs often result. Some of these initiatives reshape institutions, the great majority of them positively affect lives, and all stem from the responsibility to community that John Dewey so eloquently evokes.

Many professions might make similar claims, but there is something unusually synergistic about both education—as the means of preserving, transmitting, and evolving democracy—and the relationship between teachers and those who prepare the teachers, the professors of education. The philanthropic nature of their work warrants consideration as an act "more generously shared" (Dewey, 1934, p. 57).

In one of his earliest publications, *My Pedagogic Creed*, Dewey (Dewey & Small, 1897) identified education as "the fundamental method of social progress and reform" (p. 16). This is a profound expression of the philanthropic impulse. If one accepts such a progressive role, educators must engage their peers as a natural part of their professional lives. They share in the social consciousness of the community in a constructive manner. Individual choice is focused on creating a healthy society. Empathy is a fundamental value.

Many specializations at the university have a natural affinity for practice and application. Notably, human service professions are inevitably "applied fields of study" in which faculty activities, by definition, cross into the world of practice. Medical and nursing faculties, for example, function in the health care environment. Faculties of social work and counseling are intertwined with their peers who practice in the community. Often, however, professional faculties waver between a wholehearted embrace of their clinical and applied partners and a migration to a theoretical and research orientation. This parallels the distancing of careers from the historic concept of a "calling" (Bellah, Madsen, Sullivan, Swidler, & Tipton, 1996). Some attribute this indecision to a lack of training in "professional responsibility" in the preparation of PhDs (Kennedy, 1997).

The arts and science tradition is typically laboratory- and scholarship-oriented. When an exclusive focus on academia takes hold in professional disciplines, community institutions are often forgotten, thereby losing the chance to create beneficial partnerships between them and higher education. Lacking sufficient institutional social consciousness, the university abandons one of its primary reasons for being. Faculty turn away from direct engagement with their natural laboratory and home—the larger society. In such a manner, faculty lose the opportunity to contribute directly to the welfare of people in need who are on their doorstep—to "generously share," as Dewey framed it (Bringle & Hatcher, 2002).

The university reward system plays into this breakdown in cooperation by marginalizing community service. At the university, community engagement work is typically defined as *service*, which, in turn, is conventionally evaluated as the lowest priority for retention, tenure, promotion (RTP), and compensation. Typically, 20% or less of RTP weight is allocated to service, and rubrics for such activity are inconsistent and often vague, if they exist at all. External service that is neither on campus nor with scholarly societies is particularly neglected. Often such work is confounded with what any person might do apart from his or her employment. An example of the latter would be involvement with one's church or fraternal organization. This vagueness in definition sells community engagement short, particularly for a professional faculty. Ernest Boyer's (1990) definition of the scholarship of application notwithstanding, expertise-driven service is little heralded. Boyer emphasized that the application of disciplinary expertise was as necessary as scholarly discovery in defining the university's mission, and diverse efforts have been made to act on his challenge (O'Meara & Rice, 2005).

Constructive involvement with professionals in one's field is valuable in its own right, but, in education, these activities tie directly to faculty teaching and research. Colleges of education are a platform from which the creation of education policy and practice flows through teaching and scholarship. Service-oriented work informs and validates educational research and grounds the "teaching of teaching" in current classroom realities. Schools and parallel educational settings are the natural laboratory for educators, and they are the setting in which our value to society is most prominently demonstrated.

To those who fund and patronize the university, colleges of education are professional schools, created primarily to prepare and sustain public school teachers and administrators. The majority of full-time education faculty are at comprehensive universities, and their central responsibilities are preservice and inservice education. Within the university, however, faculty are tempted to seek status by emulating the more purely theoretical attributes of the arts and sciences in those disciplines' pursuit of knowledge. The defining characteristic of colleges of education, however, remains their use of disciplinary research and scholarship to advance the effectiveness of educators of all levels in society.

These pragmatic priorities have broad political support because a majority of the population see educational success in utilitarian outcomes such as postgraduation employment and earnings. In the popular mind, credentials from schools, and especially universities, are the most reliable foundation for good careers. This interest in the economic consequences of education has trickled down to questions about the quality of K–12 education. Market-based solutions to advancing quality include vouchers, charter schools, cyber learning, and school choice. At the same time, the public— including policymakers, elected officials, and parents—assume a competence born of their own experience in knowing "good teaching" when they see it. When it comes to education, many feel they are "experts" and most have expressed opinions. All this drives public interest in how to recognize quality in education. Out of the policy environment comes a necessity for colleges of education and their faculty to bring their insights and involvement—as *professionals*—to the public forum. It is, as Dewey (1934) said, "the responsibility of conserving, transmitting, rectifying, and expanding the heritage of values" (p. 57) that places on education faculty a duty to the public good that cannot be taken lightly.

Laboratory schools were characteristic of colleges of education during the first half of the 20th century (Clifford & Guthrie, 1990) and played a direct role in faculty engagement with the larger society as a way to develop the public good through education. After 1960, as comprehensive laboratory schools disappeared from colleges of education, a major bridge connecting the two institutions was lost. The laboratory schools provided a venue for professors to express themselves philanthropically by participating in the life of those schools. The disintegration of such organic ties has greatly weakened the link between the faculty as professionals and the public they serve.

Reclaiming the inherent public value of education can lead faculty toward a new philanthropic impulse—one that can be channeled to address the division of theory and practice within education as well as other professional fields. Increased community engagement by faculty contributes to society while potentially advancing the scholarly agenda. Through such work, faculty have an opportunity to renew a traditional mission, enhance their impact on society, and fulfill a moral purpose. Faculties of education have much to offer by participating more directly in the actual life of schools and the teaching profession. One avenue for this participation is *in-kind philanthropy*, the sharing of our effort and expertise with our community. Reclaiming the legacy described by Dewey and others, however, requires intentionality and an explicit understanding of a duty to the public good.

The initiatives discussed here illustrate ways in which education faculty reach out to the profession and the community to apply their specialized knowledge to serve students and renew our schools and universities—all with an awareness of how education makes society better, more equitable, and more inclusive. These instances are illustrative of what happens in many—indeed, most—schools of education at least in the United States and Canada; no special claim is made for these examples except to say they are representative of many ways faculty practice philanthropy.

In these case studies, the philanthropic impulse is defined by the self-aware motivations of the faculty, staff, and students who participate in the collaborations. In many instances, the contributions are not by volunteers but by compensated university persons. Voluntary action does not necessarily mean unpaid action.

In-kind philanthropy is characterized by a revision of professional priorities toward service goals and community engagement, by a conscious recognition that the work itself serves the public good and is practiced with a duty to address this larger purpose. Often there is some sacrifice of career advancement by those who follow such a path. By this definition, philanthropy is not only the work of volunteers. Instead, we see the philanthropic motive in faculty's voluntary commitment to temper a focus on career to serve the common good.

COLLEGES OF EDUCATION AND
THE MOBILIZATION OF KNOWLEDGE

One of the reasons that moral courage is lacking in the U.S. is that it is lacking in universities. As institutions, they now operate much more like ordinary corporations, fearful of bad publicity, eager to stay on good terms with the government, and focused on their bottom lines, than as boiling cauldrons of unconventional ideas sorted out through a process of disputation, debate, and occasional dramatic gestures. (Lewis, 2013, para. 2)

What follows are two case studies of specific projects intended to illustrate in sufficient detail what the abstractions of "public good" or "duty" to the public or "voluntary action" or "philanthropy" actually mean in practice. The cases are drawn from the author's experiences and are anecdotal. In the context of this volume, these examples are testimony to the way individual actions driven by conscience enable each faculty member to practice philanthropy. A concluding section identifies other examples—and resources— for enacting one's professional duty to the public good through voluntary action. *Through philanthropy.*

Your Education Matters

Many faculty are frustrated by misrepresentations of their disciplines and professions in media and politics. No Child Left Behind has dramatically illustrated the costs of such popularizations and misunderstandings of academic knowledge (Shaker & Heilman, 2008). The voice of professional educators has largely been ignored, if not silenced, in the public debate on American schools. Such manipulations of perceptions beg the question, Should faculty raise their own voice in the public forum? Could that voice disseminate research and scholarship in a nuanced, accurate manner meant to aid society?

Dewey suggests the importance of such communication in *Democracy and Education* (1916) when he writes, "A democracy is more than a form of government; it is primarily a mode of associated living, of conjoint communicated experiences" (p. 99). While I was dean of the faculty of education at Simon Fraser University (SFU) in metropolitan Vancouver, British Columbia, a colleague and I sought to place faculty in the public eye through development of a provocative television program, eventually titled *Your Education Matters* (*YEM*), for public access television (for the archives of the project, see www.youreducationmatters.ca).

This venture invited professional risk as well as satisfaction. Today's educational administrators experience pressure to conform to the views of donors, media, and political officeholders. Adding to these pressures, the Ministry of Education's relations with the British Columbia Teachers Federation have been a "wedge issue" in provincial politics for well over a decade, placing deans of education squarely between the two antagonists. Teachers are by far the primary market for faculty of education, but relevant ministers and the premier's office expect university leaders to avoid conflict with government points of view, preferably by remaining silent.

Eventually and predictably, my media presence prompted a stern protest from the government to my president and a subsequent letter of advice from his office to me. The issue of responsibility to the public good comes sharply into focus under such circumstances, and a decision to proceed according to one's conscience may be seen as philanthropic in the sense of acting for the greater good of society.

In designing our effort, we planned to serve the larger public interest. Rather than focus on safe, conventional topics, we entertained controversy and represented a point of view in the interest of serving the community. Equally significant, instead of following mainstream media conventions on equivalency or "balance," we deliberately presented the opinions of *professional* educators and elected education stakeholders while avoiding media persons, lobbyists, and self-appointed experts and consultants. *Our project aimed at going beyond our institutional self-interest to serve broader societal goals even at a cost to those university interests. We understood the risk to individual professional security because of pushback from politicians and special interests, who expected professors to speak in the classroom, not in public.*

Journalists and their editors often look for stories with conflict and simple story lines. The tension between unions and the establishment fit those needs. At the same time, teachers were often busy at school and unavailable for interviews. When teachers were interviewed, their comments would be shortened and edited. Administrators were less free to express themselves frankly in British Columbia than in the United States, since the former effectively have a dual reporting line to their board *and* the Ministry of Education. In this environment, *YEM* spoke back and presented educators' professional narratives on the abuse of testing and other K–12 and university issues. Our risk in taking such a public stance was the alienation of certain powerful individuals and their "think tanks" who sincerely—or out of self-interest—promoted an alleged accountability agenda without in turn holding themselves accountable.

YEM's focus during the first 3 months of production in 2008 was SFU faculty and staff discussing three topics: "making education decisions with your child," "market-driven postsecondary education," and "advice on entering and succeeding at university." The regional cable company hosting the program, Shaw, responded positively, particularly because the program had university "respectability," and began providing studio time in their satellite facility with a staff of interns/volunteers and a professional director, making their own community service contribution. Support also came from various funders, including the North Growth Foundation, the BC Teachers

Federation, and the Charter for Public Education (a nongovernmental organization), all of which recognized the role of faculty addressing controversial issues out of a commitment to the public good.

YEM was part of an effort by British Columbia educators to present their views in contrast to other, less public-minded but highly publicized agendas for schools, including efforts to promote ranking, standardized testing, decredentialing of teachers, vouchers/school choice, charter schools, underfunding, and a weakened teachers' federation. It is impossible to measure the program's contribution, but there is evidence of impact. Today, *The Vancouver Sun* and other media are more open to professorial points of view on schools. Politicians of the center right are less aggressive in critiquing teachers and schools. The British Columbia Teachers' Federation is rallying public support. School leaders are speaking out a bit more in public (see, e.g., Strandberg, 2014).

Perhaps what it means to be a *professional* was never clearly enough understood by the public, and even some faculty, until they actually experienced the results of speaking out on issues of societal importance. There are various dimensions to the definition of *professional*; key among them is the special societal trust and higher ethical standard that come with professional status. "The professions are important because they stand for, and in part actualize, the spirit of vocation. Professionalism promises to link performance of specific tasks with this larger civic spirit" (Sullivan, 2005, p. 38). Among its goals, *YEM* sought to reclaim the place of professional status for educators along with broader democratic values such as the commons, public goods, humanism, secularity, and multiculturalism.

For the 6 years of its production, the project challenged me as a teacher, scholar, and administrator. I had to learn technical skills; engage publically with prominent figures; articulate a rationale to a worried faculty and university administration; find financial and in-kind support; and develop ways to be accountable to a diverse group of sponsors, each with its own agenda. Nothing challenged me as much, however, as reaffirming my role as a faculty member to restore the moral courage Lewis (2013) has found so wanting among college professors and to enact the "associated living" of which Dewey speaks.

Friends of Simon

> The obligation of the intellectual has to be beyond the ivory tower. To eliminate poverty we have to be engaged, involved. (Tierney, 2013, p. 301)

Laboratory schools were a natural outgrowth of the teacher education role of colleges of education and, as noted, served for decades as experimental and demonstration sites (Butche, 2000; Ryan, 1995). They were given academic credibility and social influence by the work of scholar-activists like John Dewey, Francis Parker, and Janusz Korczak. With growth in awareness of the community engagement potential of universities, however, education faculties found other pedagogical vehicles to promote student learning that are also complementary to schools. These initiatives often focus on serving students in need with less emphasis on developing or modeling curriculum and instruction. In the previous example, *YEM*, philanthropy manifested itself in the profession's duty to the public good and individuals' intentional, voluntary action for the benefit of the greater public. In this example, voluntary action takes a different form—participants who are compensated, but nonetheless act philanthropically out of recognition of serving the greater good based on redressing inequities of society.

There is a clear philanthropic motive behind these projects, which often serve no other purpose (by academic measures) than service to the community. Professors of education, as with other human service faculty, are uniquely positioned to conceptualize and execute projects of this type because of the applied dimension of their work, ample opportunities to make discipline-based contributions to social issues, and access to the student pool of talent. The power of ivory tower idealism should not be underestimated: We have an opportunity to envision and pilot innovations not apparent to those caught in the practice of everyday life. In Dewey's (1960) words, *"The foundation of democracy is faith in the capacities of human nature; faith in human intelligence and in the power of pooled and cooperative experience"* (p. 277). University faculty have the opportunity to embody these values in their work with the community.

When I arrived in greater Vancouver in 2003 as dean of education at SFU, I carried with me the wish to continue the good work of university-student tutoring in after-school programs for youth (http://ctff.us) that had been developed at my prior institution, California State University, Fresno. A year passed, and I met a local philanthropist whose foundation was interested in school reform. Rudy North, of the North Growth Foundation, was willing to contribute Can$250,000 over 3 years to launch a tutoring initiative contingent on reciprocal actions such as the proposal being vetted by the United Way of the Lower Mainland (UWLM). The UWLM subsequently connected the SFU planners with community agencies as potential partners.

The UWLM also used its network to introduce us to officials in the provincial government who distributed federally allocated immigrant settlement funds designated for newcomers to Canada. This office—Welcome BC of the Immigrant Integration Branch of the Attorney General Ministry—joined as a partner with a Can$75,000 pledge. Throughout this fundraising, the university's reputation was a considerable asset. Agencies and individuals respected the stability and standards our institution brought to the proposal.

With an initial annual budget of Can$150,000, we opened several sites in two school districts adjacent to the SFU campus. Some locations were in after-school programs managed by community agencies; some were in agency sites themselves. All had oversight by full-time professional staff, a requirement of our program, which generally followed the fieldwork guidelines and protections of student teaching practica. We also served sites with First Nations (indigenous) children, a population that compares with newcomer students in their need for supplemental services.

The program was named Friends of Simon and was launched during the 2005–6 academic year. Tutors were paid above the minimum wage with the idea that they, like their students, needed assistance to succeed in their education. A key to the program was not volunteer labor but the high value-per-dollar that outstanding undergraduates bring to this work. With remuneration comes more accountability and professionalism, but our main motive in offering payment was to help our tutors work their way through university via highly meaningful work.

Over the subsequent years, grant support expanded, allowing the program to employ approximately 50 tutors serving several hundred children ages 8–12 in 10 sites. Program administration came from a retired teacher, a graduate student, and a senior faculty member. In 2011 the project doubled in size with the awarding of Can$600,000 over 3 years by Rogers Communications in an initiative to increase academic success among youth 12–15. As this chapter is being written, Rogers has renewed their funding and is sponsoring a pilot online tutoring version of Friends of Simon that is possible because of university technical support.

Like some U.S. research universities, SFU has staff whose charge is to promote student volunteerism and community engagement. Faculty, however, generally hold back because of the assumption that this type of activity is not central to their role and may represent time questionably spent when tenure and promotion considerations are factored in. In part, this may be a failure of imagination, since faculty can contribute to the public good from a philanthropic motive while traditional academic outcomes are also served. In his 2013 presidential address at the American Educational Research Association annual meeting, William Tierney discussed such reticence: "We emphasized research, but we defined it in a particular manner. Our focus tended to be on one another rather than those outside the academy" (p. 301). Projects such as Friends of Simon can generate research, bring in other funding, stimulate publications, and support research assistants—all while serving the public good.

In 2010, the UWLM recognized Friends of Simon with their Community Spirit Award at a gala in downtown Vancouver. This marked a coming of age for Friends of Simon and a celebratory moment after years of dedicated effort by staff and tutors. The project has become popular and beloved by many people, not least of whom are the university students themselves, who have made it a community intrinsic to their SFU experience. In a large, sometimes impersonal, university, Friends of Simon has become a focal point for many students socially and personally, generating good feelings and goodwill within and beyond the university.

With the success and expansion of the project, Friends of Simon has become a more substantial participant in defining the potential of newcomer communities. Students and faculty are seen as friendly, effective philanthropic partners in providing healthy experiences for youth, especially among a newcomer population that has many challenges, including British Columbia's highest child poverty. Faculty have worked deliberately to keep a sense of mission about their work and a spirit of service to others that exceed material rewards. It can certainly be argued that if self-interest is narrowly defined, faculty and student time could be better spent in other pursuits. When, however, self-interest is evaluated more comprehensively to include emotional rewards, the project brings considerable benefits precisely because of its philanthropic nature. Friends of Simon was created to harness SFU's (student) human capital to promote opportunity for those in need of help. This melding of university resources with community needs has brought deep personal satisfaction to those who have participated in, and on reflection awakened an awareness of the philanthropic nature of, such work.

The expertise needed to operate such programs clearly can be found in faculties of education, as well as other units, and, while professorial oversight and involvement is optimal, much of the day-to-day work is appropriately in the hands of retired teachers and other staff—the "continuous human community" of which Dewey spoke. In such an understanding of education as a vocation, there is a central place for reformist action. Dewey made this clear when he defined education as an agent of social reform. Faculties of education and teachers in this view are not to seek knowledge only for its own sake. When university personnel decide to design and execute such projects, they are serving a philanthropic interest that is at the heart of their professional identities.

AN ARRAY OF GOOD WORKS

Over the course of my career, in the six colleges and universities in which I have served, faculty and administrators have initiated and directed an array of socially valuable programs that demonstrate philanthropic motives. Their span of activity and depth of impact is impressive. In the majority of instances, those served were children, youth, and families greatly in need. At the heart of each project has been a faculty member with a passion for service and a creative approach to university-community engagement. Before considering the lens of philanthropy through which I might look at these activities, I saw them as incidental, indirect manifestations of caring people. After thinking about the nature of professional work generally and the role of education faculty specifically—in their duty to prepare teachers—I have, however, come to think of philanthropy as a useful concept that frames faculty work and makes it more accountable to the larger society. Too often we do not reflect on the more inherent, intrinsic, and fundamental role of faculty work in building and sustaining "good" societies. Brief descriptions of a number of these projects that reflect the philanthropic work of faculty in education follow in Table 14.1.

As a witness to these initiatives and as a colleague of the faculty who fostered them, I could continually see their social value. Parents and others went out of their way to thank the university and our faculty for the services we provided. From an institutional point of view, I was daily made aware of the sustaining impact this work had on our life as a school of education: The greater urgency it lent our presence and the human satisfaction that it propagated among all of us who were involved. Dewey (1934) was not offering hyperbole when he wrote, *"The things in civilization we most prize are not of ourselves. They exist by grace of the doings and sufferings of the continuous human community in which we are a link"* (p. 57). We affirm our place in society through such work and its benefits are universal.

REFERENCES

Bellah, R. N., Madsen, R., Sullivan, W. M., Swidler, A., & Tipton, S. M. (1996). *Habits of the heart: Individualism and commitment in American life.* Berkeley, CA: University of California Press.

Boyer, E. L. (1990). *Scholarship reconsidered: Priorities of the professoriate.* Princeton, NJ: Carnegie Foundation for the Advancement of Teaching

Bringle, R. G., & Hatcher, J. A. (2002). Campus-community partnerships: The terms of engagement. *Journal of Social Issues, 58*(3), 503–516.

Butche, R. W. (2000). *Image of excellence: The Ohio State University School.* New York, NY: Peter Lang.

Clifford, G. J., & Guthrie, J. W. (1990). *Ed school: A brief for professional education.* Chicago, IL: The University of Chicago Press.

Table 14.1. Selected Projects That Reflect the Philanthropic Work of Faculty in Education

Program Name and Location	Description	Origins	Outcomes	In-Kind Faculty Contributions	Philanthropic Rationale	URL
The Fresno Family Counseling Center, California State University–Fresno	A public university, public school district partnership wherein counseling student interns provide supervised family counseling to local families at a low or no cost.	Created in the 1990s by educational counseling faculty working with the public schools to meet state-mandated internship requirements while also meeting a community need to assist families with school-age children.	Local families receive needed social services. College students receive necessary internships for credentialing. Conflict resolution in families often leads to better school performance.	Faculty disciplinary expertise applied to program creation and administration. Administrator expertise and support in navigating university systems needed for implementation and program maintenance.	By creating a program that fosters student growth and serves community needs, university faculty and administrators are attending to the common good through an outreach program that they have little obligation to manage as part of their professional roles. University involvement lessens the burden on community agencies that formerly managed interns for these purposes and faculty shoulder this responsibility instead.	http://www.fresnostate.edu/kremen/centers/ffcc.html

Table 14.1. Selected Projects That Reflect the Philanthropic Work of Faculty in Education (continued)

Program Name and Location	Description	Origins	Outcomes	In-Kind Faculty Contributions	Philanthropic Rationale	URL
Turning Points Academy, California State University–Fresno	Approximately 150 sophomores from a local high school with a high immigrant population are selected to attend their high school classes and take college classes of their choice for a semester on the university campus.	Created in the 1990s by a high school principal and a professor working in concert to enhance college preparation and matriculation of a talented but high-risk secondary population, by providing them early access to the university and its resources.	At-risk high school students are more likely to matriculate to college. Community benefits from opportunity for young people and outcomes of college attendance.	Faculty disciplinary expertise applied to program creation and administration. Administrator expertise and support in navigating university systems and campus facilities needed for implementation and program maintenance.	Conceptualization and implementation of this program for high school students serves society as it does the students themselves; as the faculty involved work to support these students, they are choosing to serve in a capacity outside of the obligations of faculty work, that must necessarily be completed in addition to other obligations.	http://mclane.fresno.k12.ca.us/academics/tpa.html

Table 14.1. Selected Projects That Reflect the Philanthropic Work of Faculty in Education (continued)

Program Name and Location	Description	Origins	Outcomes	In-Kind Faculty Contributions	Philanthropic Rationale	URL
The Dowling Mentor Program, University of Mount Union	A mentoring program that pairs college students with middle-school children from low-income homes to provide opportunities for the children to participate in "middle-class" activities such as cultural events and other social outings unavailable to many low-income families.	Founded in 1985 with a philanthropic gift inspired by a local teacher, the program was instituted by education faculty members.	Young people are given experiences that allow them to develop social skills necessary in various settings. Community benefits as young people are exposed to those from different socio-economic classes. College students gain insight into the experiences of those who live in poverty.	Faculty time and expertise directed at the creation of a program that needed a university home.	Conceptualization of the program required faculty to choose to use their disciplinary and administrative expertise to envision a program that had few direct benefits to them. In doing so they engaged in reflection about their role in serving society. *Note: A small stipend is paid to the current program administrator.*	http://www.mountunion.edu/dowling-mentor-program

Table 14.1. Selected Projects That Reflect the Philanthropic Work of Faculty in Education (continued)

Program Name and Location	Description	Origins	Outcomes	In-Kind Faculty Contributions	Philanthropic Rationale	URL
Joyce Huggins Early Childhood Center, California State University–Fresno	A Kremen School of Education-based preschool and daycare for campus and community children organized around the theory of Reggio Emilia (Edwards, Gandini, & Forman, 1998).	The university's need for child care was joined with early childhood education faculty's interest in modeling exemplary practices in the 1990s when a new building was being designed.	Children benefit from a research-based educational model with extensive student intern support. Preservice teachers are able to apply in-class principles in a school-setting.	Faculty directed scholarly expertise in the creation and administration of this school to follow principles of an exemplary early childhood program.	Faculty contribute to the school in material and in-kind ways. Transformation of school from standard daycare center to research-based educational environment required faculty expertise, provided by choice and outside academic reward structure.	http://www.fresnostate.edu/kremen/centers/joyce_huggins.html

Dewey, J. (1916). *Democracy and education: An introduction to the philosophy of education*. New York, NY: Macmillan.

Dewey, J. (1934). *A common faith* (Vol. 3). New Haven, CT: Yale University Press.

Dewey, J. (1960). Democracy as a way of life [1937 speech]. In M. G. Singer & R. R. Ammerman (Eds.), *Introductory readings in philosophy* (pp. 276–277). New York, NY: Scribner.

Dewey, J., & Small, A. W. (1897). *My pedagogic creed* (No. 25). New York, NY: E.L. Kellogg & Company.

Edwards, C. P., Gandini, L., & Forman, G. E. (Eds.). (1998). *The hundred languages of children: The Reggio Emilia approach—Advanced reflections*. Greenwich, CT: Ablex.

Kennedy, D. (1997). *Academic duty*. Cambridge, MA: Harvard University Press.

Lewis, H. (2013, April 29). Moral courage in academia [Web log post]. Available at http://harry-lewis.blogspot.ca/2013/04/moral-courage-in-academia.html

O'Meara, K. A., & Rice, R. E. (2005). *Faculty priorities reconsidered: Rewarding multiple forms of scholarship*. San Francisco, CA: Jossey-Bass.

Ryan, A. (1995). *John Dewey and the high tide of American liberalism*. New York: W. W. Norton.

Shaker, P., & Heilman, E. E. (2008). *Reclaiming education for democracy: Thinking beyond No Child Left Behind*. New York, NY: Routledge.

Strandberg, D. (2014, April 25). SD 43 counters MLA comments. *Tri-City News*, A–4.

Sullivan, W. M. (2005). *Work and integrity: The crisis and promise of professionalism in American* (2nd ed.). San Francisco, CA: Jossey-Bass.

Tierney, W. G. (2013). Beyond the ivory tower: The role of the intellectual in eliminating poverty. *Educational Researcher, 42*(6), 295–303.

CHAPTER 15

Faculty Grassroots Leadership as Philanthropy

Adrianna Kezar and Sean Gehrke

Nancy has long had a passion for the environment. She worked for a government agency focused on antipollution and wildlife protection for several years and then felt it was important for her to have an even bigger impact; she decided to become a professor. She found that, in particular, these issues were not addressed with low-income populations and that future generations coming from all communities should understand the environmental challenges that face us. As a result, Nancy started working at an urban community college that serves mostly low-income and first-generation college students. Her vision for her work was to create an environmental center within the community college to help educate the surrounding community as well as the low-income students served by the college. Over a 15-year period, Nancy worked to create an environmental studies major that had not existed before she came to the college and an Environmentalism Center that has many educational programs in conjunction with the community, and she created a network of like-minded environmental faculty across the campus who are working to integrate environmental issues into general education courses to give students greater exposure.

Nancy's leadership is not unlike that of thousands of other faculty who have a passion for a particular issue and work above and beyond what is expected of them, providing a philanthropic contribution to their institutions, their students, and the broader community. These types of efforts are the focus of this chapter on faculty grassroots leadership. Faculty grassroots leadership[1] goes largely undocumented and unnoticed and is a major source of philanthropy within higher education institutions. Nancy's activism is voluntary and she receives no compensation for her additional work. Furthermore, her activity is aimed at improving the broader public good by helping to mitigate environmental degradation and to educate more students so that our planet has a better chance of supporting humankind. The recent success of service learning[2] has generated efforts to document the ways that faculty work beyond the gates of campuses to serve communities. Yet there is much leadership/activism that may not be formally tied to the classroom and is not labeled *service learning*. Furthermore, much of the leadership/activism documented and discussed in this chapter happens also on, not just off, campuses.

The purpose of this chapter is to describe faculty grassroots leadership and offer strategies to support this quieter, day-to-day form of activism for the public good. First, we define grassroots leadership and contrast it with the literature on faculty activism that demonstrates the ways that faculty have typically been understood or documented to contribute to the public good through their activism.[3] We then briefly describe the study we draw on for the examples and data for the chapter. Then we review the ways that faculty grassroots leadership is a form of philanthropy serving the public good. We end the chapter by describing strategies that administrators and other campus leaders can use to support faculty's everyday philanthropy through grassroots leadership. As many chapters in this book point out, there are increasing pressures on faculty that make it difficult for them to do work for the public good. Therefore, the final section is important in that it provides ways to support faculty in doing this important work even in an increasingly difficult environment.

GRASSROOTS LEADERSHIP VERSUS FACULTY ACTIVISM

When we think about activism, we typically think about political demonstrations, but there are many other subtle efforts (like Nancy's above) that do not hit the front pages of newspapers and therefore are less visible. In the study that informs this chapter, we decided to call this work grassroots leadership rather than activism because activism had been seen as largely episodic and highly visible in earlier literature. Also, leadership has a connotation of helping to build and be constructive, whereas activism is sometimes marginalized as something outside an organization or the mainstream. But the good philanthropic work that faculty are engaged in serves to build their campuses as well as their larger communities. In order to contrast grassroots leadership with activism, we first define what we mean by grassroots leadership. In this, we are not suggesting that faculty activism should be avoided, is not philanthropic work, and is not an essential part of serving the public good. Instead, we are arguing that grassroots leadership often goes unrecognized and is happening even more frequently than faculty activism.

Grassroots leadership is a bottom-up change process that is often collective and noninstitutionalized. Individuals who participate in grassroots leadership operate from the bottom up, pursue organizational changes that challenge the status quo of the institution, and do not have formal positions of authority. These leaders voluntarily pursue efforts and changes for which they were not hired. The work of grassroots leaders also differs considerably from that of administrative leaders. On the one hand, individuals who hold formal positions benefit from structures to enact leadership through rewards, established networks, committees, position descriptions and formal responsibilities, and delegating authority. These people are often constrained in operating from a top-down approach and may be limited to operating within the status quo. On the other hand, grassroots leaders typically create their own structures, networks, and support systems in order to challenge the status quo of their institutions. Their work consists of generating momentum and buy-in from the bottom up in order to foster long-lasting change. As we saw in the example at the beginning of the chapter, Nancy began work as a community college professor, not as a formal leader within the institution. She was not hired to develop an environmental center or improve outreach and education for lower-income students. Rather, she used her passion to challenge the status quo of her institution and worked to create new structures and networks to meet her goals.

Grassroots leadership not only differs from formal leadership; it also differs from traditional notions of faculty activism. While much of the research regarding activism in higher education has focused on student activism (e.g., Altbach & Cohen, 1990; Astin, 1975; Hamrick, 1998), others have examined the activist undertakings of faculty and staff (Astin & Leland, 1991; Bayer, 1972; Childers, Rackin, Secor, & Tracy, 1981; DeSole & Butler, 1994; Garner, 1996; Gaston-Gayles, Wolf-Wendel, Tuttle, Twombley, & Ward, 2004; Glazer-Raymo, 1999, 2000; Hart, 2007, 2008; Julius & Gumport, 2003; Safarik, 2003; Slocum & Rhoads, 2009; Theodore, 1986; Valian, 1998; Wolf-Wendel, Twombly, Tuttle, Ward, & Gaston-Gayles, 2004). In this chapter, we present a view of faculty grassroots leadership, different from these authors' conceptualizations of faculty activism, as action that is independent of social movements, internal to the institution, and the result of initial action by impassioned individuals.

First, faculty grassroots leadership is often independent of broader social movements. This conceptualization runs counter to much of the literature that examines faculty and staff activism as part of social and political movements. For example, several scholars have specifically examined the role played by faculty in the civil rights and women's movements of the 1950s to the 1980s (Astin & Leland, 1991; Bayer, 1972; Childers et al., 1981; Gaston-Gayles et al., 2004; Theodore, 1986; Wolf-Wendel et al., 2004).

Influential studies in this area have identified university characteristics that predict faculty support of unrest and protest (Bayer, 1972), the role played by female faculty in challenging sexism in order to reshape existing structures to represent the concerns of women (Astin & Leland, 1991), and the role of faculty and student affairs activists during the civil rights movement serving as advocates for change (Gaston-Gayles et al., 2004; Wolf-Wendel et al., 2004). The work of campus activists during these times not only helped develop legislation and strategized political initiatives; it also led to the creation of the first ethnic and women's studies programs. In recent years faculty activism has also been tied to broader social movements in international contexts (Rhoads & Liu, 2008; Slocum & Rhoads, 2009). In contrast with these studies of activism related to broader social movements, we provide a conceptualization of grassroots activism that can be but is not always tied to these broader movements. Further, the episodic nature of activism tied to broad social movements is in contrast to our conceptualization of grassroots leadership as an ongoing and everyday occurrence that is not necessarily tied to the temporal nature of some social movements. Nancy's example is typical of an individual working over the course of a longer period of time to accomplish overarching goals not necessarily tied to an external social movement.

Second, grassroots leadership tends to be focused on changing the activities of an institution internally. This view runs counter to much of the literature regarding faculty and staff activism as being involved solely in events and issues external to the university, whether these conditions are local, national, or global in nature. Donald Collins (2005) contends that for faculty to consider themselves true scholar-activists, their work must be drawn from and directed toward audiences external to the academic profession in order to engage in broader social change. This can involve working as a mediator between university and community interests during times of civil unrest (Wolf-Wendel et al., 2004), actively participating in public displays of unrest and protest (Rhoads & Liu, 2008; Slocum & Rhoads, 2009), or participating in international gatherings of like-minded scholar-activists (Brantlinger, 2005). Rather than participating in demonstrations and actions to advocate for change in their local and global communities, grassroots leaders focus their energy on change within the campus. While Nancy, the community college professor, helped create programs and structures that served the university and surrounding community, her efforts focused on improving internal community college structures to accomplish her philanthropic goals.

Third, while grassroots leadership often occurs in groups, it is impassioned individuals who tend to provide the initial impetus to bring people together for change. In the activism literature, scholars frequently address the role of organized groups of individuals in fostering change in university structures, with the focus being on the work of groups as whole entities. An example is unionization and advocacy for faculty and staff rights on many college and university campuses (Julius & Gumport, 2003; Peled et al., 2001; Rhoades, 1998). Unions and other organized groups have most recently garnered recognition for their work in protecting the rights of non-tenure-track faculty in higher education (Rhoades, 1998; Schell & Stock, 2001). Others have documented the role played by organizations of women faculty in either working with or pushing against administrative efforts to ensure equity for women faculty and staff (Hart, 2007, 2008; Safarik, 2003). We advance a conceptualization of grassroots leadership as philanthropy that tends to focus on the motivations and work of key individuals who are responsible for generating momentum and garnering support for change. The result of grassroots leadership is often the coming together of like-minded individuals seeking to create change on their campuses, but much of the impetus for such collaboration stems from the work of individuals to generate enthusiasm and interest in the change. We want to underscore how important individual leaders and their interests are to starting and creating change. When movements fail or lose momentum, the importance of individual leaders is often brought into our awareness. On many of the campuses studied, when a key leader got sick, priorities changed, or another obstacle got in the way, an effort stalled. As we mentioned in the above example, Nancy provided the impetus for her community college to expand its structures in support of environmental education.

In summary, the notion of grassroots leadership we provide in this chapter is of leadership activities that are ongoing, tied at times to social movements but often occurring independent of them, internally focused on campus functioning, and the result of initial efforts by individual change agents. While the terms *leadership* and *activism* will be used interchangeably throughout the chapter, this conceptualization of grassroots activism is what we are referring to as opposed to the more prevalent understanding of activism discussed in previous literature. We now describe the study that informs our understanding of grassroots leadership as philanthropy.

EXAMINING FACULTY GRASSROOTS LEADERSHIP

Through case study methodology, Adrianna Kezar and Jamie Lester (2011) followed the grassroots leadership of more than 170 faculty and staff grassroots leaders on five different college campuses. They followed individuals as well as groups working to create important changes. They identified five typical institutions of higher education representing different sectors (community college, liberal arts college, private research university, technical university, and regional public university), assuming that grassroots leadership might differ by institutional type.[4] They interviewed these individuals, collected documents from their campus about the change efforts, and conducted observations to better understand the institutional context. Faculty were interviewed with regard to the following: (a) the focus of the participants' change efforts, (b) the strategies for creating change, (c) the issues that enable and constrain grassroots leadership, and (d) the strategies for maintaining resilience and navigating power and internal conflicts.

WHAT MAKES FACULTY GRASSROOTS LEADERSHIP PHILANTHROPIC?

It is important to underscore how faculty grassroots leadership is a form of philanthropy (i.e., how it works to serve the public good) and how this was articulated within the study conducted. First, grassroots leaders on campus can act as the conscience for the organization—often bringing up ethical issues. Higher education institutions should be a model for ethical behavior, given their role in educating future generations. This ethical commitment is important for the broader public good, serving as an example to educate students about their own ethical commitments as they go out in the world and as a reminder to other types of institutions, including government or nonprofit agencies, about how to operate with integrity. Many of the change initiatives championed by faculty grassroots leaders relate to underlying ethical dilemmas found broadly in society and campus life. For example, grassroots leaders try to foster change in their institutions related to climate change, immigration rights, health care reform, and access to college. More important, faculty grassroots leaders on campus help to create dialogues so that people become more aware of ethical issues. Through these dialogues and conversations, grassroots leaders create an ethical voice and presence on campus.

Increasingly, top-down leaders who once took a position on moral and ethical issues are not taking a stand or giving voice to these issues on campus. Perhaps they simply do not have the time to dedicate to such "nonessential" activities given the crush of demands. Or they may be skittish about jeopardizing important relationships with outside stakeholders, such as key policymakers or donors, who may be important to the institution's well-being. Furthermore, board members and trustees may hold opposing points of view on ethical positions. Conflicts with those who have higher levels of authority (boards and trustees) and their direct reports may arise if leaders make public their views on issues such as the value of affirmative action. As a result, many administrators in positions of power are hesitant to be on record with any moral or ethical positions. These conflicts and concerns may be a reason that top-down leaders might support grassroots faculty leaders but are themselves becoming increasingly unable to play this broader role for the public good. Faculty grassroots leaders can articulate a moral and ethical stance that academic leaders have maintained on college campuses historically but are no longer able to express directly. Take the example of undocumented students on campus. Presidents would be hesitant to create policies in support of these students and provide a voice for them in campus discussions. However, faculty and staff grassroots leaders in our study did speak up for and provide voice for undocumented students and pushed for policies to support them.

Faculty grassroots leaders create important and needed changes that help support the broader public good. As society evolves, new issues become important on and off campus for contributing to the public good, and faculty leaders have been responsive to these outside forces and the need for changes. Many of the efforts of faculty grassroots leaders respond to the changes posed by policymakers, community groups, and other important stakeholders. These include developing greener and more sustainable campuses, integrating new technologies, preparing students for an evolving labor market, being more student centered, using alternative pedagogies, and creating greater access and success on college campuses for historically underrepresented groups. These changes to support the broader public good are typically not documented because they are not included in campus strategic plans and most of the information that is shared with policymakers or the general public comes from these types of formal documents.

Faculty grassroots leaders typically advance issues that are favorable to students and learning. Many of the changes for which grassroots leaders advocate could be considered student-centered change initiatives. In our study, faculty were deeply involved in thinking about ways to make the student experience more positive. They considered alternative pedagogies such as service, collaborative, cooperative, active, and problem-based learning. They also developed support services, such as remediation or tutoring. Faculty grassroots leaders re-envisioned the curriculum through 1st-year experience seminars, retooled individual classes, and rethought the general education curriculum. Staff and faculty worked together to revise co-curricular experiences such as leadership symposia or dialogues about environmentalism.

Faculty grassroots leaders are playing a pivotal role in helping maintain the teaching and learning orientation of campuses, long the center of their public contributions. Today's campuses face struggles that make it difficult for them to serve the broader public good. Gary Rhoades (Chapter 8, this volume) describes the rise of a neoliberal[5] philosophy that has taken hold of higher education administrators, making them focus more on revenue generation and prestige and less on the traditional teaching-and-learning mission that serves the broader public good. Grassroots leaders are developing changes that are unlikely to happen from the top down because of constraints on administrators. Various scholars suggest that administrators tend to focus on revenue generation, accountability, and prestige seeking as demanded by trustees and often in response to presidential mandates (Brewer, Gates, & Goldman, 2002; Slaughter & Rhoades, 2004). Administrators are caught between the public policy objectives of affordability, access, and quality with those of the marketplace that focus on resource acquisition and market position. As a result, the types of changes that administrators embrace often focus on a narrow set of issues related to revenue generation and prestige seeking. Certainly these are important areas where leadership efforts need to take place, but grassroots faculty leaders can supplement these leadership activities with changes that support a broader public good. If leaders in positions of power conceptualize faculty grassroots leaders as partners, they can work on different, but complementary, leadership efforts that can enhance the overall institution.

Faculty grassroots leadership also serves as a model for students about how to approach their own future work from a philanthropic stance. Faculty grassroots activities on campus model this form of leadership for students, helping them see that they too should also consider professional activities contributing to the broader public good. Students in the Kezar and Lester (2011) study noted how seeing grassroots leadership modeled by faculty was a mentoring experience and helped them to see how they themselves could be leaders from the bottom up and champion issues that serve the public good.

Equity is a primary aspect of the broader public good, and higher education institutions have often been places where issues of equity have been raised and contested as society has advanced. As noted earlier in the literature about faculty activism, higher education's prominent role in the civil and women's rights movements demonstrated its involvement in broader concerns about equity. Faculty grassroots activism is maintaining this commitment to equity, even as it has been largely abandoned or put to the side in formal leadership initiatives given the pressures of neoliberalism that make other issues the forefront for administrators on campuses. Grassroots leaders typically work to create greater equity for various communities on campus. The corporate and revenue-generating model of campus operations places emphasis on institutional goals and interests over individual members of the community. While this point is quite similar to raising ethical considerations, we make this a distinctive point as many policymakers are particularly concerned about issues of equity and do not always equate equity with ethical or moral issues. Faculty and staff from diverse backgrounds helped to create greater equality for individuals from underrepresented minority groups, women, gay and lesbian populations, and low-income individuals. In general, there was strong support for civil and human rights among the grassroots leaders and their change efforts.

While the activities discussed in this section do not form an exhaustive list, they begin to demonstrate many of the ways that faculty grassroots leaders, on a day-to-day basis, help to contribute to the public good—by raising important ethical issues, by making changes that are responsive to society's needs, by making student learning and the teaching mission central, by counterbalancing the pressures for administrators to focus on a narrow set of instrumental concerns around revenue generation, by helping model philanthropic work for students, and by increasing equity.

STRATEGIES TO SUPPORT FACULTY GRASSROOTS LEADERSHIP

We view the purpose of this chapter as twofold: first, to help document a form of faculty philanthropy that is typically invisible and unknown and, second, to build recognition of and support for this form of philanthropy and help it to become stronger on college campuses. Because such philanthropy is largely invisible, most campuses do not provide any form of support for these types of efforts. Furthermore, pressures to publish and obtain grants, and rewards for revenue-generating activities, make faculty time extremely limited for contributing to the broader public good. However, in the Kezar and Lester (2011) study, faculty grassroots leaders talked about ways campuses can and in some situations did support their efforts. We turn to these strategies in this final section.

Across the various campuses involved in the study, certain practices, policies, and aspects of institutional culture helped support faculty grassroots leadership. We highlight the ways that six strategies, including mentoring programs, creating a culture that sees questioning as healthy, and supporting professional development, can help to support grassroots leadership on campuses. Some strategies are more formal and sanctioned by the institution (e.g., supporting professional development) and others are informal practices championed by individuals (e.g., role modeling).

1. Be an Institutional Advocate

Almost every successful faculty leader mentioned a supportive department chair or faculty member (often senior) who had worked with them to understand their scholarly interests and leadership potential and shaped their leadership vision and philanthropic efforts. These supporters met with faculty on an annual basis to help them think about and plan their future, but they also occasionally met informally to check in, offer support, and brainstorm plans. Helping shape a vision was not the primary role of the supporters, though they did help alter work conditions to support faculty leadership (e.g., overcome a challenge, change or modify their role, influence those in positions of authority related to workload).

To help faculty in playing a leadership role, department chairs and other supporters can use a host of practices, such as legitimizing activities through public acknowledgment, providing resources (course releases or credit for service), and acting as institutional advocates. Despite the possibility for department chairs to help foster grassroots leadership, faculty noted that supportive department chairs are less common because they are often overwhelmed with bureaucracy, are untrained for the role, are apathetically waiting out their 2- to 3-year rotation, lack sensitivity, or have forgotten the experience of being an early career faculty. Thus, faculty recommended also looking to other support figures (e.g., associate deans, senior faculty) if the department chair is unable or chooses not to play this role.

2. Support Professional Development at Off-Campus Conferences

While faculty did not bring up traditional leadership programs, they did mention conferences they had attended, hosted by national associations (in particular the now defunct American Association for Higher Education), as extremely important to their leadership development and in increasing their philanthropic role. Conferences allowed faculty to participate in discussions of new ideas that ultimately resonated with faculty and staff on their campuses, from diversity, assessment, and environmentalism, to innovations in teaching and learning and campus and community partnerships. These conferences typically helped them foster a vision, create a network of like-minded people, learn leadership skills, and garner insight into the ways they might approach the change both on their own campuses and with external communities. Faculty noted how the conferences assisted them in developing leadership skills they were lacking but also saved time by developing key strategies and examples (so they could still play a leadership role as the workload increased and demands for publication were rising). Departments and schools that made such opportunities available for faculty, through additional funding or letting faculty know about opportunities, fostered greater leadership.

3. Develop Policies for Including Non-Tenure-Track Faculty and Staff in Governance and Leadership

Two thirds of faculty are now off the tenure track, making it more difficult for them to play this important grassroots leadership role. Contracts for the majority of non-tenure-track faculty typically address only teaching. If service is mentioned, very little detail is provided, so faculty are unclear about how their service requirements might be met and if leadership will count. Typically, non-tenure-track faculty receive little mentoring, no annual reviews, and little substantive feedback (Baldwin & Chronister, 2001). Campuses that fostered non-tenure-track leadership put new policies and procedures in place to address these deficits.

In order to capitalize on the leadership potential of this very large and growing population, some campuses created specific guidelines and policies and amended practices for their inclusion. Faculty contracts were altered to include specifics on service and leadership. Non-tenure-track faculty were included as participants on faculty senates, committees, and other governing bodies, as well as at department meetings. While some institutions may choose not to give them equal voting rights, ensuring that this significant faculty population can participate in some manner is important to developing leadership skills and creating a platform from which grassroots leadership can arise. Campuses that are unionized should address governance in union contracts. It is important that myriad issues be addressed, from representation, voting rights, inclusion in various bodies, and remuneration for governance work. Also, non-tenure-track faculty are often excluded from professional development opportunities where leadership can be fostered. At the campuses we studied, non-tenure-track faculty were encouraged and allowed the opportunity to participate in professional development. (For more details about including non-tenure-track faculty in governance and supporting their development, see Baldwin & Chronister, 2001, and Kezar, Lester, & Anderson, 2006).

4. Address Lack of Community and Dysfunctional Departments

Many faculty described how the sense of community within their departments or units allowed them to play leadership roles. They noted how many dysfunctional departments existed on campus and that administrators needed to intervene in such departments. By *dysfunctional*, faculty were generally referring to individuals or groups within departments with such significant interpersonal conflict or unwillingness to work together that work as a department on any collective initiative was virtually impossible. Faculty are more likely to take on leadership roles if they feel they can be effective and can avoid myriad interpersonal dynamics of others' making. Because time is so limited within the new academic world, with expanded professorial responsibilities and pressures to publish and secure grants, faculty appreciated administrators who helped address dysfunctional dynamics. Faculty also noted how they were less likely to play a leadership role in dysfunctional departments because it could threaten tenure and promotion. Faculty were more likely to trust that their leadership would not be used against them in the tenure and promotion process if their colleagues were supportive and collegial.

Some strategies for addressing dysfunctional dynamics were bringing in mediators, moving faculty to different departments, firing or moving supervisors, splitting or restructuring departments/units, setting up systems of accountability for the department/unit, making an ombudsperson available who is also empowered to act, providing a whistle-blowing-type hotline, and reassigning people in authority positions. These approaches were often more important among faculty with lower rates of turnover and where entrenched, dysfunctional units were more likely to emerge.

5. Foster an Environment Where Questioning Is Seen as Healthy—Not Threatening

Because many faculty and staff fear being labeled as troublemakers, which can affect their tenure and promotion (or continued employment, if they are contract faculty members or staff), campuses that are not threatened by questioning are much more likely to have grassroots leadership and, in particular, to glean leadership from non-tenure-track faculty, pre-tenured faculty, and staff. Campuses that have a strong culture in support of faculty academic freedom tend to be places where campuses see questioning as healthy. To determine if the campus was truly an environment open to questioning, faculty described looking for indicators, such as whether the administration welcomed ideas from students and community members: "You watch and see how administrators respond to student requests and community concerns; . . . these are really good barometers."

In order to create an environment that sees questioning as healthy, campus administrators can positively acknowledge change efforts that are occurring both inside and outside the institution, recognize activism as engagement in leadership, be open to addressing concerns raised by faculty and staff, and ask for input and feedback on an ongoing basis. Faculty and staff were more likely to take a leadership role when they knew that the campus was open to critique and that their comments and actions would not be used against them.

6. Support Role Models and Mentors

Perhaps the most important strategy in fostering grassroots leadership skills involved mentoring and role modeling, a strategy that often emerged organically but should also be purposeful. Because faculty are generally not socialized in graduate school to be leaders, to recognize the institution's duty to serve the public good, or even to regard any aspect of their work as philanthropic, role models and mentors serve a pivotal function in helping to create and foster leadership on campus. Positively, senior faculty informally provided mentoring to new faculty, teaching them how to create visions for change and adopt political skills, strategies, and tactics (e.g., letter writing, engaging in meetings and negotiation, working with student activists) that are effective on a particular campus. They also typically taught or modeled ways to navigate resistance and overcome barriers (again, saving faculty time within the high-stress academic environment).

While mentoring was an individual activity at many campuses, some campuses created structures that permeated a department or even the campus. Several campuses established formal faculty networks that included a mentoring function. Examples include groups for women faculty in the sciences, faculty of color, gay and lesbian faculty, and faculty committed to sustainability. In addition, campuses ensured that faculty professional development opportunities (learning communities, committees, forums) included both senior and junior faculty, maximizing opportunities for cross-generational mentoring and contact.

CONCLUSION

Our goals in this chapter were to describe a form of philanthropic faculty leadership and provide strategies for campus administrators and leaders to foster this type of activism. Grassroots leadership for the public good is an ongoing, day-to-day form of campus activism that serves many purposes, including addressing ethical concerns in a university community, serving as a model for students to learn to serve the public good, and fostering structural changes to support learning. By using appropriate strategies and developing campus communities that foster this grassroots leadership, campus officials can provide a setting for faculty like Nancy, from earlier in the chapter, to thrive in their leadership efforts and contribute to an evolving perception of faculty as contributors to the public good.

NOTES

1. In this chapter we use the terms *leadership* and *activism* interchangeably. While we foreground leadership because of the role these individuals play in creating important changes, *activism* is another term used for this work.

2. Service learning is a pedagogy that includes integrating community service work into academic courses.

3. However, in much of the literature and historically, activism has been associated with more episodic changes and often ones that happen outside organizational context.

4. Although we anticipated differences based on institutional type, few emerged.

5. *Neoliberalism* refers to a global economic ideology that foregrounds privatization of public institutions, individual over community, greater centralized control and managerialism, among other values and practices. This ideology has become pronounced across societies globally and is shaping the way government and other public institutions are conceived and run.

REFERENCES

Altbach, P., & Cohen, R. (1990). American student activism: The post-sixties transformation. *Journal of Higher Education, 61*(1), 32–49.

Astin, A. (1975). *Power of protest.* San Francisco, CA: Jossey-Bass.

Astin, H. S., & Leland, C. (1991). *Women of influence, women of vision.* San Francisco, CA: Jossey-Bass.

Baldwin, R. G., & Chronister, J. L. (2001). *Teaching without tenure.* Baltimore, MD: The Johns Hopkins University Press.

Bayer, A. E. (1972). Institutional correlates of faculty support of campus unrest. *Sociology of Education, 45*(1), 76–94.

Brantlinger, P. (2005). Faculty activism: Utopian universities and international activism. *Academe Online.* Available at http://aaup.org/AAUP/pubsres/academe/2005/ SO/Feat/bran.htm

Brewer, D. J., Gates, S. M., & Goldman, C. A. (2002). *In pursuit of prestige: Strategy and competition in U.S. higher education.* Brunswick, NJ: Transaction Press.

Childers, K., Rackin, P., Secor, C., & Tracy, C. (1981). A network of one's own. In G. DeSole & L. Hoffmann (Eds.), *Rocking the boat: Academic women and academic processes* (pp. 117–127). New York, NY: Modern Languages Association of America Press.

Collins, D. E. (2005). The ivory tower and scholar-activism. *Academe. 91*(5), 26.

DeSole, G., & Butler, M. A. (1994). Building an effective model for institutional change: Academic women as catalyst. In S. M. Deats & L. T. Lenker (Eds.), *Gender and academe: Feminist pedagogy and politics* (pp. 217–229). Lanham, MD: Rowman and Littlefield.

Garner, S. N. (1996). Transforming antifeminist culture in the academy. In V. Clark, S. N. Garner, M. Higonnet, & K. H. Katrak (Eds.), *Antifeminism in the academy* (pp. 201–217). New York, NY: Routledge.

Gaston-Gayles, J., Wolf-Wendel, L., Tuttle, K., Twombley, S., & Ward, K. (2004). From disciplinarian to change agent: How the civil rights era changed the roles of student affairs professionals. *NASPA Journal, 42*(3), 263–282.

Glazer-Raymo, J. (1999). *Shattering the myths: Women in academe*. Baltimore, MD: The Johns Hopkins University Press.

Glazer-Raymo, J. (2000). The unfinished agenda for women in American higher education. In R. Bohr & J. Longnion (Eds.), *Shaping a national agenda for women in higher education*. Minneapolis, MN: University of Minnesota.

Hamrick, F. (1998). Democratic citizenship and student activism. *Journal of College Student Development, 39*, 449–460.

Hart, J. (2007). Creating networks as an activist strategy: Differing approaches among academic feminist organizations. *Journal of the Professoriate, 2*, 33–52.

Hart, J. (2008). Mobilization among women academics: The interplay between feminism and professionalization. *NWSA Journal, 20*, 184–208.

Julius, D., & Gumport, D. (2003). Graduate student unionization: Catalysts and consequences. *The Review of Higher Education, 26*(2), 187–216.

Kezar, A. J., & Lester, J. (2011). *Enhancing campus capacity for leadership: An examination of grassroots leaders in higher education*. Stanford, CA: Stanford University Press.

Kezar, A., Lester, J., & Anderson, G. (2006). Challenging stereotypes that prevent effective governance. *NEA: Thought and Action, 221*, 121–134.

Peled, E., Hines, D., Martin, M. J., Stafford, A., Strang, B., Weingarden, M., & Wise, M. (2001). Same struggle, same fight: A case study of university students and faculty united in labor activism. In E. E. Schell & P. L. Stock (Eds.), *Moving a mountain: Transforming the role of contingent faculty in composition studies and higher education* (pp. 233–244). Urbana, IL: National Council of Teachers of English.

Rhoades, G. (1998). *Managed professionals: Unionized faculty and restructuring academic labor*. Albany, NY: State University of New York Press.

Rhoads, R. A., & Liu, A. (2008). Globalization, social movements, and the American university: Implications for research and practice. *Higher Education: Handbook of Theory and Practice, 24*, 277–320.

Safarik, L. (2003). Feminist transformation in higher education: Discipline, structure, and institution. *The Review of Higher Education, 26*(4), 419–445.

Schell, E. E., & Stock, P. L. (2001). *Moving a mountain: Transforming the role of contingent faculty in composition studies and higher education*. Urbana, IL: National Council of Teachers of English.

Slaughter, S., & Rhoades, G. (2004). *Academic capitalism and the new economy: Markets, state, and higher education*. Baltimore, MD: The Johns Hopkins University Press.

Slocum, J., & Rhoads, R. (2009). Faculty and student engagement in the Argentine grassroots rebellion: Toward a democratic and emancipatory vision of the university. *Higher Education, 57*(1), 85–105.

Theodore, A. (1986). *The campus troublemakers: Academic women in protest*. Houston, TX: Cap and Gown Press.

Valian, V. (1998). *Why so slow? The advancement of women*. Cambridge, MA: MIT
    Press.
Wolf-Wendel, L. E., Twombly, S. B., Tuttle, K. N, Ward, K., & Gaston-Gayles, J.
    L. (2004). *Reflecting back, looking forward: Civil rights and student affairs*.
    Washington, DC: National Association of Student Personnel Administrators.

CHAPTER 16

Community Engagement

An Expression of Faculty Philanthropy?

Jia G. Liang, Lorilee R. Sandmann, and Audrey J. Jaeger

Many faculty choose, at their own discretion, to engage in activities that benefit others and the community, work that approximates a definition of philanthropy as "voluntary action for the public good" (Payton, 1988, p. 3). Without special attention paid to the philanthropic dimensions of teaching, research, and service, such contributions by faculty may become either casualties of efficiency or a pretext for denouncing "voluntary action" as time and effort ill used (see Genevieve Shaker, Chapter 1, this volume). At this critical time of demands for accountability and relevancy from higher education, establishing an understanding of the philanthropic value and nature of faculty work can bring clarity and accuracy to discussions about the professoriate and academe. Exploring community-engaged faculty work as philanthropy thus offers a possible new lens on faculty motivations and values.

Through the voices of faculty, our study explores the benefits of and challenges to using the concept of philanthropy to discuss faculty's community-engaged work. We realize that the conceptualization of one's professional responsibilities and contributions are a product of contextualization. As the meanings of being a faculty, being an engaged scholar, and doing philanthropic work in the academy (and even being a citizen) change, we can respond with reconsideration and redefinition. Further, efforts to find boundaries for defining these roles bear the risk of oversimplification and arbitrariness; nevertheless, it is important to start that conversation, seek a deeper understanding of the nature of faculty's engaged scholarship with philanthropy, and strive for intentionality regardless of disciplinary and institutional classifications.

We begin our analysis with an introduction of Robert Payton's conceptualization of philanthropy, followed by a brief review of relevant literature on faculty engagement. Next, we describe the methodological aspects of our study, including participant selection, data collection and analysis techniques, and methodological strengths and limitations. We then present findings around five major themes and offer implications for practice, research, and policy.

PAYTON'S CONCEPTUALIZATION OF PHILANTHROPY

Payton's conceptualization of philanthropy as "voluntary action for the public good" serves as the theoretical foundation for this study. Although by no means the only definition of this term, it has been widely accepted within the literature of philanthropic studies (see Michael Moody, Chapter 2, and Dwight Burlingame, Chapter 9, this volume). According to Payton (1988), philanthropy is a *tradition* that has common roots, themes, practices, and values and is also dynamic and changing. Philanthropy embraces community and compassion as its central values where community relates to that which brings us and holds us together, with an emphasis on mutuality, sharing, and common values that outweigh self-interest and competitiveness. Payton argues that having compassion gives us charity only, but having community *and* compassion gives us philanthropy.

This conception of philanthropy, grounded in community and compassion, seems simplistic; however, the discussion is complicated by skepticism regarding whether the philanthropic endeavor is truly *voluntary* when initiated by corporations or the state (Payton, 1988). One could argue that shareholders, employees, or taxpayers (and, we might add, tuition payers) were not given an opportunity to decline to participate when their money was collected and transferred into corporate, institutional, or government philanthropic initiatives. Does the absence of this voluntary dimension in mobilizing these resources negate their philanthropic nature? Also blurring the discussion is the conflict within philanthropy about the concern for others and one's self. Can philanthropic work be truly devoid of any self-interest and selfishness? A philanthropic end product, Payton noted, does not secure a philanthropic motivation. According to Payton, love is an accepted philanthropic motivation, fear (such as fear of divine retribution or of loss of self-esteem) probably is not, and greed never is. Nevertheless, Payton was certain that all philanthropic transfers are one-way; that is, they are gifts without return, gifts that may bring satisfaction but no compensating material benefit. Last but not least, despite the complexity and arbitrariness, philanthropy can be a powerful lever for social change.

To summarize, Payton's (1988) definition of philanthropy is anchored in a sense of community and voluntarism. The dynamic nature of philanthropy speaks to various methods (monetary or nonmonetary), participants (individual, state, or corporation), and impacts (immediate relief, development, or social change) involved under this broad cause for human betterment.

COMMUNITY ENGAGEMENT IN HIGHER EDUCATION

The history of engagement in higher education can be traced back to the inception of the institution in the 17th century. Knowledge production and application for the common good has been a fundamental principle of American colleges and universities (Veysey, 1965). However, over the years, the expert model of knowledge delivery, which prioritizes prediction and control, has come to dominate the discourse and practice of university–community relations (Deetz, 2008). Many colleges and universities have drifted away from their original roots in resolving societal problems, and higher education has lost its standing in society as a valued public good (Fitzgerald, Bruns, Sonka, Furco, & Swanson, 2012; Saltmarsh & Hartley, 2011). Late in the 20th century, a movement for institutions of higher education to be more relevant to society revived the conversation about higher education's public purpose and pushed for engagement grounded in a reciprocal and mutually beneficial model that underscores partnerships with co-created solutions (Fitzgerald et al., 2012). Scholars (among them Boyer, 1990; Votruba, 1992) as well as major commission reports (such as the Kellogg Commission on the Future of State and Land-Grant Universities, 1999) challenged higher education to renew its historic commitment to resolving social, civic, economic, and moral problems, thereby calling on it to regain its potential as a powerful lever for social change. The goals of higher education institutions are similar to Payton's (1988) six main areas of philanthropic work: education, welfare, religion, health, culture, and civic/community affairs. Most would agree that these emphases are also connected to the missions, expectations, and demands of higher education institutions, in all their diversity.

According to the Carnegie Foundation for the Advancement of Teaching (n.d.), "Community engagement describes the collaboration between institutions of higher education and their larger communities (local, regional/state, national, global) for the mutually beneficial exchange of knowledge and resources in a context of partnership and reciprocity," and it can involve partnerships and coalitions that help mobilize resources, influence systems, and serve as a catalyst for initiating or changing policies, programs, and practices. Community engagement is distinct from the more familiar terms *public service*, *outreach*, and *extension*, as defined in an influential report on the duty of higher education to the public good:

> Engagement goes well beyond extension, conventional outreach, and even most conceptions of public service. Inherited concepts emphasize a one-way process in which the university transfers its expertise to key constituents. Embedded in the engagement ideal is *a commitment to sharing and reciprocity* [emphasis added]. By engagement the Commission envisioned

partnerships, two-way streets defined by mutual respect among the partners for what each brings to the table (Kellogg Commission, 1999, p. 9).

These qualities of community engagement manifest themselves organizationally through the engaged campus and academically through engaged scholarship (Glass & Fitzgerald, 2010). The development of an engaged campus takes institutional efforts, involving both administrators and faculty. Engaged scholarship is primarily scholarly work produced by faculty. The institutionalization of community engagement stands on its own merits; nevertheless, given the study's focus on faculty, we limit our review to engaged scholarship only.

ENGAGED SCHOLARSHIP

The notion of engaged scholarship was conceived by Ernest Boyer (1990, 1996), in his call for multiplicity in scholarship as an appreciation of the full range of scholarly expression that highlights blurring the distinctions among discovery, learning, engagement, and integration, *a border-crossing* type of scholarship (Fear, Rosaen, Foster-Fishman, & Bawden, 2001). Over nearly 2 decades, a wide range of terminology has been used to describe engaged scholarship (and engaged scholars) by various institutions, associations, and disciplines for their specific audiences and contexts, such as publicly engaged academic work, public scholarship, and civically engaged scholars, to name a few (Doberneck, Glass, & Schweitzer, 2010; Sandmann, 2008; Schomberg & Farmer, 1994). The proliferation of terminology signified "a welcome maturing and deepening of the engagement movement in the disciplines" (Doberneck et al., 2010, p. 6). Today, the conceptualization of the scholarship of engagement has grown toward being "heterogeneous, multidirectional, collaborative, highly participatory, and of service to multiple audiences" (Sandmann, 2006, p. 81; see also Gibbons, 2001; Gibbons et al., 1994). Nevertheless, the versatility of engaged scholarship by no means suggests that all community engagement activities conducted by faculty constitute scholarship (Sandmann, 2006). Engaged scholarship is scholarly work through collaborative inquiry with an essence of boundary crossing over disciplines and faculty research, teaching, and service (Driscoll & Lynton, 1999; Fear et al., 2001; Fear & Sandmann, 2001).

Faculty performing engaged scholarship are "to be *in* the world rather than *about* the world" (Deetz, 2008, p. 289). Engaged scholars are meant to *take moral responsibilities* and *maintain mutual growth* between scholarly and everyday life communities by using engaged scholarship grounded on cogenerative theorization (Deetz, 2008). Engaged scholarship has shifted paradigmatically the nature and purpose(s) of the scholarly functions, roles, and activities that faculty perform and undertake. The *being* (of faculty) serves a bigger purpose—connecting scholarship and practice to address problems that are significant to citizens, institutions, and society, that is, serving for the public good (Bloomgarden & O'Meara, 2007; Colbeck & Drago, 2005; Fear et al., 2001).

It is undeniable that a consideration of public good is not only at the very heart of philanthropy but also deeply rooted in the founding principles of higher education in the United States. Research on faculty's motivation for engaged scholarship speaks to a voluntary aspect. Overlapping and interacting personal and contextual factors are involved in faculty's motivation for engagement. Specifically, the primary forces behind faculty's involvement in and commitment to engaged work are those traditionally called intrinsic factors, such as personal values, sense of responsibility, and feeling that one's work has purpose, rather than the extrinsic (or contextual) factors such as rank, appointment, or discipline (Colbeck & Weaver, 2008; O'Meara, 2008; Wade, 2008; Ward, 2010). Thus, conceptually, faculty's engaged work and philanthropy could reflect a shared note of moral responsibility and volunteerism. Could this commonality be an entry for applying a philanthropic lens to faculty engagement work? As scholars from both fields—philanthropy and community engagement—seek better understanding and increased clarity in definitional issues, our study takes an important step by considering faculty's perception of philanthropy and their engaged work.

Researching Perceptions of Engagement and Philanthropy

The purpose of this exploratory research was to better understand the faculty's perspective on viewing their community-engaged work as philanthropy. We posed three research questions:

1. How do engaged faculty define community engagement?
2. How do engaged faculty define philanthropy or philanthropic work?
3. To what extent do engaged faculty view their engaged work as philanthropy?

We studied engaged faculty, here defined as faculty of community-engaged or service-learning fellows programs in two higher education research institutions, for three reasons. First, these are faculty recognized by their peers and supervisors for their engaged work and then recommended and selected to the programs; therefore, their commitment to engagement is more likely to have entailed a substantial period of involvement. Second, because the selection spans a wide range of departments within the institutions, these faculty represent various disciplines and provide a spectrum of faculty involved in engaged scholarship. Third, given the nature of these programs, faculty participants are likely to have a more comprehensive understanding of community engagement and engaged scholarship conceptually and empirically, which was essential for our study on possible connections or disconnections between engagement and philanthropy.

Potential participants were contacted through email, and with follow-up phone calls to further solicit participation in the study. The final sample included five engaged faculty, an appropriate number of participants in exploratory qualitative research (Gaskell, 2000). With IRB permission from both institutions, a 1-hour interview was conducted with each participant. Interviews were recorded and transcribed and pseudonyms were assigned.

HyperRESEARCH software was used for *in vivo* coding from the interviews. In vivo coding is an analytic process of examining data and generating concepts using the words of the respondents when these words are so descriptive of what is going on that they become the designated concepts (Corbin, 2004). In vivo coding, therefore, generates indigenous categories. Content analysis (Roulston, 2010) was used to identify major themes for addressing the research questions. The descriptive and in vivo coding process allowed the researchers to adhere closely to the data where the themes emerged (Charmaz, 2006); nevertheless, readers should be cautious in making broader generalizations from the findings.

The first-round coding and content analysis was conducted independently by each of the researchers. Then we convened and discussed each other's codes and themes, noting agreements and disagreements. Each researcher took time to reflect independently, returned to the data to recheck, and decided if changes should be made to individual first-round results. The whole process involved three rounds of such independent and convened work. In addition, follow-up emails containing a particular quotation (or quotations) were sent to participants when clarification of data was needed. We reached the final codes and themes through consensus.

Faculty Views of Engagement and Philanthropy

Our participants were faculty from five disciplines: school psychology, soil science, public health, veterinary science, and horticulture. Two were assistant professors, two were associate professors, and one was a full professor. The sample included three males (James, Justin, and Jack) and two females (Anna and Linda).

Five major themes emerged from the data. The first two themes speak to the first research question, that is, how engaged faculty define community engagement. The third theme responds to the second research question, that is, how engaged faculty define philanthropy. The fourth and fifth themes are related to the third research question, investigating the extent to which engaged faculty view their engaged work as philanthropy.

Theme 1: The Essence of Community Engagement—Commonality and Mutuality

Despite their different disciplinary backgrounds, our faculty participants held definitions of community engagement that were similar in that all considered the essence of community engagement as working for a common goal, fulfilling a need, and achieving mutuality (as reciprocally beneficial) in the process. Examples of their most concise definitions of community engagement follow.

> *Anna:* Community-engaged work is really through my work as a faculty, my teaching, trying to meet or address community needs [for] organizations and individuals who don't have resources to do it on their own, and so using my time, energy, knowledge, and expertise to help to meet these needs . . . probably also that reciprocity occurred. So working with the community partner, that is not just [a] one-shot deal; you try to develop a relationship.
> *Linda:* [For engagement], there is a mutual understanding and mutual benefit of the work that we are doing together; this is a feel of a team.

Along with the shared knowledge of core components of community engagement, participants varied in terms of the scope and depth of their understandings. Also, the variation seemed to be associated with faculty's understanding of what it means to be a professional and the awareness there is of professional duty to serve the public good. The difference can be partially explained by our second finding.

Theme 2: The Inseparability of Personal Experiences and Community Engagement

Rather than being an abstract or fixed concept, participants' views of community engagement were closely related to their personal experiences with engaged work and had evolved over time. For instance, Jack shared that his definition of community engagement had changed over time as he learned more about the field and the work. For him, community engagement started with personal interest in community projects; then progressed to the integration of engagement into curriculum, to encourage more hands-on experiences for students; and then advanced into changing his ways of doing engaged work by involving a more diverse group of people. Jack's narrative revealed that his understanding of community engagement had grown into one that included working *in* the community, *with* community partners, connected to service learning particularly, and taking into consideration the interests of all parties involved (especially students and the community).

Anna also talked about how her idea about community engagement had evolved over the years:

> When I first realized that faculty could work with community to meet needs, it was defined to me as service learning. Now, I understand more; that's a category within the community engaged work. But for many years . . . my window into community engagement was through service learning, and it is only now I feel like I am starting to expand that, that definition of it.

Justin had recently left private practice to join academia. His premise differed somewhat from that of the other participants but reflected a close connection between his personal experiences and his view of community engagement. His view of community engagement was based on the notion of "I have the ability to help and they need help; they get help." Justin indicated that becoming a faculty member was his way of "giving back to a profession and a community that have been giving [him] so much." In the transition to an institutional setting, however, the notion of engaged work as scholarship had caused a "personal struggle" as he started doubting his goal and motivation in doing service learning or community engagement against the prevailing academic reward structure.

> Now, [on] the ground of academia, are my intentions really pure, or is there part of my brain going, yeah, there is some reward here. . . . I am not in it for myself, but every time I talked to somebody, it's a matter of how can we make this work because you are on tenure. . . . We should be allowed to [pursue] that in our 40, 50, 60 hours' work, [and] we should have resources available to us. There should be recognition that you are doing this, so that you are not wasting your time; I think that's fine, but . . . as soon as the reward system comes out . . . I am not saying it's incorrect, but that becomes a personal struggle.

Theme 3: Faculty's Commonsense Definitions of Philanthropy

In general, faculty's definitions of philanthropy were in accordance with a conventional understanding of "philanthropy as rational, large-scale giving by foundations and individuals to enhance the quality of life in the community" (Payton, 2000, para. 6). In contrast to Payton's definition of philanthropy, faculty's views were less accommodative, as they excluded actions such as volunteer service and association. Faculty emphasized different components underlying the conventional definition of philanthropy. For James and Justin, the prominent characteristic of philanthropy was the purpose behind giving: more about fulfilling others' needs than about personal recognition, return, or gain.

> *James:* [Philanthropy] is some type of humanitarian interest in bettering humanity, and I would say, through some type of charitable work, again, that's going towards something that's either local, national, or international concerns. . . . I think of it in terms of giving something to the community to solve some type of issue or problem that individuals are having, whether [an] individual has a little money, or other economic means, to be able help a school.
>
> *Justin:* My definition of philanthropic work is somebody who does what they are doing without any sense there is going to be recognition, payback, reward; you do it because it's what you want to do, it's the right thing to do. The other component of philanthropy from my perspective is that it is not directed to your self-enjoyment. . . . It's a gift . . . ; it's the right thing to do. There is a need and needs to be fulfilled, and I happen to be in the right place, at the right time, with the right tools, there it is.

Anna and Jack spoke more about forms of giving as an important defining trait of philanthropy. For them, philanthropy usually meant giving money, but it could be donation of time, energy, or expertise when money is not available.

> *Anna:* Philanthropy to me has always been this just donation of large amounts of money to organizations to meet a need. And if I think of philanthropy, what I believe the historical root is more of something is going to help humans do better, human needs. . . . So, going from there, when I then connect to the philanthropic work, I say, okay, this is not necessarily a big donation of money, it's something else, and what is it? Well, it's donation of . . . time, knowledge, resources that we have access to.
>
> *Jack:* I would think philanthropy is more like Carnegie, something a little bit bigger, because I am not establishing any grants or anything like that. But if I add up all my time, especially if I add up my time based on university salary there's probably been a sizable contribution that has been made.

It is possible that the variation in faculty's definitional focus of philanthropy was related to their disciplinary training and prior knowledge about or experience with philanthropy.

Theme 4: Faculty's Defined Responsibilities Separate Engagement from Philanthropy

Faculty's view of their engaged work as philanthropy related to their perceptions of what it meant to be a faculty member. Those perceptions were influenced by personal beliefs and institutional cultures. Faculty participants considered engaged work philanthropic when it went beyond their job responsibilities. For example, James stated, "With philanthropy, I kind of feel that it's going beyond what your job role is. . . . People are involved with philanthropy that has nothing to do with their actual professional jobs." Anna said something similar: "Philanthropic work is something [that] not necessarily falls within my bounds of job responsibilities." Linda spoke from more of an institutional angle, noting that the absence of institutional reward for faculty engagement enabled her to view her engaged work as philanthropy in that she was giving with no expectation of return from the institution.

Although some of the participants acknowledged that engaged work could lead to philanthropic work, they did not consider the extra time, energy, and expertise (whether acknowledged or valued by institutional standards) that they put into their engaged work to be philanthropic, if it provided what they perceived as long-term professional benefits. James explicitly stated the distinction between community engagement and philanthropy:

> I do think they are very different. I don't know if I would [have] thought of it as philanthropic or even not philanthropic, when I started doing engagement scholarship; I just would not even necessarily connect the two. But, as I am thinking about it now, I think that engagement scholarship might promote almost a unique or maybe novel pathway towards philanthropy . . . in a simplified term, almost like an opportunity to do a lot [of] pro bono work, kind of thing. In some cases, that pro bono work could lead into more research, could lead to something like that, so it is hard to define—is that then philanthropic if there is some type of intermediate gain? . . . That's how I would see them [as] separate, but I think they are related some way.

Theme 5: Community Engagement and Philanthropy— The Directional Opposition

Faculty's comfort level in considering their engaged work as philanthropic was rooted in the directionality of the constructs: community engagement as reciprocal and two-way and philanthropy as giving, unidirectional, and unconditional. Linda's interview provides a vivid example:

> When I think of philanthropy, I think of someone giving to something in need. . . . I will have something that this organization does not have, so I am giving with no anticipation of being given back to. . . . When I give my knowledge of evaluation, I learn from who I've been giving information to about how to apply to in that setting. So with mutual giving, I can see sort of mutual philanthropy but not one-side format of philanthropy where I feel like I am giving to a person or an organization in need and I am the higher person.

Likewise, Anna shared that community engagement demands reciprocity and it lives through developing a relationship with the community partner(s). She cherished and sought "feeling good about myself" in doing engaged work but felt "guilty of" this "gain," when it was put in the context of philanthropy when no self-benefit is supposed to be expected. In agreement with Anna, James also considered such personal satisfaction a benefit disqualifying his engaged work from being framed as philanthropy. He related philanthropy to the idea of altruism—one-way giving—but clearly portrayed community engagement as a relationship built on mutuality and reciprocity. Like Linda, James was troubled by the implicit superiority of the giver in the "give to the given" interpretation associated with philanthropy and found it in opposition to his view of engaged work, which was grounded in relationship building with multiple parties.

Justin presented his views somewhat differently but still struggled with seeing engaged work as purely philanthropic:

> Philanthropy, as I see it . . . has no buy-in [on my part]; I am not looking for a long-term relationship; if that happens, that's great, but this is almost a gift to. The word *gift* just has too many negative connotations for me, but it's like I have this, I can give it to you. I give it to you, and I walk away, that's how I perceive philanthropy. . . . So coming to the how do I perceive the [engaged] work we plan to do or try to do, I'm really struggling with that. There's part of me that feels it's good work, it needs to be done, but I don't really want to start putting a page and half in my CV to make it sound [good], that's where I am struggling with it. So, is it philanthropic? Yes, I saw it being that, but now it's getting muddied. The ground of academia, are my intentions really pure, or is there part of my brain going, yeah, there is some reward here.

Like the other participants, Justin showed resistance and discomfort when viewing his engaged work as philanthropy because of the perceived directional opposition between the two concepts. This oppositional view suggests that a richer conversation about faculty participants' perspectives would be valuable.

COMPARING ENGAGEMENT WITH PHILANTHROPY

Our findings revealed that in comparison with their perceptions regarding philanthropy, our faculty participants had an understanding of community engagement that was clearer and aligned with current literature. Their engaged work and scholarship were an inseparable part of who they were personally and professionally. In contrast, philanthropy was viewed as a more detached concept, with the conventional idea of philanthropy as a monetary donation or charity—one-way giving. The unidirectionality in particular, while only one component in Payton's (1988) conceptualization of philanthropy, was the key rule for our faculty participants' identification of philanthropy (or philanthropic work). The perceived lack of mutuality in philanthropy, with its largesse or works of "mercy," connotes power disparities between the giver and the receiver that troubled our faculty participants, preventing them from fully viewing their engaged work as philanthropy. To a great extent, faculty participants' views were aligned with the earlier literature on philanthropy, which conceptualized philanthropy and charity as equivalent. The current field of philanthropy has moved from a concept of charity to one that emphasizes equality. A possible explanation for the disparity between our faculty participants' understanding of philanthropy and the current state of philanthropy scholarship is disciplinary expertise: Engaged faculty are more likely to have current knowledge of community engagement scholarship than of philanthropic studies scholarship.

Faculty participants showed a basic understanding of philanthropy but lacked a strong connection with the concept. Although the interview offered them an opportunity to explore the possible linkages between engagement and philanthropy under a broader notion of public good in the academy, participants reacted to the term with hesitation and resistance. We postulate that the extent of hesitation and resistance depend on faculty's conceptual maturity around community engagement and the pervasiveness of their practice of engaged scholarship. In the cases of four of the five participants, the more experienced they were and the more able to frame their engaged scholarship as an integration of teaching, research, and service, the more reluctant faculty were to label their engaged work as philanthropy.

For many participants the interview was probably the first time they had considered viewing their engaged work as philanthropy. These faculty were students and champions of community engagement. Not surprisingly, the idea of community-engaged scholarship as a possible expression of philanthropy was novel to them. As many learning theories indicate, when an individual encounters a new idea, his or her reaction is dependent on prior knowledge and experience of a subject of study (Lave & Wenger, 1991; Merriam & Bierema, 2014). Most of our participants came from disciplines that have a longer history of community engagement and stronger prevalence of faculty involvement in community engagement, such as education and public health (Glass, Doberneck, & Schweitzer, 2011). These disciplinary traditions/cultures could have helped reinforce their adoption or acceptance of the new paradigm of community engagement. In contrast, Justin's initial contact with community engagement took place in private practice. Philanthropy, with its notion of giving without expectation of return, paralleled his work of giving back to the veterinary profession and the people in it. The resistance or reluctance faculty exhibited toward the idea of engaged work as philanthropy did not necessarily represent an antagonistic view; rather, it might be explained as part of the learning process that our faculty participants had experienced and manifested in their responses.

Our findings suggest that faculty perceived a directional opposition between community engagement and philanthropy, the former being reciprocal and the latter being unidirectional. Faculty's differentiation of the two constructs echoes the literature of both community engagement and philanthropy. In that case, wouldn't the answer to the question of "faculty engaged work as philanthropy" be no? We would argue, not necessarily. Let us present our argument by going back to Payton's conceptualization of philanthropy. Payton's (1988) notion of philanthropy, with the general public in mind, is broad enough to include every sector in society; however, with this universal inclusiveness comes decontextualization, so that the framework cannot address the actualization of philanthropy operated locally in various sectors or fields. Philanthropic activities in the broader society, those associated with foundations, organizations, and business in particular, often involve transfers of money that conform well to Payton's description of philanthropy as one-way transfers where the return is not expected and actually rarely occurs. Faculties do their engaged work voluntarily without expectation of receiving in return.

Given the voluntary initiative or intention behind giving as key to Payton's claim of one-way philanthropy, wouldn't faculty's community engagement be one-way as well? We would argue that faculty's engaged work is one-way because of the voluntary dimension; and it is also two-way because of its direct linkage to the fields or disciplines woven into faculty's daily lives and professional and personal identities. In contrast to Payton's sector/field-nonspecific definition of philanthropy, faculty's definition of community engagement (which is aligned with current literature of community engagement) is contextualized within higher education and speaks to the distinctive characteristics of faculty's involvement. Instead of money, faculty's community engagement mainly involves expertise, time, and participation. The cogeneration of knowledge is more pronounced when knowledge is at center stage for engaged scholarship than it would be for other sectors such as business or industry when such a close connection is unlikely. In their interviews, our participants indicated on multiple occasions that learning was mutual. Nonetheless, such a distinction does not deny the connections between faculty engaged work and philanthropy. As our findings revealed, the attention and work that faculty had given to serving the needs and purposes of society do speak to compassion and community, the two fundamental values of philanthropy, and some faculty noted that our interview had expanded their views of what community engagement could be.

Last, although we did not start out with a research question about motivation, our participants' narratives were consistent with the literature of faculty motivation for community engagement (Neumann, 2005; Neumann & Peterson, 1997; Neumann, Terosky, & Schell, 2006; O'Meara, 2008). We will not have an expanded discussion here, but understanding motivation will help explain faculty participants' initial learning angle or scope about community engagement (or philanthropy) and their developmental paths of engaged scholarship. Overall, our faculty participants' motivations fell within the first three of the seven sources identified by O'Meara (2008), as motivation to facilitate student learning and growth; motivation grounded in the perceived fit between the discipline and the engagement; or motivation grounded in personal commitment to specific social issues, people, and places. Some overlap in the motivation for community engagement and for philanthropy is evident. We believe acknowledging commonality and difference is only the first step; critical to the conversation about philanthropy and community engagement is how we move forward knowing the terms are both similar and in opposition.

IMPLICATIONS FOR THE FUTURE

This exploratory study found that engaged faculty perceived their community engagement as similar to philanthropy in that both involved volunteerism and social change. For these faculty, however, the mutuality with community partners distinguished community engagement from philanthropy. The study participants held conventional views of philanthropy, but their stories about their engaged practice reflected an approach congruent with Payton's description of philanthropy as community and compassion.

Moreover, through mutual and combined effort, the faculty and community partners collectively were engaged in philanthropy, voluntary action for the public good.

Our study raises questions for future work about espoused theories and theories in use. Future research should consider how faculty, as learners, can encounter, interact with, and integrate seemingly paradoxical yet interconnected ideas in multidisciplinary community engagement. Given the elite sample in this study, replicative studies on a larger scale or using an expanded pool of types of faculty would help test the pervasiveness of these findings. What about the flip side—the philanthropic faculty, those who have been very involved personally in philanthropic work but not community engagement, like serving food regularly at a soup kitchen? Do their views resemble or differ from those of our engaged faculty? Do our international faculties hold a more integrated view of their engaged work as philanthropic? Do faculty members from some disciplines tend to have a more integrated view of their engaged work as philanthropic than their colleagues from other disciplines? A further investigation of these questions is warranted.

Implications for policy lead us initially to the institutional efforts to bridge philanthropy and community engagement. First, faculty often participate in institution-wide philanthropic initiatives or projects such as fundraising for organizations like the United Way. Such unidirectional actions of faculty donating money or participating in charitable fundraising events, however, are unlikely to yield community connections. It is important for institutions to provide faculty with philanthropic activities, such as campus days of service, that can also serve as openings for community engaged work. Second, implications for policy point to the need for concern with faculty development in higher education institutions. It is not enough to appreciate the importance of providing professional development opportunities; increased attention in tailoring them to more diversified faculty members is also called for.

For the field of community engagement and the field of philanthropy, this study offers prospects for rethinking in both disciplines as well as openings for beneficial conversations between the two fields: If community engagement is boundary crossing, where are the boundaries it can cross to bridge engaged scholarship and philanthropy? If the unidirectionality in Payton's definition of philanthropy truly does not speak to the work of community engagement or even the current state of philanthropic scholarship, could this definition and older views of philanthropy be further challenged so the two constructs and scholarships can build on each other with a common ground of the shared values of community and compassion?

We conclude with reflective thoughts: Does considering and framing work in community engagement as philanthropic actually matter? Yes and no. If philanthropic work is unidirectional, then it should not be used for community engagement, but if the definition of philanthropy can be more definitively expanded or the two fields can find common ground to build on, then perhaps it introduces the possibility of bringing others into the community-engaged world through their work that is not connected to their jobs, and vice versa. Perhaps the theory base of engagement could be expanded to allow for the collective work of faculty and their community partners to be seen as the philanthropic act, toward the improvement of the public good. As society demands more of higher education, it is critical that we connect all our resources (ideas, energy, and funding) to discovering interconnections within faculty work so that philanthropy and community engagement are mutually supporting rather than oppositional ideas.

REFERENCES

Bloomgarden, A. H., & O'Meara, K. (2007). Faculty role integration and community engagement: Harmony or cacophony? *Michigan Journal of Community Service Learning, 13*(2), 5–18.

Boyer, E. L. (1990). *Scholarship reconsidered: Priorities of the professoriate.* Princeton, NJ: Carnegie Foundation for the Advancement of Teaching.

Boyer, E. L. (1996). The scholarship of engagement. *Journal of Public Service and Outreach, 1*(1), 11–20.

Carnegie Foundation for the Advancement of Teaching. (n.d.). *Classification description: Community engagement elective classification.* Available at http://classifications.carnegiefoundation.org/descriptions/community_engagement.php

Charmaz, K. (2006). *Constructing grounded theory: A practical guide through qualitative analysis.* London, UK: Sage.

Colbeck, C. L., & Drago, R. (2005). Accept, avoid, resist: How faculty members respond to bias against caregiving . . . and how departments can help. *Change, 37*(6), 10–17.

Colbeck, C. L., & Weaver, L. D. (2008). Faculty engagement in public scholarship: A motivation system theory perspective. *Journal of Higher Education Outreach and Engagement, 12*(2), 7–32.

Corbin, J. (2004). In vivo coding. In M. Lewis-Beck, A. Bryman, & T. Liao (Eds.), *Encyclopedia of social science research methods* (pp. 529–530). Thousand Oaks, CA: Sage.

Deetz, S. (2008). Engagement as co-generative theorizing. *Journal of Applied Communication Research, 36*(3), 289–297.

Doberneck, D. M., Glass, C. R., & Schweitzer, J. (2010). From rhetoric to reality: A typology of publicly engaged scholarship. *Journal of Higher Education Outreach and Engagement, 14*(4), 5–35.

Driscoll, A., & Lynton, E. A. (1999). *Making outreach visible: A guide to documenting professional service and outreach.* Washington, DC: American Association of Higher Education.

Fear, F. A., Rosaen, C. L., Foster-Fishman, P., & Bawden, R. J. (2001). Outreach as scholarly expression: A faculty perspective. *Journal of Higher Education Outreach and Engagement, 6*(2), 21–34.

Fear, F. A., & Sandmann, L. R. (2001). The "new" scholarship: Implications for engagement and extension. *Journal of Higher Education Outreach and Engagement, 7*(1&2), 29–39.

Fitzgerald, H. E., Bruns, K., Sonka, S. T., Furco, A., & Swanson, L. (2012). The centrality of engagement in higher education. *Journal of Higher Education Outreach and Engagement 16*(3), 7–27.

Gaskell, G. (2000). Individual and group interviewing. In M. W. Bauer & G. Gaskell (Eds.), *Qualitative researching with text, image, and sound: A practical handbook* (pp. 38–56). London, UK: Sage.

Gibbons, M. (2001). *Engagement as a core value for the university: A consultant document.* London, UK: Association of Commonwealth Universities.

Gibbons, M., Limoges, C., Nowotny, H., Schwartzman, S., Scott, P., & Trow, T. (1994). *The new production of knowledge: The dynamics of science and research in contemporary societies.* London, UK: Sage.

Glass, C. R., Doberneck, D. M., & Schweitzer, J. H. (2011). Unpacking faculty engagement: The type of activities faculty members report as publicly engaged scholarship during promotion and tenure. *Journal of Higher Education Outreach and Engagement, 15*(1), 7–30.

Glass, C. R., & Fitzgerald, H. E. (2010). Engaged scholarship: Historical roots, contemporary challenges. In H. E. Fitzgerald, C. Burack, & S. D. Seifer (Eds.), *Handbook of engaged scholarship: Contemporary landscapes, future directions: Vol. 1. Institutional change* (pp. 9–24). East Lansing, MI: Michigan State University Press.

Kellogg Commission on the Future of State and Land-Grant Universities. (1999). *Returning to our roots: The engaged institution.* Washington, DC: National Association of State Universities and Land-Grant Colleges. Available at http://www.aplu.org/NetCommunity/Document.Doc?id=183

Lave, J., & Wenger, E. (1991). *Situated learning: Legitimate peripheral participation.* Cambridge, UK: Cambridge University Press.

Merriam, S. B., & Bierema, L. L. (2014). *Adult learning: Linking theory and practice.* San Francisco, CA: Jossey-Bass.

Neumann, A. (2005). Observations: Taking seriously the topic of learning in studies of faculty work and careers. In E. G. Creamer & L. R. Lattuca (Eds.), *Advancing faculty learning through interdisciplinary collaboration* (New Directions for Teaching and Learning 102, pp. 63–83). San Francisco, CA: Jossey-Bass.

Neumann, A., & Peterson, P. L. (1997). *Learning from our lives: Women, research, and autobiography in education.* New York, NY: Teachers College Press.

Neumann, A., Terosky, A. L., & Schell, J. (2006). Agents of learning: Strategies for assuming agency, for learning, in tenured faculty careers. In S. Bracken, J. Allen, & D. Dean (Eds.), *The balancing act: Gendered perspectives in faculty roles and work lives* (pp. 91–120). Sterling, VA: Stylus.

O'Meara, K. (2008). Motivation for public scholarship and engagement: Listening to exemplars. *Journal of Higher Education Outreach and Engagement, 12*(1), 7–29.

Payton, R. L. (1988). *Philanthropy: Voluntary action for the public good.* New York, NY: American Council on Education/Macmillan.

Payton, R. L. (2000). Hofstra's most distinctive virtue. In *Philanthropy: Voluntary action for the public good* (Part 2, chap. 4). Available at http://www.paytonpapers. org/output/ESS0023_1.shtm

Roulston, K. (2010). *Reflective interviewing: A guide to theory and practice.* London, UK: Sage.

Saltmarsh, J., & Hartley, M. (Eds.). (2011). *"To serve a larger purpose": Engagement for democracy and the transformation of higher education.* Philadelphia, PA: Temple University Press.

Sandmann, L. R. (2006). Scholarship as architecture: Framing and enhancing community engagement. *Journal of Physical Therapy Education, 20*(3), 80–84.

Sandmann, L. R. (2008). Conceptualization of the scholarship of engagement in higher education: A strategic review, 1996–2006. *Journal of Higher Education Outreach and Engagement, 12*(1), 91–104.

Schomberg, S. F., & Farmer, J. A., Jr. (1994). The evolving concept of public service and implications for rewarding faculty. *Continuing Higher Education Review, 58*(3), 122–140.

Veysey, L. R. (1965). *The emergence of the American university.* Chicago, IL: The University of Chicago Press.

Votruba, J. C. (1992). Promoting the extension of knowledge in service to society. *Metropolitan Universities, 3*(3), 72–80.

Wade, A. M. (2008). *Faculty and the engaged institution: Toward understanding motivators and deterrents for fostering engagement* (Doctoral dissertation). Available at http://etd.ohiolink.edu/view.cgi?acc_num=osu1227558125

Ward, E. C. (2010). *Women's way of engagement: Explorations of gender, the scholarship of engagement and institutional rewards policy and practice.* Available at http://0-eric.ed.gov.opac.msmc.edu/?q=%22%22&ff1=souProQue st+LLC&ff2=subContent+Analysis&pg=15&id=ED521096

Part V

THE PUBLIC GOOD AND THE
FUTURE OF ACADEMIC WORK

CHAPTER 17

Reflections on the Public Good and Academic Professionalism

R. Eugene Rice, John Saltmarsh, andWilliam M. Plater

In this concluding chapter, I have invited three of the nation's leading think-ers about higher education and practitioners of engaged scholarship to reflect on the culminating issues of public policy and the public good. In different ways over several decades, they have shaped much of our thinking about the professoriate, the changing academic workforce, and the role of higher education in renewing democracy. Here they engage in a thoughtful dialogue, exploring what this book might mean for the future of American higher education.

—Genevieve G. Shaker, editor

William (Bill) M. Plater: Many excellent people have contributed to this volume. In reading their chapters, it is clear—at least to me—that there is something crosscutting in their analyses of what motivates, even defines, the academic workforce in all its changing forms. But is *philanthropy* the core of this amorphous, yet compelling, sense of *good* underlying faculty work? And so what, even if it is? Is philanthropy the best, or even an especially use-ful, framing with which to address the urgent policy issues facing academics but also the public that relies on higher education for economic, social, and spiritual well-being?

The chapters that compose this volume contain an extraordinary range of opinion and purpose. Yet everyone has taken philanthropy as a starting point for reflection and analysis. Is it possible to extract from this diversity a few key principles or ideas for action that might help the United States prepare for the new ecology of higher education, one where the United States is no longer the inevitable world guarantor of innovation, democratic principles, and human progress through education?

This book has been based in large part on Robert Payton's (1988) defi-nition of philanthropy as "voluntary action for the public good" (p. 3). His is a sweeping and abstract concept, one that offers a nearly blank slate for explaining those key words—*voluntary*, *action*, and *public good*. Even *for* has contextual relevance.

Surely this openness accounts for much of the appeal Genevieve Shaker has seen in applying the concept to the professoriate specifically and to the academic workforce broadly. She has recognized a useful framing for the *discretionary* use that many faculty make of their time, often directing their actions to purposes and tasks that contribute directly to making society better. Certainly teaching and research by themselves qualify as—mostly—constructive elements in improving society; when contributions to communities through civic engagement are added to the mix, there is an understandable feeling that faculty are doing more than their job, more than they are paid to do, in the contributions they make to society.

The chapter authors write about philanthropy as moral action, as the loving of humankind with a duty to act on their behalf, as a way of life saturated with public value, as an inherent force of integration, as a counterweight to the unbundling of faculty roles, as a nuanced continuum of possible activities shielded from criticism by a pretense of intent, as a way to counteract past social wrongs, and more. Such concepts and interpretations lend themselves to reflections on the work faculty do—even if they are a bit self-serving. And each author has given a unique spin on the seemingly clear and simple six words of Payton's definition.

Shaker has not asked the authors or readers to accept blindly the "truth" or the certainty of this approach to considering faculty work, but instead she has held it up as a mirror—to require each of us as writer, indeed, as reader—to ask what public good there is in faculty work and then to articulate a rationale for why the professoriate might continue to claim a place of social privilege, respect, and authority from the public as a reflection of the good they contribute. She asks us how to preserve the important dimension of faculty work that is committed to the public good and that relies on the choices individuals make about their own work and their own priorities.

But, in this very concept, there is a fly in the ointment of feeling good about faculty work. Payton's formulation inherently relies on individual action, not collective action and collective purpose. It actually reinforces a centrifugal force both of you have thought deeply about—the tendencies of faculty to act on their own behalf, to seek the gains that come from aligning with their disciplines instead of their institutions. Faculty, as educational entrepreneurs, are creative and innovative, and often do things to benefit society, but they act as individuals rather than as part of a community. This tendency is a barrier to engagement with the community, and it reinforces the idea that the university is an "ivory tower"—free from any connection to societal needs.

Tenure is based on the mutual responsibility between individual and institution (and vice versa). Yet in recent years, we have seen a shift toward a lopsided expectation from faculty that tenure is about benefiting the individual with scant attention to the community that supports the individual—at a time when barely 25% of the academic workforce can ever expect the privilege of tenure—just as society is seeing tenure as an ill that prevents a more productive, cost-effective academic workforce.

So, I put it to you, John, is a focus on the philanthropic work of faculty a useful framing for either informing or shaping public policy? Does it have value for how faculty themselves think about their work? How might policymakers respond to the conditions that are driving the faculty toward a "workforce" instead of a professoriate—a profession with its defined duty to the public good? And, Gene, might you comment on what is most at risk in preserving the profession of "professing"—the professoriate as distinct from an academic workforce?

John Saltmarsh: I find it very helpful that this volume invites us to interrogate the definition of philanthropy as "voluntary action for the public good," looking critically at each word of the definition and the implications for meaning and action in the context of the faculty. I want to start and end my comments with the last part of the definition, "the public good."

One way to think about the relationship of faculty to the public good is within a historical context. In the late 19th and early 20th century, when the modern university was emerging, disciplines were forming, and faculty were professionalizing, there were efforts to define what the faculty role would look like, what faculty rights and responsibilities would be, and what kind of academic culture would best advance new knowledge and prepare democratic citizens. In the context of the United States, the purpose of higher education has historically been both academic and civic. From my perspective, a key document in defining this faculty role was the "1915 Declaration of Principles on Academic Freedom and Tenure," which marked the founding of the American Association of University Professors (AAUP).

To Bill's point, in discussing the "nature of the academic calling," the declaration states that the "conception of a university as an ordinary business venture, and of academic teaching as a purely private employment, manifests also a radical failure to apprehend the nature of the social function discharged by the professional scholar" (AAUP, 1915, p. 294). It is that larger social responsibility that led to the profound notion affirmed in the document that "the responsibility of the university teacher is primarily to the public itself" (p. 295). What this suggests is that there is a longstanding and important cultural tradition within the academy for faculty to engage in scholarly work that has public relevance.

Thus, faculty public work is very much within the culture of profes-sionalism and the strictures of academic freedom that define the profession. Part of faculty culture includes extraordinary latitude on the part of faculty to determine lines of inquiry, in shaping curriculum, and in constructing and disseminating knowledge through teaching and research. Foremost, because of disciplinary graduate training, faculty develop epistemological assumptions that form the core of their faculty roles—they identify them-selves as scholars in terms of how knowledge is constructed, how knowledge gets generated, and how knowledge is used and by whom. Related to this is how faculty think about and shape a professional identity around how stu-dents learn and construct knowledge, and the role of teaching in facilitating learning. Faculty's service role has been associated with the faculty role in shared governance, but it also reflects a professional identity associated with institutional citizenship.

In all these roles, faculty navigate often complex and unstated cultural norms that lead to acknowledgment, advancement, status, and power—as well as personal fulfillment, ideally where personal values align with profes-sional practice. Also, faculty navigate their roles in ways that can often allow them to integrate their research, teaching, and service commitments. The way faculty shape their professional identity relates to generating knowledge more effectively, teaching more successfully, and shaping institutions to cre-ate environments where knowledge generation and learning take place.

For some faculty, this work leads to community-engaged teaching and research, and service commitments that are external to the campus. But I do not see this as philanthropic work—I don't see it as "voluntary action for the public good." If some amount of faculty work is undertaken to aid oth-ers and the community, as is a key contention in this book's framing, within their faculty roles, then they are doing it because there is some benefit—for knowledge generation, for teaching and learning, or for a larger sense of institutional citizenship—for which they are "rewarded" within academic culture. That faculty do public work as part of their roles is not mandated, but within the wide autonomy of faculty culture, in which little is actually prescribed. Public work, even if not formally rewarded at many institutions in the reward structure, still has its place within faculty assignments and has professional rewards that serve as incentives for doing such work. As Ann Austin wrote so clearly, it is work that is "core to what [she] understand[s] to be the long-established essence of being a member of the academic profes-sion" (Chapter 4, this volume).

One concern that I have is that framing public work as voluntary activity could lead to a response that says that it should not be formally sanctioned or rewarded because it is something that faculty can do on their own—something like Stanley Fish's 2008 argument that faculty should save the world on their own time. I think that faculty can do public work legitimately as academic professionals. It is their practice as democratic professionals that allows them to, as Albert Dzur (2008) writes, legitimately act to facilitate collaborative production of knowledge with community partners and with students through the democratic values of task-sharing and lay participation to build a wider public culture of democracy. This is their professional work—it is not work that they choose to do outside their professional practice as gestures of goodwill.

It also seems to me that there is a subtext to this entire discussion about faculty work as private philanthropy. It appears that it is symptomatic of the effects of neoliberalism in higher education. To be clear, what I am suggesting is that approaching faculty work for the public good as private acts of philanthropy enacts a kind of highly individualized, privatized, market-driven faculty practice that reshapes faculty work away from a public obligation and responsibility to one of private choice. Part of neoliberalism's impact is in approaching faculty as a managed workforce without protections (tenure), academic freedom (rights), or public responsibilities (duty) as part of the faculty role—hence work for the public good can be construed only as a private choice. As a counterweight to neoliberalism's effects on faculty work, I would prefer that we not reinforce what Sheila Slaughter and Gary Rhoades (2004) call the "academic capitalist knowledge/learning regime" of the neoliberal university and instead create a public-engagement regime with core academic norms such that faculty work addressing public problem-solving with the purpose of advancing an inclusive, collaborative, and deliberative democracy is an expectation.

Gene, what is your take on the framing issues about the public nature of faculty work?

R. Eugene (Gene) Rice: I deeply appreciate the way John draws on his own disciplinary orientation in anchoring our discussion of the changing faculty role and the public good in a well-informed historical context. He underscores the larger social responsibility of the faculty as a profession—a primary responsibility to "the pubic itself"—that was a critical part of the vision of the new American university as it emerged during the opening of the 20th century.

It was a vision that has structure and content—a part of the process of professionalization—that Talcott Parsons (1968), by the middle of the 20th century, could describe as "the most important single component of the structure of modern societies" (p. 545). This leading social theorist then went on to argue that the keystone in the arch of the emerging professionally-oriented society is the modern university and "the professional *par excellence* is the academic" (p. 545).

It was a professional vision that would later prove to have flaws with its siloed departments, narrowly specialized disciplines, and hierarchical status system driven by a debilitating prestige economy. But it was a professional vision that called for academic freedom, individual autonomy, shared governance, and honoring scholarly creativity and innovation in a way that continues to be identified around the globe as "the envy of the world." It was a conception of the academic professional—or the academic as a professional—that became firmly institutionalized through graduate school preparation and built into longstanding policies of most colleges and universities. It was a professional understanding of academic work that was widely shared and rooted in a call to serve the public good.

By the opening of the 21st century, American higher education had moved into a new era, as most of this book indicates; we are living in a profoundly different period with a radically different workforce, student population, and technological base. It is now time for a new vision of the academic profession that is, as John urges, publicly engaged and aimed at "advancing a more inclusive, collaborative, and deliberative democracy."

During the past 4 decades the faculty role itself has transformed—becoming unbundled and confused. The public–private boundaries have lost their definition. The dominance of the research-oriented universities—what Christopher Jencks and David Riesman described in 1968 as the academic revolution—led to the rise of a faculty that rather than being publicly engaged became increasingly individualistic and aggressively entrepreneurial. Attention to teaching and learning eroded, student well-being was neglected, institutional citizenship moved to the margins, and any professional notion of the responsibility for the public good lost its meaning.

The recent changes have been so dramatic that a national conversation—surfacing on the margins—now needs to be vigorously cultivated. As the boundaries between public and private are rearranged and deteriorate, and as entrepreneurial universities emerge globally, the faculty voice needs to be heard.

E. J. Dionne, Jr., university professor at Georgetown, Rhodes Scholar, and public intellectual, has written a significant book, *Our Divided Political Heart* (2012). In it he analyzes the careful balance America has struggled to sustain between individual liberties and a strong commitment to community. It was these polar strengths that were set forth in the professional self-understanding identified in the AAUP 1915 declaration. For example, it called for the rights of academic freedom and responsibility. Individual creativity was valued and protected; the cultivation of an unfettered imagination and innovation were honored. At the other end of the spectrum, civic engagement and social responsibility—the building of vital community—were expected. It was this tension that was written into the professional role of the faculty in the earlier part of the 20th century.

As we moved into the 21st century, the social fabric shaping this consensus had unraveled. The pendulum has swung as faculty—particularly at the norm-setting research universities—now see themselves as independent entrepreneurs. The unbundling of the faculty role and the commercialization of the academy have encouraged this development. Freeing the imagination and cultivating innovation have had their obvious benefits. Visiting the universities of China and the Middle East—witnessing their absence—makes this immediately evident. But the pendulum has swung too far. As Ernest Boyer (1990) was fond of reminding us, American higher education has gone through a fundamental shift, from functioning in the interests of the public good to being primarily concerned with private benefit. Regrettably, the academy—including the faculty—is being perceived by the public as making this shift. Greater attention to community engagement and the public good are urgently required to restore this critical balance.

The creative tension between individual freedom and community responsibility needs to be restored in the American idea, as Dionne (2012) argues, but I want to contend—if it is not too far a reach—that leadership on this important point must be established in the nation's colleges and universities, and particularly in the professional understanding of faculty at the core of the changing academic workforce.

Before the contemporary faculty—as diverse as it is—can go very far in addressing the public good and being socially responsible, it needs to speak to the gross injustices in the academic workplace itself, especially the discrepancy between the full-time tenure-track faculty and those regarded as contingent, those Bill identified earlier as the 75% majority of the instructional staff in our colleges and universities.

In a recent issue of *The Chronicle of Higher Education*, Jeffrey J. Williams (2013), professor of English at Carnegie Mellon University, attacks what he calls the "great stratification" in the American professoriate. He finds the shape of academic labor as "profoundly unbalanced," introducing "its own harsh class structure" (paras. 26 and 24). Others, such as David Scobey (2002), describe this blatant exploitation of the majority of what was once regarded as a community of scholars as being about more than salary and benefits; they see it as a moral issue. Williams compares the way the medical profession has dealt with its professional stratification issues—as bad as they are—with what has emerged in the American professoriate. The comparison renders what is happening in the American academic workplace a public embarrassment. The restructuring of the academic profession might well begin here.

Academic freedom, a hallmark of the professional understanding of an earlier time, needs to be rethought. It is not just freedom to pursue one's own intellectual interests and independent goals—as important as these are—but also to ensure that the permanent faculty, of whatever form, have responsibility for the academic freedom for the whole academic workforce, including those who are on the full-time tenure track but not yet tenured. Ironically, these are the ones who often have the least academic freedom under the present system.

To return to the core discussion, the philanthropic theme introduces to the professional role of faculty the expectation that to be professional means that the privilege of autonomy and academic independence is intertwined in the long run with the obligation to attend to the public good. This is what faculty should practice and model throughout their professional work; this is especially true of their role in preparing students as civic agents in a democracy.

Plater: So, what now? How can we—all who have contributed to this volume—address what is clearly a critical transition, maybe even a tipping point, in the role of the academic profession within U.S. society? It seems to me that each of us has made the case in different ways that there is a bargain, a contract, among academics as professionals (both as individuals and collectively as "the faculty"), the institutions that hire and retain the faculty, and society at large—the "public" whose good we have been discussing. Perhaps it is only me, but I infer from your comments and many of the chapters in the volume that the only party to the bargain that is thinking much about this issue is the faculty itself, and not many of them, although the media is devoting more space and time to issues related to costs, the rise in numbers of contingent faculty (and related issues), and the (largely economic) value of degrees. The near absence of other parties from this reflection is disappointing and disheartening, as is the media's recognizing institutions' and society's duty to the public good through education. While the lack of leadership from college and university provosts, presidents, and trustees is concerning, the faculty bear partial responsibility for the lack of an adequate institutional response. And so far, the public response—as represented by the media and elected officials—seems mostly about finding blame or addressing costs.

As a public policy issue, the changing nature of the academic workforce and its duty to the public good through the social contract you have both articulated looms in my mind as the most important policy issue of higher education—more than access, cost, or regulation. The issue is about *quality* and the *purpose* of higher education. I think we all agree that higher education is essential to a sustained democracy, an equitable society, and economic prosperity. Yet the promise of the profession itself—its sense of a duty to the public good—seems to be disappearing with the emergence of a largely contingent academic workforce where the bargain between society, the institutions, and the individuals who work in the academy has weakened to the point that it cannot long endure.

Framing the exchange that is inherent in the AAUP formulation of tenure with its reciprocal responsibilities among the three parties as "philanthropy"—something voluntary—poses a risk, as John points out. Yet the role of faculty as contributors to the public good out of their own sense of profession is already at greater risk than raising the issue to the level of an explicit debate among policy officials and the larger society. Is the contribution of *all* faculty—regardless of tenure status or percentage of appointment or duration of contract—to the public good through their work within the academy voluntary, necessary, or optional? Who decides? Who enforces by what means, however subtle or direct? If a contribution to the public good were either a real duty of the profession or an obligation of the institution, would not accrediting bodies require evidence of the performance of this duty as a condition of accreditation? Would not the Department of Education require such evidence as a qualification for eligibility for federal aid, as an explicitly required return on the public's investment in education?

What I believe the contributions to this volume illustrate is that we have a nation at risk, but the risk is the disappearing *expectation* of a duty to the public good through teaching, research, and community engagement. We can no more legislate "doing good," whether voluntary or required, than we can legislate the weather. But if acting for the public good is voluntary and faculty of all types so engage, they should be recognized and celebrated. I think the only way we can come to terms with a duty to the unenforceable is through a new social contract between the three parties—the public, the "faculty" (in all their variety), and the institutions that employ them—based on a new concept of tenure, a new set of reciprocal responsibilities to each other. Only when all the parties are at the table and agree can there be any certainty about academe's contribution to the public good, whether voluntary, an expectation of employment, or the duty of a profession. Risky as it is, legislators, governors, unions, associations, accreditors, governing boards, foundations, and the media need to talk about whether the faculty's contribution to society is philanthropic and if it is not, then define the social contract for preserving it. How do we make this discussion of the public good public?

Saltmarsh: If we want to catalyze a public policy debate about the "quality and purpose of higher education" in a democracy, I am highly skeptical that the best way to do that is by arguing for what Shaker calls "the unfamiliar framework of philanthropy." Bill, I hear in your words a similar skepticism. I have the words of Oliver Wendell Holmes Jr. ringing in my ears—that hard cases make for bad laws. The hard case of faculty contingency is compelling and urgent, which you and Gene and many authors in this volume have addressed. But the solution of conceptualizing faculty commitment to the public good as a philanthropic choice or gift is not, from my perspective, a solution or a viable way of instigating action on public policy.

I would argue instead for a public dialogue on why it is that higher education is a public good, how faculty—tenure track or non–tenure track—as a condition of employment and as a professional duty should contribute to the public good, and, fundamentally, what is the faculty we need for the society we want? If the society we want is one in which private self-interests overwhelm any sense of collective well-being, then an academic workforce of contingent faculty with philanthropic sensibilities is what we need. If, instead, the society we want is where the collective well-being in a diverse democracy is deliberately balanced with individuals' interests, then we need a faculty with job structures, rewards, and public sensibilities that will prepare students as engaged civic actors.

What I would like to see is a vigorous and inclusive dialogue on campuses about faculty rewards for *all* faculty. Since the mid-1990s there has been work on many campuses across the country to revise faculty reward policies to specifically include rewards for community engagement, not as exclusively service work but as core to the research and teaching roles of faculty. Bill, you were in the mix of that work at Indiana University–Purdue University Indianapolis for over a decade. Gene, you were central to this work while at American Association for Higher Education and even before that at the Carnegie Foundation. At present, I see two things happening. One is that the conversation about rewards for community engagement as core faculty work across the faculty roles has risen to a higher and more intense level. Second is that the conversation of community engagement has contributed to a widening discussion about new forms of scholarship.

On the first point, we have the example of the Carnegie Foundation's Community Engagement Classification, which asks campuses for evidence of how community engagement is valued as core faculty work, through campus reward policies. On the second point, campuses like the University of North Carolina at Chapel Hill have in their current strategic plan the goal of revising their faculty rewards to address new forms of scholarship, identified as digital scholarship, interdisciplinary scholarship, and community-engaged scholarship. What is happening in a 21st-century world of networked knowledge generation is that there are new epistemic assumptions about how we know what we know, how knowledge is generated, and what is legitimate knowledge in the academy. These epistemic assumptions, as much as anything else, will define not only our faculty but also the quality and purpose of higher education.

I say all this because when a university, like Syracuse University, revises its faculty rewards, it is in recognition of new forms of scholarship, that the core scholarly work of the campus has and should have wider social impacts, and that a commitment to the public good is the central work of the university, not a gift or a choice. At Syracuse University, the faculty manual explains that the university is

> committed to longstanding traditions of scholarship as well as evolving perspectives on scholarship. Syracuse University recognizes that the role of academia is not static, and that methodologies, topics of interest, and boundaries within and between disciplines change over time. The University will continue to support scholars in all of these traditions, including faculty who choose to participate in publicly engaged scholarship. Publicly engaged scholarship may involve partnerships of university knowledge and resources with those of the public and private sectors to enrich scholarship, research, creative activity, and public knowledge; enhance curriculum, teaching and learning; prepare educated, engaged citizens; strengthen democratic values and civic responsibility; address and help solve critical social problems; and contribute to the public good. (Syracuse University, 2009, sec. 2.34, 2009, para. 6)

As Tierney and Perkins observe in this volume, reward structures that do not value new forms of scholarship, such as community-engaged scholarship, inhibit the ability of faculty and the institution to contribute to the public good. Here is where policy could shape deeper engagement and deeper social impact. They write that "academic work needs to have an impact in order to provide a return on society's investment and the privilege accorded to those who seek truth and knowledge" (Chapter 13, this volume).

Evolving perspectives on scholarship bring with them evolving perspectives on impact. The question of impact as it is related to the generation of knowledge is best understood in the context of the National Science Foundation's framing of "broader impacts" of research. Academic impact is conceived as "knowledge and activities that contribute to the achievement of societally relevant outcomes" (National Science Foundation, 2013, chap. II. C. 2. d. i) and is shaped by examining the nature of the system within which knowledge is transformed into public policy or social action and how scholars engage others to transform research into actionable and useful knowledge. This same goal of impact is being sought by other federal agencies—the National Institutes of Health, the Centers for Disease Control and Prevention, and the Department of Health and Human Services.

What this evolving perspective could mean on campuses is that faculty are asked to provide, in their personnel review materials, not only a personal statement, but also an "impact statement," articulating how their work as a scholar has had impact, on whom has it had an impact, and how they know it has had an impact. This might include publishing in top-tier journals with high-impact factors, but it could also mean that publication is not the best way of evaluating the impact of one's scholarly work. Social impacts would be an expectation of faculty work and would be considered core to the professional role of faculty, not as philanthropic service or as a gift.

Finally, I would suggest that faculty contingency needs to drive public policy considerations. My sense is that when we do things like frame faculty public commitments as philanthropy, we are positioning contingency in a way that is reactive and accommodationist. I agree wholeheartedly with Shaker that "what is at stake is nothing less than the nature of faculty work in the coming decades" (Chapter 6, this volume)—and, I would add, nothing less than the role of higher education in a diverse democracy. To get there, I would suggest, we need to bring together efforts at examining higher education's public commitments and efforts at addressing the form of faculty work.

One example of how this might be done is with mechanisms like the Carnegie Community Engagement Classification. There is a poignant irony in the story of Maria Maisto, in 2008 a non-tenure-track, part-time faculty member at the University of Akron. It was the circumstances of the university's receiving the Carnegie Community Engagement Classification that year that led Maria to write an op-ed to the local Akron paper raising the question of what community engagement meant at a campus where more than half the faculty were off the tenure track and where issues were being raised not only about salary disparities and equity but also about the importance of the quality of education and its purpose. That op-ed was Maria's entry into advocacy. She is now president of the national organization the New Faculty Majority and is working to catalyze a public policy debate about equity and social justice and about the public commitments of academic professionals. At the 2014 annual meeting of the Association of American Colleges & Universities, Maisto presented with colleagues at a session called "Democratic Engagement and Academic Integrity." In the op-ed she wrote, Maria congratulated the university on its recognition by the Carnegie Foundation. But she also raised the question of why the classification requires no information about contingent faculty. What I hear in her question is, How can we advance community engagement as a core commitment of higher education if we don't at the same time work to shape the faculty we need for the society that we want?

Rice: John, your call for shaping the "faculty we need for the society we want" reminds me of the earlier imperative of the Carnegie Foundation for realigning faculty priorities with the institutional missions of American colleges and universities. It was that urgent concern that led to the influential report *Scholarship Reconsidered* (Boyer, 1990), the formation of a decade-long national forum on faculty roles and rewards, the press for greater community engagement, and the launching of a host of other reform efforts over the past 30 years focusing explicitly on the changing role of faculty.

Despite these gallant initiatives, we find ourselves in a period of crisis, as Bill put it, a new era triggered by a number of external and internal changes, each one "disruptive." In this book much has been written about the radical expansion of the use of contingent faculty, their blatant exploitation, and the decline in the number of tenured faculty. Technological changes have disrupted the fundamental way we go about research, teaching and learning, and community building. A new epistemology is being called for; the global context and the kinds of students turning to the American university for higher learning are dramatically different. The escalation of costs, the decline of public support, and the stratification of our diverse system of higher education are constant sources of public concern and complaint. Older, venerable images, such as the ivory tower, are no longer useful—in fact, they are a source of derision.

Yet American higher education still receives a kind of global admiration as an institution: "the bulwark of democracy" and even "the envy of the world." The university continues to be credited with sustaining the freedom of inquiry, the open exchange of ideas, and a climate for fostering innovation and the generation of new knowledge. Faculty in our flagship research universities, however, see themselves as primarily individual entrepreneurs engaged in a kind of academic hustle, and community college faculty competing simply to survive—all focusing more on "my work" than "our work."

In this conversation, indeed across the chapters of this book, an agreement is emerging that the social commitments to the common good are withering away. There was a time when a social compact held the faculty together and provided a sense of what it meant to be professional. That earlier consensus is no longer viable even in the most affluent and prestigious of our institutions.

This era requires a different social compact that goes beyond autonomous individualism to a firmly institutionalized vision of what it means to be professional. Payton's definition of philanthropy as "voluntary action for the public good" is not enough.

Some will want to return to an older, formerly established way of proceeding. The changes have been so dramatic and diffused, however, that a new professional vision is called for, one that builds on the best of what we have and takes advantage of our environment, technological skills, innovative processes, and learning strategies.

Not only has the academic context changed, but the faculty itself is being transformed also. In most institutions, the faculty are no longer full-time, tenure-track academics who see themselves as primarily content specialists, the experts in charge of organizing and dispensing knowledge. The faculty role has been, in fact, "unbundled": Teaching and learning has become a complex, challenging process involving a wide range of contributors; research is now largely interdisciplinary and cross-cultural; community engagement is beginning to honor the wisdom of practice and require that the walls of the university become more permeable, with knowledge flowing in multiple directions; and practitioners are starting to emerge as genuine colleagues when involved in the learning/action enterprise.

This wide spectrum of scholars—with *scholarship* being defined more broadly—will need to be included in an academic profession where shared values and responsibilities are incorporated into a common vocation, a calling. At the heart of the social compact would be a commitment to maintaining the university as a special place in the society where academic freedom is sustained, a public forum—a commons—where open, critical deliberation is possible and the creative imagination is nurtured. This commitment would extend to all the actors in the learning endeavor. The permanent contributors (tenure equivalents) would have as their primary responsibility maintaining and protecting the academic freedom of all participants.

Those making up the profession would learn how to work collaboratively and commit themselves to doing so, to foster a different kind of individuation, creative freedom, and, most important, the professional autonomy of the institution itself. Institutional responsibility would take on new meaning. Responsibility for protecting academic freedom would extend beyond the individual to others, and particularly those genuinely disadvantaged—with less prestige and power. In the complex, global world of the future, collaboration will be required for the pursuit of excellence. Academic success will need to be redefined. The new faculty I envision would be not only collaborative and engaged but also more inclusive, moving beyond the walls, silos, and prestige rankings that separate the present faculty from one another and the larger community.

REFERENCES

AAUP. (1915). 1915 declaration of principles on academic freedom and academic tenure. Washington, DC: American Association of University Professors.

Available at http://www.aaup.org/file/1915-Declaration-of-Principles-on-Academic-Freedom-and-Academic-Tenure.pdf

Boyer, E. L. (1990). *Scholarship reconsidered: Priorities of the professoriate.* Princeton, NJ: Carnegie Foundation for the Advancement of Teaching.

Dionne, E. J. (2012). *Our divided political heart: The battle for the American idea in an age of discontent.* New York, NY: Bloomsbury.

Dzur, A. W. (2008). *Democratic professionalism: Citizen participation and the reconstruction of professional ethics, identity, and practice.* University Park, PA: Pennsylvania State University Press.

Fish, S. (2008). *Save the world on your own time.* New York, NY: Oxford University Press.

Jencks, C., & Riesman, D. (1968). *The academic revolution.* Garden City, NY: Doubleday.

National Science Foundation. (2013, November). *Proposal and award policies and procedures guide: Part 1—Grant proposal guide* (NSF 14-1). Available at http://www.nsf.gov/pubs/policydocs/pappguide/nsf14001/gpgprint.pdf

Parsons, T. (1968). Professions. *International Encyclopedia of the Social Sciences, 12,* 536–547.

Payton, R. L. (1988). *Philanthropy: Voluntary action for the public good.* New York, NY: American Council on Education/Macmillan.

Scobey, D. (2002). Putting the academy in its place. *Places, 14*(3), 50–55.

Slaughter, S., & Rhoades, G. (2004). *Academic capitalism and the new economy: Markets, state, and higher education.* Baltimore, MD: The Johns Hopkins University Press.

Syracuse University. (2009). Faculty manual, section 2.34, areas of expected faculty achievement: Teaching, research, and service. Available at http://provost.syr.edu/faculty-support/faculty-manual/2-34-areas-of-expected-faculty-achievement-teaching-research-and-service/

Williams, J. J. (2013, December 2). The great stratification. *The Chronicle of Higher Education.* Available at http://chronicle.com/article/The-Great-Stratification/143285/

About the Contributors

Ann E. Austin is professor of higher, adult, and lifelong education at Michigan State University, where she holds the Mildred B. Erickson Distinguished Chair. Her research concerns faculty careers and professional development, teaching and learning in higher education, the academic workplace, organizational change, and doctoral education. She is a fellow of the American Educational Research Association (AERA) and past president of the Association for the Study of Higher Education (ASHE), and she was a Fulbright fellow in South Africa (1998). She is the co-PI of the Center for the Integration of Research, Teaching, and Learning (CIRTL), funded by the National Science Foundation, and the co-PI of an NSF-funded ADVANCE grant to study organizational change strategies that support the success of women scholars in STEM fields. Her work is widely published, and includes *Rethinking Faculty Work: Higher Education's Strategic Imperative* (2007) and *Educating Integrated Professionals: Theory and Practice on Preparation for the Professoriate* (2008), as well as other books, articles, chapters, and monographs concerning higher education issues in the United States and in international contexts. In 2011, she wrote a commissioned paper for the Board on Science Education of the National Research Council titled "Promoting Evidence-Based Change in Undergraduate Science Education." She has worked with colleagues at the national and institutional levels on higher education issues in a number of countries, including Australia, China, Egypt, Finland, Malaysia, Oman, Thailand, the Philippines, South Africa, the United Arab Emirates, and Vietnam.

J. Herman Blake is the inaugural Humanities Scholar in Residence at the Medical University of South Carolina (MUSC) in Charleston. He earned a BA in sociology from New York University and an MA and a PhD in sociology from the University of California–Berkeley. At MUSC, Dr. Blake works in the Offices of the President and Provost. Dr. Blake serves as professor in the College of Health Professions and Dental Medicine and lectures in the Colleges of Dentistry, Health Professions, and Medicine and the Graduate School. He also coleads special workshops in ethics and end-of-life care for students, as well as seminars on humanism in medical education for faculty.

Dr. Blake served as the founding provost of Oakes College at the University of California–Santa Cruz, director of African American Studies at Iowa State University, vice chancellor for undergraduate education at Indiana University–Purdue University Indianapolis, and president of Tougaloo College in Mississippi. He served for 2 years as the Eugene M. Lang Visiting Professor of Social Change at Swarthmore College. Dr. Blake has a substantial publication history with over 50 contributions and a book titled *Revolutionary Suicide* with Huey P. Newton (Harcourt Brace Jovanovich, 1973). Dr. Blake has been awarded six honorary doctorates and two presidential medals.

The United States Secretary of the Interior appointed Dr. Blake as a founding member of the Gullah Geechee Cultural Heritage Corridor Commission (2007) where he also serves as acting executive director.

Dwight F. Burlingame is the director of the Indiana University Lilly Family School of Philanthropy's master of arts program and holds the Glenn Family Chair in Philanthropy. He has been active over the past 25 years in developing philanthropic education at Indiana University and for the field of civil society education globally. He also serves as an active member of the national Association of Fundraising Professionals' Research Council; the Association for Research on Nonprofit Organizations and Voluntary Action (ARNOVA), where he is currently the treasurer; and the International Society for Third-Sector Research (ISTR) and is a board member for Learning to Give.

Dr. Burlingame is an expert in the field of philanthropy and fundraising and spent 6 years as editor of the *Nonprofit and Voluntary Sector Quarterly*, the journal of ARNOVA. He is the coeditor of the Philanthropic and Nonprofit Studies book series for Indiana University Press and has written or cowritten 10 books, nearly 60 articles, and more than 100 book reviews. Dr. Burlingame also is the editor of *Philanthropy in America: A Comprehensive Historical Encyclopedia*, published in 2004.

He is active in the nonprofit community as a board member and volunteer and is a frequent speaker, consultant, and author on topics relating to philanthropy, corporate citizenship, nonprofit organizations, and fundraising.

Denise Mott DeZolt has worked for over 20 years in higher education in both campus-based and distance education. She earned her PhD in school psychology from Kent State University, her MS Ed in counseling from the University of Dayton, and her undergraduate degree in behavioral science from the State University of New York, Plattsburgh. She is currently chief academic officer at Laureate Education in the Global Products and Services group. DeZolt's community and professional service activities include participation on a number of college/university and community organization boards, involvement in professional organizations, coordination of faith formation programs, and engagement in chairing and serving on human participants in research review boards. She has conducted research on multicultural, gender, and diversity issues in education; use of story and narrative inquiry; and spirituality and professional practice. Her presentations at international, national, state, and local professional conferences have been in the areas of accreditation and quality assurance, higher education in the for-profit sector, distance education, gender, and education. She has also been the primary or co–primary investigator on a number of federal, state, local, foundation, and university grants related to service delivery to diverse populations of children and adolescents. Additionally, she worked in private practice and consulting for 10 years.

Sean Gehrke is a doctoral candidate and researcher in the Pullias Center for Higher Education at the University of Southern California. His research focuses on organizational issues in higher education relating to social networks, leadership, and organizational change, as well as how the college environment and student experiences influence learning and development. His research has been published in the *Journal of College Student Development* and *Educational Policy*, as well as in edited volumes relating to leadership and college student spirituality. He earned his MEd in counseling and personnel services from the University of Maryland, College Park, and his BA in psychology from Lewis & Clark College, and he has worked in higher education and student affairs for over a decade as an administrator and scholar.

Audrey J. Jaeger is a professor of higher education and Alumni Distinguished Graduate Professor in the Department of Leadership, Policy and Adult and Higher Education at North Carolina State University. She also directs the National Initiative for Leadership and Institutional Effectiveness (NILIE), an organization focusing on campus climate survey administration. Dr. Jaeger's research examines relationships and experiences among faculty and students that illuminate issues of transition, access, climate, agency, and civic and community engagement. Additionally, her research explores how various aspects of the environment, from labor market conditions to institutional policies, affect faculty and students. Dr. Jaeger teaches courses in organizational theory, foundations of research and scholarship, governance of higher education, and student affairs. Prior to NC State, she worked in higher education administration at New York University's Robert F. Wagner School of Public Service and Bucknell University. She was also an adjunct professor at Baruch College, City University of New York. Her professional experience includes both academic and student affairs positions. She received her PhD from New York University.

Dr. Jaeger is an associate editor for *Research in Higher Education* and on the editorial boards of the *Journal of Higher Education* and *Journal of Higher Education Outreach and Engagement*. Her own work has been published in the *Journal of Higher Education*, *Research in Higher Education*, *Educational Policy*, *Community College Review*, *Journal of College Student Development*, *Journal of Higher Education Outreach and Engagement*, and other journals.

Adrianna Kezar is professor of higher education at the University of Southern California and codirector of the Pullias Center for Higher Education. Dr. Kezar is a national expert of non-tenure-track faculty, change, governance, and leadership in higher education. Her recent books include *Embracing Non–Tenure Track Faculty* (Routledge, 2012) and *Understanding the New Majority of Non–Tenure Track Faculty* (Jossey-Bass, 2010).

Jia G. Liang is a doctoral student in the Department of Lifelong Education, Administration and Policy at the University of Georgia. She has taught students at various levels and courses in English, human development, and educational psychology. She has research experience in the areas of school leadership, community engagement, faculty-engaged scholarship, and professional development for math and science teachers. She was awarded as the David L. Clark Scholar by the University Council for Educational Administration and Divisions A and L of the American Educational Research Association in 2013. Her research interests include assessment of educational leadership and teacher education programs, faculty engagement and civic leadership, and disciplinary and institutional equity for women and racial minorities.

Elizabeth Lynn directs the Institute for Leadership and Service at Valparaiso University and the Center for Civic Reflection, an innovative national resource center for humanities-based discussion founded in 1998 with generous support from the Lilly Endowment. She also teaches in the field of philanthropy and service and conducts research on the role of the humanities in American civic life. Lynn holds a PhD in religion and literature from the University of Chicago and is a past recipient of a Mellon Fellowship in the Humanities. Coeditor with Adam Davis of *The Civically Engaged Reader* (Great Books Foundation, 2006), she is the author most recently of *An Ongoing Experiment: State Councils, the Humanities, and the American Public* (Kettering Foundation, 2013). Active in her own community and state, Lynn serves on the Valparaiso Board of Zoning Appeals, the governing board of Indiana Humanities, and the advisory board for the Lake Family Institute on Faith and Giving at Indiana University.

Michael Moody is the Frey Foundation Chair for Family Philanthropy at the Dorothy A. Johnson Center for Philanthropy at Grand Valley State University. As Frey Chair, he works with a network of partners to pursue a comprehensive program of applied research, teaching, professional development, and public engagement, all designed to advance and promote the field of family philanthropy. Dr. Moody was trained as a cultural sociologist at the University of Chicago and Princeton University and previously served as faculty at Boston University and the University of Southern California. He has been actively working to understand and improve philanthropy and nonprofit organizations for 25 years, both inside and outside the academy. He is coauthor of *Understanding Philanthropy: Its Meaning and Mission* and has written numerous other publications about family foundations, next-generation giving, donor education, ethical giving, venture philanthropy, giving as "giving back," nonprofit advocacy, the meaning of the public good, and many other topics.

Emily L. Moore is professor emerita in the Department of Educational Leadership and Policy Studies, Higher Education, College of Human Sciences at Iowa State University. She served as provost and vice president for academic affairs at Dillard University in New Orleans, where she led faculty in rebuilding and reinvigorating academic programs devastated by Hurricane Katrina. She also served as vice president for academic affairs and dean of faculty at Concordia University in St. Paul, Minnesota. She is the former director of the Master's in Health Administration (MHA)—Global program, Medical University of South Carolina. She retired as associate dean for academic and faculty affairs and chair and professor, Department of Health Studies, College of Health Professions, Medical University of South Carolina.

Her scholarly interests include health education intervention in HIV/AIDS in sub-Saharan Africa, China, and rural populations in the Sea Islands of South Carolina; health behaviors among the rural Gullah Geechee elderly; and college teaching. She is editor of the monograph *Student Affairs Staff as Teachers*, in the series New Directions for Student Services. Her current research project is an analysis of life perspectives of Gullah residents collected through oral histories.

Thomas F. Nelson Laird is an associate professor in the Higher Education and Student Affairs Program at Indiana University, Bloomington. He was that program's coordinator from 2010 to 2014 and was interim director of the IU School of Education Center for Postsecondary Research in 2014. Tom received a BA in mathematics from Gustavus Adolphus College (1995), an MS in mathematics from Michigan State University (1997), and a PhD in higher education from the University of Michigan (2003). His work focuses on improving teaching and learning at colleges and universities, with a special emphasis on the design, delivery, and effects of student experiences with diversity. He directs the Faculty Survey of Student Engagement, a companion project to the National Survey of Student Engagement, run through the Center for Postsecondary Research. Author of dozens of articles and reports, Tom has published in key scholarly and practitioner publications. He also consults with institutions of higher education and related organizations on topics ranging from effective assessment practices to the inclusion of diversity into the curriculum.

Jason F. Perkins is a 5th-year PhD student whose dissertation focuses on increasing the admission rates of first-generation and underrepresented college students. His previous publications and research interests center on the impact of technology on postsecondary education, learning through digital media platforms, the effects of the Bayh-Dole Act on higher education research, and college access for low-income students.

William M. Plater is Chancellor's Professor Emeritus of public affairs, philanthropy, and English at Indiana University and executive vice chancellor and dean of the faculties emeritus at Indiana University–Purdue University Indianapolis (IUPUI), where he served as chief academic officer for 19 years. Plater has been actively involved in civic engagement activities, locally, nationally, and internationally, which have been recognized with the establishment of the Plater Award for Civic Engagement by the Association of American Colleges and Universities, the first national award of any kind to recognize provosts. Students graduating from IUPUI—from bachelors to PhDs—with outstanding records of community involvement are awarded the Plater Medallion for Civic Engagement. IUPUI also established the Plater International Scholarship Program, providing 10 entering undergraduates a 4-year tuition scholarship, residency in the International House, and a study-abroad opportunity. Plater has been awarded honorary doctorates by Purdue University, Indiana University, and the National Institute of Development Administration in Thailand.

Gary Rhoades is professor and director, Center for the Study of Higher Education at the University of Arizona's College of Education. His work focuses on the restructuring of academic institutions and professions, as evidenced in his two books, *Managed Professionals: Unionized Faculty and Restructuring Academic Labor* (SUNY Press, 1998) and (with Sheila Slaughter) *Academic Capitalism and the New Economy* (The Johns Hopkins University Press, 2004).

R. Eugene Rice is senior scholar at the Association of American Colleges and Universities. He received his PhD in religion and society from Harvard University and is a graduate of Harvard Divinity School. For 10 years he served as director of the Forum on Faculty Roles and Rewards and the New Pathways projects at the American Association for Higher Education (AAHE). Before moving to AAHE he was vice president and dean of the faculty at Antioch College, where he held an appointment of professor of sociology and religion. Earlier, Gene was program executive and senior fellow at the Carnegie Foundation engaged in the national study of the scholarly priorities of the American professoriate and collaborating with the late Ernest Boyer on the Carnegie Report *Scholarship Reconsidered*. His work on that topic is available in the New Pathways Working Paper Series in an essay titled "Making a Place for the New American Scholar" (Stylus) and appears in the book *Faculty Priorities Reconsidered: Encouraging Multiple Forms of Scholarship*, edited with KerryAnn O'Meara (2005). Gene's special interest is in the scholarship of engagement, and recently he has taken this work internationally, to, for example, Brazil, Liberia, the West Bank, Saudi Arabia, and the United Kingdom. In *Change* magazine's survey of leadership in American higher education, Gene Rice is recognized as one among a small group of "idea leaders" whose work has made a difference.

John Saltmarsh is the codirector of the New England Resource Center for Higher Education (NERCHE) at the University of Massachusetts, Boston, as well as a faculty member in the Higher Education Administration Doctoral Program in the Department of Leadership in Education in the College of Education and Human Development. He is the author of an edited volume, *"To Serve a Larger Purpose": Engagement for Democracy and the Transformation of Higher Education* (2011) and a book with Edward Zlotkowski, *Higher Education and Democracy: Essays on Service-Learning and Civic Engagement* (2011). He is also the author of numerous book chapters and articles on civic engagement, service learning, and experiential education and is the coauthor of the *Democratic Engagement White Paper* (NERCHE, 2009). He is an associate editor for the *Michigan Journal of Community Service-Learning* and is on the editorial board of the *Journal of Higher Education Outreach and Engagement*, *Metropolitan Universities Journal*, and the *E-Journal for Public Affairs*. He also serves on the boards of Imagining America and the International Association for Research on Service Learning and Community Engagement. From 1998 through 2005, he directed the national Project on Integrating Service with Academic Study at Campus Compact. He holds a PhD in American history from Boston University and taught for over a decade at Northeastern University and as a visiting research fellow at the Feinstein Institute for Public Service at Providence College.

Lorilee R. Sandmann is professor in the Department of Lifelong Education, Administration, and Policy at the University of Georgia and editor of the *Journal of Higher Education Outreach and Engagement*. Her research, doctoral advisement, and teaching focus on leadership and organizational change in higher education with special emphasis on the institutionalization of community engagement, as well as faculty roles and rewards related to community-engaged scholarship. She is recipient of the Distinguished Researcher Award by the International Association for Research on Service Learning and Community Engagement and the UGA's Outstanding Faculty Scholarship of Engagement Award. She serves on the National Advisory Panel for Community Engagement of the Carnegie Foundation for the Advancement of Teaching. Dr. Sandmann holds a PhD from the University of Wisconsin–Madison in adult education and business management.

Genevieve G. Shaker is associate dean for development and external affairs in the Indiana University School of Liberal Arts at Indiana University–Purdue University Indianapolis (IUPUI) and assistant professor of philanthropic studies in the Indiana University Lilly Family School of Philanthropy. She is one of the few academicians who is also a practicing advancement professional.

Shaker completed her PhD in higher education at Indiana University–Bloomington, and her MA in philanthropic studies from the Lilly Family School of Philanthropy's predecessor, the Center on Philanthropy. Her research focuses on the changing nature of the American professoriate as well as on higher education advancement, particularly the philanthropic giving of faculty and staff. She is the author of peer-reviewed articles and book chapters for both the scholarly and practitioner communities. The quality of her research has been recognized with the Bobby Wright Dissertation of the Year Award (2009) from the Association for the Study of Higher Education, and with her co-authors, the Robert Menges Award for Research in Educational Development (2009) by the nation's primary group of faculty development professionals (Professional and Organizational Development Network), and the Best Paper Award from the Association for Institutional Research (2013).

Paul S. Shaker is a career educator who has served as teacher, teacher educator, and dean in five states in the United States and in Asia and also in Canada, at Simon Fraser University of British Columbia, where he is professor emeritus. An alumnus of The Ohio State University, Dr. Shaker has sought to advance our social democratic legacy in public schools and higher education through scholarship, leadership, and media activism. He has developed and directed independently funded projects such as Friends of Simon, an outreach to immigrant and refugee children that provides university students as after-school tutors. Professor Shaker also hosted, for 6 years, *Your Education Matters*, a television program widely cablecast in British Columbia. He is a fellow of the National Education Policy Center.

Paul Shaker has been recognized as a Fulbright Senior Scholar in Kuwait, by the American Association of Colleges for Teacher Education Outstanding Writing Award for *Teachers and Mentors*, and by the American Educational Research Association Division K Award for Exemplary Research in Teaching and Teacher Education for the coauthored book *Reclaiming Education for Democracy: Thinking Beyond No Child Left Behind.*

Paul Shaker's writing and speaking center on the application of contemporary theory to education politics and policy and to the enrichment of meaning in schools and in teacher education. He has been particularly active in defending the integrity of professional educators and their values, including as they pertain to self- and social realization.

Marty Sulek holds a PhD from the Indiana University Lilly Family School of Philanthropy, where he also completed his MA. As a member of the first cohort of the school's PhD program, he feels particularly privileged to have been one of the last students of its founder, the late Robert Payton (1926–2011). Dr. Sulek now serves as a faculty member at the school, teaching the ethics and values of philanthropy. His primary scholarly interests are in the philosophical and historical dimensions of philanthropy, particularly during the classical age of Greece, and the early modern era. Prior to pursuing graduate studies, he worked as a nonprofit development professional in Canada, (what was then) Czechoslovakia, and the United States, and for every major type of charitable nonprofit organization. He earned his BA (1990) at Mount Allison University, in Sackville, New Brunswick, Canada, with honors in political science and philosophy. Dr. Sulek currently serves as chair of the board of trustees of the Winchester Presbyterian Church and on the board of the Randolph County YMCA.

William G. Tierney is university professor and codirector of the Pullias Center for Higher Education at the University of Southern California. His research focuses on equity on and access in higher education and the role of the academic in the 21st century.

Richard C. Turner is emeritus professor of English and philanthropic studies at Indiana University–Purdue University Indianapolis. He taught a range of courses in English and philanthropic studies, including a graduate seminar in philanthropy and literature. He has published on Milton, Swift, the teaching of literature, interdisciplinarity, philanthropy and literature, and faculty development.

Index